Pray for Lu—

Christmas 1959

SAINT JEAN-MARIE VIANNEY:

Curé of Ars

Saint Jean-Marie Vianney: *Curé of Ars*

MARGARET TROUNCER

SHEED AND WARD – NEW YORK

Nihil obstat:

John R. Ready
Censor Librorum
November 28, 1958

Imprimatur:

† Robert F. Joyce
Bishop of Burlington
November 30, 1958

To
all my French friends
both new and old
with my love and gratitude

CONTENTS

PREFACE

What a joy it is to write about the saints! One wanders in places enchanted by their memory, discovering their secrets with a surprise like that of a child finding Easter eggs hidden in long grass. One makes new friends—and above all, wonderfully and mysteriously, one finds oneself being received into the friendship of the saint himself. This happened to me when I was finding out about St. Margaret Mary and St. Bernadette. And now it is the Curé of Ars. I have spent long hours at Dardilly, Chantemerle, Ecully, Lyons, Roanne, Les Noës and Ars.

There is nothing like the company of the saints. Farewell loneliness. First of all, they are kind and loving to us; secondly, they lead us into a spacious world of light peopled by other gracious beings like themselves, whom we come to know through them.

I must express my gratitude for the help I have had in the writing of this book. Monseigneur Trochu kindly allowed me to make use of references of his extracted from the sworn testimonies of the canonization procedures. The Abbés Pagnoux and Balavoine gave me advice, lent me volumes of the Curé's sermons, and drove me around to his haunts in the neighbourhood of Ars and even to Les Noës. My warmest thanks are due to Mother Bede of the Assumption for correcting my tendency to think in French and putting some of my translations into more respectable English.

And now I bid my reader farewell, so that the Curé may speak for himself. Like the medieval scribe in his cloister, all I ask is to be remembered in your prayers.

Margaret Trouncer

PART I

1. A FARMHOUSE NEAR LYONS

THE VIANNEYS OWNED A SMALL, COMPACT FARMHOUSE AT THE ENtrance of the village of Dardilly, on the heights above Lyons. The windows of the farm kitchen faced southwest, and Mont Blanc could be seen even on stormy days.

Marie and Mathieu Vianney farmed several acres of wheatfields, hayfields, vineyards and woods. They also possessed three cows and a little grey donkey which carried logs to the poor and corn to the mill. This family friend lived to the age of thirty: he was loved by the toddlers, for he was their only means of transport. On his back they ambled to the fields at noon to bring their father his meal.

Before the Reign of Terror had begun six children were born to the Vianneys: Catherine in 1780; Jeanne-Marie in 1882 (she died four or five years later); François in 1784; blue-eyed Jean-Marie on May 8th, 1786; Marguerite, nicknamed Gothon, in 1787; and lastly, in 1790, the younger François, nicknamed Cadet to distinguish him from his elder brother of the same name. They were all born in an alcove of the main room on the ground floor of the farmhouse, under a picture of the Blessed Virgin.

Jean-Marie, the future saint, had only to look at his parents to learn lessons of Christian love and virtue. The Vianneys lived frugally in order to help the poor. Often they shared their meals with beggars, who flocked to their door, having heard that they would not be sent away. Hospitality to vagrants was a family tradition with the Vianneys; under the rags of the destitute they recognized Christ.

3

Jean was his mother's especial favourite. He had been born towards the hour of midnight. The midwife, who went to the door to look at the night sky, said the stars foretold that the child would be either a great saint or a great sinner. Before he had learned self-discipline, Jean was an impetuous, quick-tempered child. It was remarkable that he was so obedient to his parents, for he could have been extremely obstinate.

In the rhythm of the seasons and the enjoyment of country delights, he built up the foundations of that health which resisted all the strain of his later asceticism and labour. He grew strong and wiry, full of nervous energy. Later on, he was able to endure for over thirty years the vitiated air of a confessional, sometimes for more than sixteen hours a day, just because he was a country man. He had known March ploughing and sowing, seen plover plunging down to the newly tilled furrows of brown earth; in June he had raked and tossed hay in the sweetly scented air; he had ridden great haycarts rumbling along the sleepy lanes; and at Lammastide he had helped with the reaping and binding of heavy stooks of golden corn. Towards Michaelmas came vintage time; and in October he picked chestnuts and acorns. In winter there was rest for man and beast. During the long evenings around the hearth, while the logs crackled against the beautiful fire-back with its delicate pillars and crowns of flowers, the Vianneys mended tools and cracked nuts. The lives of the saints were read to the family and the farm hands. The year ended with the convivialities of Christmastide.

Before the Reign of Terror began, little Jean-Marie had already taken part in the Corpus Christi processions through the sunlit village street, listened intently to sermons, watched priests planting crosses in the fields at Rogationtide, worshipped at the Christmas crib. It all made a deep impression on him: he loved to enact the part of the preacher, imitating the voices and gestures he had observed. Then came the day when his mother swept away the familiar statues of the saints, the crucifix and the missals. Catherine, who was old enough to have some understanding of the event, wept.

In those days before swift communications, country folk were often bewildered by conflicting reports and opinions. Terrible things might be happening in Paris and they would not know. Or they might hear of them weeks later from hawkers and pedlars. The nearness of Dardilly to Lyons, where the fighting was fierce, meant that the Vianneys had heard of some of the main events of the Revolution even before marauding soldiers were seen stalking through the hamlet.

In the years 1793–94 Lyons was under a reign of terror, the rebellion of the anti-Jacobins, at first successful, having been repressed with inexorable severity after the city had been under siege by the forces of the Paris Convention for two months. The Vianneys must have heard the roar of bombardment, received wounded fighters seeking dressings and refuge for the night. Reports must have reached them of the trials of suspected persons at the rate of twenty an hour; the executions by firing squad and guillotine at the rate of twenty-eight a day; the mass shootings of December 4th, 1794. They must have heard of the Festival of Reason staged by the former Oratorian Fouché, who found the extirpation of fanaticism especially congenial, in the Church of St. Jean—the very church in which Jean-Marie was one day to receive minor orders.

On All Souls Day of 1789 the clergy were despoiled, and church property was nationalized. On July the 12th, 1790, the Civil Constitution of the Clergy was declared, and in November of the same year, priests were made to choose between swearing to uphold this Constitution or being turned adrift into exile, or even worse. After that it was death to harbour a non-juring priest.

At Dardilly M. Jacques Rey, who had been Curé for thirty-nine years, was replaced by a friend of Mirabeau, a Monsieur Lamourette, who had sworn allegiance to the Civil Constitution of the clergy.

On the surface Dardilly's parochial matters looked exactly the same as before. How should these simple country people suspect that the Civil Constitution would lead to schism and heresy?

It was the Vianney's eldest daughter, devout, ten-year-old

Catherine, a lover of saints' lives, who noticed odd things in church which aroused her suspicions: she said to her mother: "Mamma, why does the new curé talk about citizens all the time? Why does he criticize Monsieur Rey? Why does he say all the curés before him were bad? He says people like them are no more curés than his old shoe! And how is it that the benches in church are full of people I've never seen at Mass before?"

Her mother was surprised and puzzled. But now on her guard, she was prepared to listen when a relative from her native hamlet of nearby Ecully told her that the old curés were being persecuted and forced to flee for their lives, and that some had escaped death only by going into exile. The new curé had separated himself from the Church by his vow. The Vianneys decided to stop going to church.

A witness has observed that little Jean "showed his horror for sin from the day when he began to flee from the juring curé."

How brave those Vianneys were! Although they knew quite well that any Judas who denounced a non-juring priest would receive a hundred livres reward, and that the person who gave him asylum would be deported, they often hid hunted priests in their farm, and even arranged for them to say Mass. It is extraordinary that the family was not denounced.

On December the 8th, 1793, the celebration of Sunday had been abolished by law. And now every tenth day, called Decadi, was to be the holiday for working people. Any girl who did not keep this godless new Decadi might have all her hair shaved off. It is easy to picture the painful scenes which ensued when feminine jealousy found excuses to betray girls with lovely hair. One is glad to hear that in the neighbourhood of far-away Ars, the betrayers had scalding water poured over them. Similar incidents occurred at the end of the German occupation of France, in the last war, when so many women collaborators had to wear turbans because their hair had been shaved off by the Resistance Movement.

The faithful now began a life very like that of the early Christians. There were two heroic priests in the neighbourhood

who fulfilled their duties to their flock at the peril of their lives:
Abbé Groboz, who disguised himself as a cook, carrying his sauce-
pans and frying pans on his back, and travelled by night, and Abbé
Balley, who became a travelling carpenter, and also went about
laden with the tools of his trade. They would send their trusted
agents around to give the message that Mass would be said at
midnight in such and such an isolated farmhouse or barn. The
faithful would walk there in the darkness, at the mercy of any
treacherous servant who wanted money. Seven-year-old Jean always insisted on going along with the family, even though his little
legs grew tired walking such distances long after bedtime. The
others complained, he never did. Their mother used to urge them
on by saying: "Now imitate Jean-Marie. He's always so eager."

The martyrs of Rome began to fill the child's imagination. He
loved those early morning hours in hidden attics where only a
night-light was allowed lest their presence should be betrayed.
Everywhere lay dark shadows, broken only by the tiny flickering
flame playing on the tired face of the hunted priest who had nowhere to lay his head. Jean was impressed by the grave looks of
the faithful: the old who had lived all their lives with the consolations of faith, the young children half asleep, and the watcher at
the door, on the alert for the click of the lifted latch and the
stealthy footfall on the stairs which meant treachery.

Then the return home, still in darkness. When they reached a
crossroads they would pause for a moment, sorrowfully, remembering the cross before which it had been their custom to bless
themselves, now smashed and taken away by men from Lyons.
Jean would slip his hand into the pocket of his blouse and clasp
the little wooden statue of the Virgin Mary which his mother had
given to him some time before. It was his most precious possession.
Many years later he told his friends that the Virgin Mary had been
his first love: "I loved her even before I knew her." The gift of the
statue had come about in this way.

When he was only four, his young sister, Marguerite—"Gothon"
—had suddenly taken a fancy to his rosary. He could hardly bear
to think of parting with it, even though he was so little and

couldn't quite master the intricacies of telling his beads. So brother and sister had a scrap and a tussle. In tears, Jean rushed to his mother for advice. She said, "My little one, give the rosary to Gothon. Yes, give it for the love of God." Jean obeyed, sobbing aloud. To console him, his mother then gave him the roughly carved wooden statuette which he had always admired above the hearth. Seventy years later he was to say, "Oh, how I loved that statue! I could not be separated from it day or night, and I would not have slept in peace if I hadn't had it by my side in my little bed. . . ."

Occasionally he would put the statue on a chair in a corner of the room and pray before it. One day he had disappeared, and his mother, growing anxious lest he should have fallen into the pond in the yard, looked for him everywhere; she found him at last in the stable, praying before the statue. Like Mary she "pondered all these things in her heart." She began to understand that her son had a vocation. Often she would say to him, "My little Jean-Marie, if I saw you offending God, it would grieve me more than if it were another child of mine." When he was only a tiny child, he learned to pray at her feet. He would join his hands and slip them between hers.

As she went about her work in house, farmyard or field, he would trot after her and she would teach him his faith. He drank it all in thirstily, and with love. Hardly was he out of the cradle when she taught him how to make the sign of the cross before his bowl of broth. One day he refused to open his mouth; she could not understand the reason for this, because she knew he was extremely hungry. Only after she had guided the little hand to make the cross on his forehead would he eat. This reminds one so much of plump, determined St. Thomas Aquinas as a baby, refusing at bath time to unclench the fist holding a parchment scrap on which was written the name of Mary.

Jean-Marie's mother taught him to bless each hour by a prayer to the Queen of Heaven. When he was an old man, somebody congratulated him on having loved prayer at such an early age, and he replied, with tears in his eyes, "After God I owe this to my mother. She was so good! Virtue slips easily from the hearts of mothers into the hearts of their children. . . . A child who has the good fortune to possess a good mother should never look at her or think of her without emotion."

Often he told his friend that it was his mother who came to wake each child, every morning, to make quite sure that his first waking thought should be of God.

2. *A SAINTLY BEGGAR AND THE SHEPHERD OF MONTMERLE*

ONE HOT NOONTIDE IN THE MONTH OF JUNE DURING THE REIGN OF Terror, Mathieu Vianney, who as usual had been up since cockcrow, was having a much-needed rest on the doorstep of his house. It was cooler there than under the oak tree or the ancient apple tree, where he usually took his midday siesta. And the flies were less bothersome. He was talking to two hawkers whom he knew well. One of them, Ignace, had just returned from Italy, where he had been for some years.

Mathieu was a quiet man, rather severe-looking. He had a strong sense of justice and a dry sense of humour. To a neighbour who had filched his firewood and then invited him to sit by his fire, he said: "Yes, willingly. When one provides the wood, one might well warm oneself!" He suffered agonies from rheumatism. When Jean was older, he used to bribe him for permission to go to church with the promise that he would pray for him, asking relief from his attacks of "the screws."

That hot afternoon he had bad pains, particularly in his toil-worn hands. One of the hawkers, Blaise, newly come from Paris, was offering him a present of some special balsam to ease them. Jean was in the house, sitting in a corner, trying to mould a statue of St. John the Baptist out of clay. He was so clever at these statues that his little friends were always begging him to give them away as gifts. There was one wonderful day when his father, much pleased with his work, had baked a statue for him, and it became a treasured ornament in the house.

Mathieu Vianney turned and looked uneasily at the boy. "You must hide that Saint John the Baptist if you hear footsteps," he said. "Do you understand? We can't be too careful."

"No," agreed Blaise.

"Why, he wouldn't be sent to the guillotine for that?" exclaimed Ignace, the one who had just come back from Rome.

"Oh," cried Blaise, "one can see you've been out of the kingdom for some time."

"Hush," said Mathieu. "You don't call it a kingdom any more. We call it a republic now. You and I are not Christians: we're citizens."

He gazed at the blue line of hills which could be glimpsed in the distance.

"Yes," said Blaise, turning to Ignace. "Things seem quiet here at the moment. I can see that you haven't heard very much about what has been happening." And in a low voice he went on to give a vivid account of the storming of the Bastille, of the King's attempt to escape and his ignominious recapture, and the terrible procession through the streets of Paris, with the royal family imprisoned in the coach. He described the dreadful silence of the crowds on that bitter January day when the King was guillotined, the horror of the good people of Paris who loved him; the execution of the Queen, broken by humiliation and pain, riding with her hands behind her back to the scaffold. He himself had sat near the fish-wives on the steps of St. Roch. He spoke of the rumours about the death of the little Dauphin, of the execution of young Madame Elizabeth, the King's only sister, driven in a tumbril and looking like an angel in her white dress.

"Ah, the poor Queen," said Mathieu in a whisper, "and yet some of the people of Lyons hated her. They said she caused the downfall of the silk trade by her passion for muslins."

He paused a moment. "But tell me, Blaise, how is it with the faithful in Paris? Are they ever able to receive Holy Communion in secret?"

"Oh, yes," replied Blaise. "You mustn't think that you people in the Lyonnais have got the monopoly on heroic priests. There are

plenty of them in Paris. And strangely enough, the mob attacking
the Tuileries cried out to the King, 'Hand us over the priests you
are hiding in your attics, and we will leave you alone.' I have seen
niches behind sliding panels in some old houses in Paris where
these good priests crouched in the dark for days on end, afraid
of being betrayed by a servant. They would slip out at night to
give Holy Communion to some of their penitents. There was one
I knew, disguised as an old-clothes dealer, so that he could go
into many houses unchallenged. Then there was one—I think he
was the Papal Nuncio—who lived in the Bois de Boulogne. He
cooked in the open on a little stove which he carried about with
him."

As the men talked, Jean's eyes began to flash with excitement.
How he would like to be with those hunted priests of Paris! How
he longed to save many souls! What great work priests could do
for God!

Blaise continued, "But, you know, the people of Paris wouldn't
be put down by the revolutionary tribunal. I remember I was
quite near the Halles market one day, when I saw a priest bringing
Viaticum to a poor man: what was my amazement when I saw
some armed *sans-culottes*, apparently from the dregs of the people,
give him military honours and go with him to the door of the
dying man; and then wait to escort him back to church. Everybody was kneeling. That's heroism, isn't it?"

Ignace exclaimed, "Yes, I have heard that the revolutionary
tribunal is very capricious. (I have heard more than you think.)
It will let that sort of thing pass, and yet I know of two humble
creatures from the Artois who were sent to the scaffold just because
some relics of the beggar Benedict-Joseph Labre were found
among their possessions. He's the patron of persecuted French
Catholics."

Mathieu Vianney started. "What! Say that name again. Did you
say Benedict-Joseph Labre? Why, surely I've told you about him.
He was the beggar who came here when I was a boy of seventeen.
Oh, a long time ago. I was much struck with him, he was so gentle
and refined-looking. Yes, now I come to think of it, he did come

from the Artois. He'd just left the Trappists. We gave him food and shelter for the night, and he wrote us a courteous letter of thanks. I have it here in the oak cupboard by the clock."

"Well, I should hide that," said Blaise. "If they came to search here and found it, you'd end your days on the scaffold."

"Ah well, we're all in the hands of God," said Mathieu imperturbably. "Our death won't come before we are ripe for the harvest."

Jean put down the statue he was modelling and said to his father, "Do tell us all about him again! I do wish I'd met him."

"Oh," said his father smiling, "it was a long time before you were born. Perhaps he brought a blessing to our house, who knows?"

Ignace, who had been waiting to put a word in, said: "I knew him in Rome."

"Did you really?" said Mathieu. "Tell us about him. I've always wondered what became of him."

"Well," said Ignace, "he's dead, you know—or hadn't you heard? He died about ten years ago—in Holy Week, to be exact, in the church of the Madonna dei Monti. The priest had been chanting the Passion, and just as he reached the word 'exspiravit' Benedict-Joseph Labre grew faint. He staggered out of the church and collapsed on the steps. A butcher picked him up and took him back to his house to die.

"As soon as word got about that he was dead, the children began to run about the streets crying 'The saint is dead! The saint is dead!' Everyone knew him. He used to spend his days praying in the Colosseum and at all the shrines and churches all over Rome. He was very quiet, very humble. The poor people all thought he was a saint—another Saint Alexis. During that last week he'd been seen at Saint Praxedes' before the column of Our Lord's Scourging. He had a great devotion to the Sacred Passion and would climb the Scala Santa on his knees in all weathers.

"After he died they opened the satchel he was carrying and found some books of devotion and a few hard crusts of bread. I went to see him lying in state on Easter Day and he looked very beautiful and peaceful. But oh, those Italians, how they quarrelled over his relics! I bought some pictures of him from another hawker by the church. I've got them in here rolled up in some sheepskin. Very dangerous! I'll let you have one as thank-offering for your good wine, M'sieu Vianney," he added, "but you'd better hide that too."

Jean came to lean over his father's shoulder and gaze at the rude lithograph of the saint who had come to this very farm when his father was a boy. Here was the beggar in rags, and not too clean— a living indictment of all the luxury which had preceded the Revolution. His thin hands were crossed on his breast and his eyes, the eyes of a contemplative, were downcast. He reminded Jean of an Ecce Homo statue he had seen in church—Christ wounded for our iniquities, Christ carrying the weight of our griefs. The Passion of Christ had been bequeathed to him. It was said that when little boys threw stones and struck him, he would pick up the stones and kiss them as the blood trickled from his cuts. The hardships of his pilgrimages surpassed any of the mortifications in the Trappist Monastery of Sept-Fonts which he had left.

"Please, Father," Jean repeated, "will you tell us about him once again?"

The two hawkers drew closer to their host, and Mathieu began:

"Oh yes, I remember him very well. It was in July. He had been ill. And I seem to remember he told us he had been to Paray-le-Monial to pray at the Visitation convent of a nun whose name I can't recall now. She had spread devotion to the Heart of Our Lord. Some nursing nuns were very kind to him and cared for him in their little hospital. He was on his way, he told us, to Assisi, to pray at the tomb of Saint Francis. I remember he wore a dreadful three-cornered hat and a novice's tunic; his buckled shoes were falling into holes. What was so strange, I remember, was that his attacks of despair in the monastery, so he told my father, had led his prior to dismiss him. But the despair always seemed to leave him when he was on the road again. So he must have thought it was his vocation to live as he did on the highways of Christendom. He knelt down with us when we said family prayers at night with the other poor men. He ate very little at our table. When he was at his prayers I couldn't take my eyes off him. It was easy to pray when he was there. Yes, I'm sure, now, he left a blessing on this house. How wonderful to hear that the people of Rome acclaimed him as a saint! We have had a saint at our table!"

In the distance the clock struck the hour. Mathieu rose painfully from the step and stretched himself.

"I must go back to work now. Come and see us again when you are passing this way."

The pedlars wished him farewell and disappeared down the road.

"What can I do for you, Father?" said Jean.

"You want to help me, child? Well, the best thing you can do is to take the flour to the mill on the donkey. Don't hurry him. It's a very hot day and I don't want either of you to get sunstroke."

Just then a playmate of Jean's came into the yard. Her name was Marion Vincent.

"May I come too?" she asked. "I want to lead the donkey by the bridle. I'm old enough to help Jean now."

"You needn't bring the donkey home at once," said Mathieu. "I think you could take him to graze at Montmerle. You'll find your sister there with the cows."

While his father was loading the donkey, Jean went in again to fetch the knitting he was always supposed to take with him, and his beloved wooden statue of Our Lady. Also a hunk of bread from the bread bin. Then he set out with Marion.

If St. Benedict-Joseph Labre had prayed with all the roads of Christendom as his chapel, little Jean Vianney used the field of Montmerle as his private oratory. That afternoon he could think of nothing else but the pedlars' stories and the tales of heroic priests in Paris. It seemed to him that the greatest vocation in the world was to be a priest and save souls from the Devil.

How he envied Benedict-Joseph Labre for being able to pray for days on end in the Colosseum surrounded by memories of the martyrs. Then he thought of the persecution of Christians at Lyons long ago, of young St. Blandina, who endured every imaginable kind of torture, amazing everyone by her courage. The old records said of the martyrs of Lyons: "The confessors march, brimful of alacrity and joy, their faces shining with glory and beauty. Even their chains seem noble adornings, like a bride's robe, with gold-embroidered fringes; the martyrs diffused the sweet odour of Christ, so that many of the onlookers thought they were perfumed. The tortures which were inflicted upon them were varied, like numberless flowers woven into crowns and offered to the Father."

As the stench of burning flesh floated up in the arena, the young girl Blandina, after enduring all manner of anguish, was tossed by a bull, and at length, while she was still breathing, they strangled her.

And then in the second century there was St. Irenaeus, from Asia Minor, a disciple of St. Polycarp, who repeated untiringly what the Apostle John had taught him about Jesus. This St. Irenaeus, later Bishop of Lyons, never forgot that the first commandment of Jesus was to love. Jean Vianney knew that Lyons, like Rome, had its Catacombs, and he longed one day to explore them, in order to love God in union with the hearts of those early martyrs. It was from those strange underground haunts of death that the flame of hope sprang forth.

As Jean gazed into the distance, lost in his thoughts, Marion Vincent became impatient. She tugged at his smock. "Hurry, Jean," she said, "or we'll never be there before sunset."

As they walked along Marion kept looking up at Jean, a little worried by his abstraction. He was a thin, agile boy with deep blue eyes and dark brown hair, a determined jaw and chin and a sensitive nose, already rather long. He loved to chaff and tease, though not unkindly. He was extremely observant, and had he been less loving, he might have been inclined to mockery. But even in those early days there was a kindliness about his expression which was beyond his years.

It was extremely hot on the dusty white road that afternoon. They stopped by an oak tree and Marion said hesitatingly, "Let's sit down for a moment, Jean. I'm a little tired."

"Yes, if you like. It is hot, isn't it, Marion?"

So they tethered the donkey and sat down together. Then she looked up at him with her innocent eyes and said, rather tremulously, "Jean-Marie, if our parents agreed, we could pledge our betrothal."

He looked very much surprised.

"Oh, no, never," he replied with conviction. "No, do not speak about that, Marion." He rose quickly and unleashed the donkey, and the two children set off again towards the windmill.

Sixty years later, Marion, still unmarried, was at the door of her house with her distaff when she was questioned by the commission enquiring into the heroic qualities of her old play-fellow Jean, and she told them of this vanished idyll with tears in her eyes.

When the flour had been delivered, Marion went home alone, rather pathetically, and Jean took the donkey to Montmerle. The descendants of the blackbirds which gave their name to this valley are there to this very day, but there are fewer trees than there were a hundred and fifty years ago. Montmerle was a quiet, green, gently curving valley, lovely with wild roses, alders and aspens. In the dip meandered a slow, sedgy stream. On one of the gentle slopes grew three willow trees, which have been preserved until now. The one that Jean especially loved had been split in the middle, either by lightning or by age; he could get into this cleft and pretend it was a little chapel. The niche, prepared by nature, he filled with moss, flowers, sweet herbs and leafy branches, making a small oratory for his wooden statue.

Jean's sister Gothon was always glad of his company, for he told her such lovely stories. On that hot afternoon he had much to tell her about the beggar who had once come to their house, and about the martyrs of Lyons. After a while he begged her to do some knitting on his sock for him. "I want to pray near the brook," he said. He meant that he was going to kneel down inside his tree and say his rosary.

In a nearby copse, overlooking the valley, crouched a man in ragged clothes. His grimy face was haggard and hungry-looking, his hair unkempt and dishevelled. He remained utterly still, for he must stay concealed till nightfall. He watched the little boy curiously. The gentle summer breeze lifted the silver alder leaves, and they glittered in the late afternoon light of this enchanted place. A blackbird sang Vespers from an oak tree. A little cloud of mosquitoes buzzed in the heat haze, the stream murmured timelessly, as the boy let the beads of his rosary slip through his fingers and his mind dwelt on mysteries, joyful, glorious and sorrowful.

After a while his sister came to join him. She said: "I see our friends coming. Supposing we make up a Corpus Christi procession? Can you remember a few of the hymns they used to sing before they closed the church?"

The other shepherds were called André Provin, François Duclos and Jean Dumond, and there was a fourth boy (his name is not recorded), who carried a stick. He was rather a bully, and often hit Jean on the legs. He stood by sniggering while the children lined up to form a procession. Jean, of course, played the part of the curé. He made a cross from two branches, and they all sang hymns to Our Lady, *Alma Redemptoris Mater,* and some of the Eucharistic hymns like the *Pange lingua gloriosi,* which they remembered from the days before the Reign of Terror.

The beggar in the bushes watched them.

However, the little boys didn't like praying for long. Quite soon Jean's flock scattered to play a game of quoits.

Seventy years later André Provin recounted that Jean was skilful at this game and he often won. This saddened the others, and when he saw how upset they were, he would say, "Well, you shouldn't have played." And then to console them, he would give them back what he had won, and even a sou or two more.

When it came time to eat, Jean would share his large hunk of bread with one of the poorer shepherds. The little Duclos boy remembered how Jean said to him: "Come now, I've got plenty: we'll share it." If some of the children swore or lost their tempers with each other or fought with sticks, he would scold them gently. Then the bully with the stick would strike Jean, assured of course that he would not hit back.

Abbé Monnin said that "the air around him was filled with a

secret enchantment." Even in those early days of his boyhood,
Jean was able to captivate others. He would speak to them of Our
Lady, and fill their hearts with love. Strange to think that in the
Reign of Terror, in this quiet, hidden spot in the depths of the
French countryside, there should have been a little apostle to those
children who had been brought up in religious ignorance.

It was at Montmerle that Jean-Marie gathered his lifetime's store
of the beauties of nature. As Monseigneur Trochu has pointed out,
there is not one of his catechism instructions in which he does not
several times mention brooks, forests, trees, birds, flowers, dew,
lilies, balm, perfume or honey. He remembered these things during
the years when he was a prisoner between the hard boards of his
confessional. As a boy, he had known pure air and the light of the
sun. He had gazed on flights of birds, on little fishes swimming in
brooks; he had breathed in the scent of flowers and the balmy
breezes of spring. Francis Thompson said that nature is God's
daughter, and she reveals herself most fully to her Father's friends.

But to return to that afternoon. While the children played, the
man in the copse kept to his place of concealment. He was a priest
disguised as a carpenter. He was very tall, very, very thin and
exhausted-looking. (It was no doubt after looking at priests like
him and at Abbé Balley that Jean in later life defined saints as
"skin thrown over an armful of bones.") He had been in hiding all
day from the *sans-culottes*. He had just heard of the martyrdom of
some of his fellow priests.

Jean, with Gothon, was the last to leave Montmerle. The priest
gave a long, low whistle. Jean knew the signal, and when he was
quite sure that the other boys were out of earshot he answered. At
last the priest ventured out of the copse. Night had fallen in the
wonderful opaline, heliotrope glow of the Lyonnais sunset, and the
distant hills of Mont d'Or were bathed in golden light: it was the
hour between hawk and buzzard.

The priest's satchel was slung over his shoulder. Beneath the
mallet and plane and the other tools of his trade, he had concealed
the holy oils for the sick, the chalice and other vessels for Mass.

The patriots never guessed about the hard and dangerous life this carpenter led, how he might be up all night, walking long distances from one barn to another—saying Mass, attending a deathbed, teaching children in secret—always in peril of betrayal and a terrible death.

"Ah," said Jean, "there's no moon. You'll be quite safe. The boys went home some time ago. Have a piece of my bread! I saved it for you. Let me carry your tools. There will be some good soup when we get home, and I know there are some peaches we picked for you. I know what you're hiding there! We've got some Mass wine for you too. How I wish I were old enough to receive Holy Communion! When will that be?"

After half an hour they reached the house of the Vianneys. Jean went on ahead and looked in, in case there should be strangers about. The priest came last, tottering with fatigue.

The room he entered was square. The door was in the middle, with windows to the right and left. In the far left-hand corner was the parents' bed in an alcove, and the priest noticed above the bed a simple picture of the Blessed Virgin Mary. Against the wall opposite the door was a huge old cupboard, and the big grandfather clock. On the right-hand side was the hearth, and on the left of that the oven for baking. In the middle of the room was a long narrow table with a bread-bin attached. There were benches on either side—long enough to accommodate as many as twenty beggars.

The priest was given water to wash in, and a member of the family bathed his feet. He was given a fresh shift smelling of the lavender hedge on which it had dried during the hot day, and he was made to drink some warm, spiced wine. He was almost too tired to speak.

Madame Vianney bustled round, trying to feed all her children at once. Jean-Marie must have been thinking of his mother when he said, long afterwards, "The Virgin Mary is like a mother who has many children and is continually occupied in going from one to another." Imperceptibly, sweetly, the love of Mary had been born in his heart through his love for his mother.

"The heart of Mary is so tender towards us, that the hearts of all mothers in the world are like icicles compared with hers. . . . I have often drawn from that source. There would have been nothing left of it long ago, had it not been inexhaustible."

And he had also learned God's love from his own father: "When He sees us coming, He leans His heart very low towards His little creature, just like a father who bends down to listen to his little child speaking to him."

"In the morning we must do as a baby in his cradle does; as soon as he opens his eyes, he looks quickly about the room to see his mother. When he sees her, he smiles. When he cannot see her, he cries."

Speaking about the priest giving the Eucharistic Bread, he compared it to the mother who says to her child, "Here you are, my little one, eat."

"A child, when he sees his mother, springs towards her. He struggles with those who hold him back; he opens his little mouth and stretches forth his little hands to embrace her."

And when in later life he had reached the heights of mystical prayer, he could find no sweeter comparison of the love of God for the soul than a mother taking her child's head between her hands and covering it with kisses. He says in one of his catechism instructions: "Oh beautiful life, beautiful union of the soul with Our Lord! . . . The inner life is like an ocean of love into which the soul plunges. God holds the soul, when she has reached this state, just as a mother clasps the head of her child to cover it with kisses and caresses. Our Lord is hungry for her!"

But Marie Vianney, the saint's mother, unlike many mothers, had room in her wide heart for others besides her own children. Not only for the beggars who flocked to her door asking for charity, but also, at great peril to her life, for the priests in hiding. On that evening, however, the lights were dimmed and the door was locked even against beggars, lest they should be spies and the priest should be betrayed. All the members of the household rested for a while. When the old clock struck midnight, the room was arranged as a chapel. Two candles were lighted and an altar-stone in the form of a slate was placed on the long table.

The children were waked up in the room over the barn. (The barn is still standing, but it has been condemned as unsafe.) They came down the narrow staircase rubbing their eyes. Jean alone was not sleepy; his great blue eyes were glowing with joy.

When his mother and father and Catherine went to Communion, his eyes followed them avidly. A thick black cloth had been drawn across the windows so the lights would not betray them. With what dread Madame Vianney listened for any footfall outside!

In those penitential years of the Reign of Terror, Jean's vocation was formed. His heart overflowed with pity for the children who were too young to remember the happy days of Corpus Christi processions, or the blessing of Sunday Mass. Young though he was, he had a heart like his parents'. He foresaw the future when many more children would be born who would never even hear of the love of God, and he longed to devote himself to their service.

3. THE DEEPENING OF A VOCATION

IN LATER YEARS, JEAN SAID THAT HE HAD LONGED FOR SOLITUDE FROM the age of eleven. It is interesting to note that it was when he was eleven that he made his first confession. Abbé Groboz, the priest who went about disguised as a cook, once came to call at the farm of the Vianneys. After blessing the children he turned to Jean.

"How old are you?"

"Eleven."

"How long since you have been to confession?"

"But I have never been to confession," replied the child.

"Ah, well, let us hear you at once."

"I shall always remember it," he used to say. "It was at home under our clock."

Two years afterwards, at haymaking time in 1799, Jean, who had acquired the nickname "*le petit Gras*" ("little Fatty") from his school friends ("Look at *le petit Gras* wrestling with his good angel"), received his first Holy Communion in the house of the one-time Dame de Pingon, near Ecully. His sister Gothon, who was there too, still remembered it after his death.

It was all done with the greatest secrecy, in the darkness before daybreak. Hidden under their long cloaks, the mothers brought veils for the girls, white armbands for the boys, and candles. For fear that lights might be seen from outside, a great haycart was drawn up before the shuttered windows. (This room, looking out on an old-fashioned courtyard, has been preserved.)

Jean had prayed hard in the retreat which preceded the great

23

event. He remembered this Communion all his life. No doubt he was thinking of it when he said that when a Christian rises from the holy table he leaves with all heaven in his heart.

His sister Marguerite recounts: "I was there . . . my brother was so happy that he did not want to leave the room where he had had the joy of receiving Communion for the first time."

In the autumn of that year, hope for relief from religious persecution arose in the person of General Bonaparte, who now led the destinies of France. Soon this hawk-eyed young Corsican would devastate Europe with his ambitions. First the years of victory, and then the price to pay. But the details of his rise to power would not be known by those humble peasants of the Lyonnais. They lived according to the rhythm of the seasons, and their lives were governed by good or bad harvests, by rainfall or sunshine.

Jean was loved by the villagers for his open countenance and his charming courtesy. He greeted everyone he met. He was a strong, wiry, well-knit lad and a willing worker. Soon after the time of his First Communion he was treated as an adult, assuming a large share of the farm work. His biographer Joseph Vianey, who got his information at first hand, testifies to the variety of the chores he did and remarks: "By observing so many varied aspects of nature, he was unconsciously quickening his powers of observation. He was laying up a store of picturesque imagery, for later his sermons were full of apt expressions: they sparkle, in spite of constructions which can hardly be considered grammatically correct. Above all, he strengthened his faith in Divine Providence, which seems to have ordained that the farmer should be forced to recognize its presence everywhere by depending for success in the fields on the marvellous interplay of many factors."

Of course the responsibilities which the boy assumed on the farm ruled out the possibility of his having further education; in fact, he reached the age of seventeen without having had more than a year at school. But we must not make the common mistake of identifying intellectual development with formal education. The Italian poet Jacopone da Todi says: "I leave you the syllogisms, the verbal traps and the subtle calculations. . . . I leave you the art of which Aristotle had the secret. A simple and pure intelligence will soar, unaided by philosophy, and will reach the presence of God."

The women of that remarkable peasant family must have had their moments of intuition about Jean. When Catherine, the eldest sister who died young, was on her deathbed, she spoke of an angel hovering over the head of her brother Jean.

And the beggars, tramps and vagrants would have their tale to tell. On his way back from working in the fields, Jean would collect everyone he met. It was well known that no man was ever turned away from the Vianneys' farm. He could wheedle articles of clothing from his mother, who, to please him, would open the door of the cupboard and look through her shelves. The more repulsive these vagrants looked, the more tenderly did Jean care for them. He cleansed them of dirt and vermin. He washed their ragged clothing and put it to dry in the oven, on a hurdle which he made especially for this purpose. After he had installed the men comfortably on a bed of hay in the barn, he would carefully sweep and scrub the places where they had sat in the kitchen, as his father had done before him.

Mathieu Vianney, hard-headed notwithstanding his great generosity, would become lavish to the point of extravagance when his son begged. He would tell Jean to take wood on the donkey's back to poor people in the village. Yes, he could take as much as the donkey would carry.

But Jean's care was not solely for the bodies of the poor. He would try to teach them prayers or would read the catechism or the gospels to them, or tell them stories of the saints, so that they would leave the Vianneys' hearth strengthened and comforted in their troubles.

The tramps of those revolutionary years must have been quite alarming, and one does not blame some of the farmers for refusing to open their doors to those disquieting creatures of the night. But there was no fear in the hearts of the Vianneys.

"The mercy of God is like an overflowing torrent. It sweeps all hearts along on its way."

Jean always saw human beings, whether clothed in rags or silk, as hungry souls to feed. One day he confided to his mother, "If I were a priest, I would want to win many souls."

Before he was sixteen, that is, on April the 18th, 1802, Notre Dame de Paris was opened again for public worship. Church bells long silent pealed joyfully. Crosses were put up again at crossroads. Corpus Christi processions began again—those processions, so beloved by the people of France that even during the Reign of Terror in Paris the humble folk complained that they missed them; garlands of box were placed outside houses, and white sheets stuck with little bunches of field flowers hung down from windows. Rose petals strewed the village street. And here again were all the village people, men bareheaded and women veiled, walking in procession, two by two, in the sunlight, holding lighted candles and singing the *Pange lingua gloriosi*. And here was the priest under the silken canopy again, holding the shining monstrance so long hidden.

Out came the statues, crucifixes and holy water stoups which had lain in the depths of farmhouse cupboards. And now Jean would not have to hide any more when he was making his little clay statues of saints: these were useful to him, for when his friends took his share of the work so that he could go to Mass, he would give them statuettes in payment. Naturally he was teased by his work fellows. Although François, his kindly elder brother, blushed for him, he would be very loyal about him behind his back. He knew that the only thing this younger brother loved was prayer. He guessed that during the midday siesta under the oak tree, instead of sleeping like the others, Jean would lie with his face to the ground and pray, pray as if his life depended on it. At night they shared a bed in the stable. Sometimes François was kept awake by Jean's light, for he often read the lives of the saints and the Gospels far into the night, thus beginning a lifelong habit of stealing time from sleep.

Jean could have held his own with the village lads who twitted him, for he had keen powers of observation and a mordant wit. But out of charity he muffled his wit and kept silent when he could have won the day with repartee. Like St. Francis of Assisi, he was glad to be counted a fool for Christ's sake.

St. Thomas Aquinas says that "the soul is the form of the body and imprints its own beauty on it." The other lads must have known, as they watched that spare, austere form and looked into those blue eyes brimming over with kindliness, that Jean was not like them. They searched for a chink in his armour. They did all they could to make him lose his temper, for they sensed that he was impetuous. But they did not succeed. When he was away for his few moments in church, they would play practical jokes on him and hide his work tools in hedges and ditches. When he returned he had only to look them straight in the eyes to learn who had done it. Then he would thank the guilty one very kindly and amusingly for having taken such great care of his tools. It was his engaging personality and charming manners, that gentleness which is so especially gentle when it is built on the foundation of impetuosity, which won them in the end.

Jean took his farm work very seriously. He was impatient with himself for not being able to work as fast as François in the vineyard. One night he came home exhausted and said to his mother that he had tired himself out trying to keep up with his brother. The following morning a nun from Lyons called at the farm. She gave a holy picture to each of the children, says Marguerite, but she kept the choicest treasure to the end for Jean.

"She had a little statue of the Holy Virgin in a case. We all wanted that statue. But she made a present of it to Jean-Marie. The day after that he went to work with François. Before starting his task, he devoutly kissed the feet of the statuette, then he threw it in front of him as far as he could. When he'd reached it, he picked it up with respect and repeated his first action. . . . When he came back to the house in the evening he said to my mother, 'Always put your trust in the Blessed Virgin. I prayed to her so hard today, and she helped me very much. I was able to keep up with my brother without getting tired.'"

Years afterwards, in one of his loveliest homilies, he spoke of Our Lady as a worker in the vineyard, which is the state of grace: "O *la belle ouvrière!*"—"Oh, what a blessed and beautiful labourer! The good God might have created a more beautiful world than this, but He could not have given existence to a creature more perfect than Mary. She is the tower built in the midst of the vineyard of the Lord."

4. JEAN MAKES A FRIEND

THE YEAR 1830: JEAN WAS NOW SEVENTEEN. HIS SISTER CATHERINE had married and there had been all the expenses connected with her dowry and the wedding. Moreover, Mathieu Vianney had been obliged by the military authorities to purchase François's release from conscription. With all this, and the added worry of taxation, Mathieu was in a most anxious frame of mind during that summer.

But a vocation is not ruled by time or the convenience of mortals. One day Jean got his mother by herself and told her what she already knew: "I want to become a priest."

She wept a little, but after a while she wiped away her tears on her apron. "Now you speak to your father. Do it during the afternoon siesta. He can't make an excuse to do some other job. He'll have to listen to you."

Trembling with fear (for Mathieu could sometimes be formidable), he spoke to his father.

"No!" cried Mathieu. "It's quite impossible! What with your sister's marriage and having to buy François's exemption. . . . Who would be left at the farm to help me with the work? And then my rheumatism is worse. I can't afford the wages of a new farm worker. No, don't mention it again. I won't hear of it."

For two long years Mathieu went on saying no, and Jean, who believed in Divine Providence, made no complaint. He continued to work for him with all his might, not fully realizing, perhaps, that his work and obedience were part of his training for the priesthood.

In the meantime, in the neighbouring hamlet of Ecully Abbé
Balley was installed as Curé. He had been a monk before the Revolution. Now, at fifty-two, he was prematurely aged and broken in
health as the result of ascetical practices combined with the difficulties of his ministry during the Reign of Terror. But he had lost
none of his priestly zeal; his first thought, once he had been appointed Curé, was to open a school for future priests in the presbytery. He taught them himself.

This wonderful priest should be made the patron saint of friendship under difficult circumstances; for, indeed, had he not be-
friended Jean when everything seemed against him, Jean would
not have become a priest. In the comparatively new church of
Ecully there is a wall painting of Abbé Balley receiving his last
Communion from Jean. He has the face of a contemplative.

Abbé Balley was the youngest of sixteen children. He had a long
bald head rather like St. Bruno's, a Roman profile, an aquiline
nose; the whole expression of his face was aspiring and eager. The
motto of the religious Order to which he belonged was "*Supere-
mineat caritas*"—"Charity above all"—and the arms of the congregation showed a hand holding a flaming heart. He was very tall
and should have eaten well to support such a large frame. He
wore a hair shirt, iron chains and took the discipline. An old
parishioner of his described him in this way: "He was a great big
person who seemed to be only skin and bones. He looked as if he
never ate enough to meet his needs." He wept as he said his Mass,
and merely to hear him exclaim, "My God, I love you!" filled one
with devotion. Though he appeared severe and imposing, his eyes
were kind. When he came to Ecully, he brought his sister with him
as housekeeper. She had been a nun before the Revolution had
closed her convent. Devout and intelligent, she still kept to the
ways of the Soeur Marie Joseph Dorothea she had been.

One day Madame Vianney, accompanied by her sister Marguerite Humbert, both very nervous and apprehensive, came to the
Curé's door. They rang the bell and were admitted by the housekeeper. Plucking up their courage, they begged him to accept nine-

teen-year-old Jean as a pupil. He said he was too busy to take even
one more pupil. And so the interview ended.

Then Catherine's husband went to see him and persuaded him
at least to interview the candidate. When Monsieur Balley saw
Jean, the thin, pale, austere-looking boy with the wonderful smile,
he took him instantly into his heart and into his life: he said at
once, "All right, as for that one, I accept him."

Jean went to live with his aunt Marguerite Humbert at Ecully,
and every day he had lessons with Monsieur Balley. His troubles
now began in earnest. He who was so good a workman in vineyard
and field, so clever at fashioning clay statues, who could tell the
most marvellous stories to his brothers and sisters and knew the
Gospels and the lives of the saints by heart—when it came to learning his Latin declensions he was entirely nonplussed. He could
read and write, but how could he possibly master Latin grammar
when he hardly knew the grammar of his native tongue?

The other pupils—all younger than he—began to look down
on him and laugh at him. In fact, one twelve-year-old called
Mathias lost patience with him altogether and struck him in the
face in front of the others. Jean made a heroic act of self-mastery.
He knelt down before this child and begged pardon for his stupidity. They became friends for life.

Jean had a large appetite (in fact, his penances with regard to
food in later life suggest that he imagined himself inclined to
greed). Now, as a mortification to spur himself on with his studies,
he begged his aunt to pour his soup on to his bread before she had
added butter. If she forgot, he would look mutinous as he swallowed his soup; in fact, as if, his aunt reported, each mouthful were
choking him.

He continued his prodigal almsgiving. When his father had
given him a pair of good new shoes, Jean gave them to a beggar he
met on the road: he was soundly scolded when he came home bare-
foot.

And here the wise Monsieur Balley intervened. He noticed that
Jean was not eating the amount of food absolutely essential to a
boy who was still growing. He said to him: "No doubt one must

pray well and do penance, but one must eat enough to preserve one's health."

In 1806 Jean was twenty, and no further advanced in his Latin declensions and verbs than he had been a year before. Very much discouraged, he went to Monsieur Balley and said, "I want to go home. It's no good."

Monsieur Balley talked to him like a father. He warned him that if he went home now he would never be a priest: and then it would be "*adieu les âmes*"—farewell to souls.

During those arduous years of study by the light of an uncertain lamp Jean found himself unable to master the simplest rules of grammar. He became convinced of his own intellectual incapacity. That was not a bad thing. ("He hath filled the hungry with good things, and the rich He hath sent empty away.") His soul was to be scoured by a deep and fierce humility and invaded by something much deeper and more luminous than earthly learning— the light of the Holy Spirit, the stirring of mystical perception. There came to him all the gifts of wisdom and counsel which fill the heart of a saint.

And all this time the country districts, especially those furthest removed from the towns, were without priests. When villagers flocked to Cardinal Fesch at Lyons and begged for priests, he was heartbroken, for he could do nothing to help them. And then one day Jean made a vow. He would go to the sanctuary of La Louvesc and pray at the tomb of Francis Regis, the apostle of Velay and of the Vivarais; he would go the whole distance of a hundred kilometres (around sixty miles) on foot, and beg for his bread on the way. (In those days of stage coaches, before the coming of the railways, the average man travelled as great distances on the roads of Christendom as his mediaeval ancestor on pilgrimages to far-off Rome and Compostella. It was the age of speed which restricted men's journeyings!)

Early one morning Monsieur Balley saw him off. He carried a staff and his rosary. As he walked, his mind was concentrated on a single thought: souls to be saved, souls to be saved. The hot summer sun rose high over the horizon, and soon he left the highway and mounted to the higher altitude of the mountain paths. At twilight he breathed in the evening sweetness of flowers. He revelled in the fields, the meadows in full bloom, and the pine forests with the lofty peaks of the Alps behind them in the distance.

As he climbed peaks and skirted ravines, he thought of St. Francis Regis himself in those early years of the seventeenth century, consumed with zeal for souls as he walked tirelessly in snow and against piercing winds to minister to the peasants of these regions. From time immemorial the mountains, with their ravines and granite slopes, have nurtured contemplatives. St. John of the Cross led his novices to mountainous places and encouraged them to separate, to pull up their hoods over their heads and learn to pray in the solitude by the murmuring streams.

In the distance Jean could see bright yellow broom glowing on the hillsides; its bitter-sweet scent came to him on the wind. He heard the canticle of wild torrents. He gazed at shuddering leaves, glittering in the sun—lovely sycamores, and pine trees, like seven-branched candelabra, swayed by Pentecostal winds.

Towards evening he had not yet eaten. He came to a cottage. The door was open and he could hear the family saying their prayers. Remembering how his own family always gave hospitality to all and sundry, he knocked timidly and asked for a crust of bread and a place in the barn for the night. The father of the family came to the door and looked at Jean suspiciously. "Clean, properly dressed and strong enough to work—aren't you ashamed of yourself?" he said. "You idler, you glutton. There's plenty of work for strong arms like yours. If you don't clear off at once I'll set the dogs on you, or I'll call the police."

That was what happened to him all the way. But he kept to his vow that he would walk to La Louvesc as a beggar. He drank from streams, he ate roots and grass.

That night, his hunger unassuaged, he fell into the sleep of exhaustion on the bare ground under the stars. He awoke at dawn, feeling lightheaded. As he rose to his feet, everything turned black and he thought he was going to faint. At length he recovered enough to stagger to the nearest hamlet. There he saw a house with a woman at the door, unwinding a skein of wool. She looked kindly enough. He went up to her and asked for a piece of bread. She gave him a keen glance but made no reply to his request. Instead she presented him with the end of the thread and asked him to pull it back from the doorway into the garden. He took the thread and stepped back. As soon as he was across the threshold, she slammed the door in his face.

Tramps along the road were kinder, and two or three of them gave him a few dry crusts. At long last he reached La Louvesc, exhausted but triumphant. At once he went to pray at the shrine where the bones of St. Francis Regis were enclosed in a walnut reliquary above the high altar. He knelt down and looked upward. "Oh, great, good saint," he prayed, "give me the grace to learn enough Latin to pass my theology."

After spending a day there in prayer and in visiting all the hallowed places, he made his confession and asked the Jesuit who heard him to commute his vow to journey as a beggar. He could not, he felt, return in the way he had come. In later life he was to say, "I would never advise anyone to make a vow of begging."

On his return to Ecully his prayer to St. Francis Regis was answered. He now progressed sufficiently in his studies for Abbé Groboz, who had become the Cardinal's private secretary, to put him on the list of those aspiring to the priesthood.

In the Lent of 1807, just before he was twenty-one, he was confirmed, on a very snowy day, by Cardinal Fesch, Napoleon's uncle.

In order to catch up with the arrears of the Revolution the Cardinal had to confirm great numbers of candidates together. In 1807, for example, he confirmed no fewer than 30,000 people, and as the churches would not hold such crowds, he had to do it out of doors. Jean added the name Baptiste to Jean-Marie. We are inclined to become friendly with the saints who suit our temperaments. That is probably why we choose their names. The Baptist, that greatest among the sons of men, was indeed a twin-soul of Jean's—he who had left his parents in early youth, who fed on locusts and wild honey and whose great cry was "Repentance." And when one puts oneself under the patronage of a certain saint, *noblesse oblige* enters in—he is under a kind of spiritual obligation to grant us particular graces to do God's work. This will be seen more clearly after Jean goes to Ars as Curé. Speaking in later life of the Holy Ghost, Jean was to say: "The Holy Spirit rests in the soul of the just like the dove in her nest. He hatches good desires in a pure soul, as the dove hatches her young."

For two years he lived in the peace and strength of the sevenfold gift and then disaster—at least, so it would seem to mortal eyes—came. In the autumn of 1809 a sergeant appeared at the door of his father's farm with Jean's calling-up papers.

5. *A YEAR IN HIDING*

JEAN ARRIVED AT THE LYONS BARRACKS ON OCTOBER THE 26TH WITH his fellow recruits. His life of mortification had not prepared him for soldiering, and almost immediately he fell ill with a fever. On the 28th a doctor had him moved to the hospital. He was there for a fortnight and his whole family came to see him. On the 12th of November, he was well enough to leave with his convoy in a cart, but it was so cold that when he reached Roanne he was again shivering with fever. They put him in the hospital of the Augustinian nuns; there he stayed for six weeks, and the nuns did their best to spoil him. At length, by the 5th of January, he was considered fit to leave for Spain. He was to report to Capitaine Blanchard that afternoon. On the way he passed the church (it is still standing), and that visit was providentially his undoing. He slipped in to say a prayer, and as he later said, "All my troubles melted like snow in the sunshine." And of course he forgot the time. When he got to the barracks, it was too late. The door was shut.

He went to report again next morning, the feast of the Epiphany, still feeling shaky. The captain, outraged, threatened him with all kinds of punishments. Jean began to picture himself in the place of the miserable deserters he had seen, with two policemen on either side swearing and storming. But the captain only ordered him to rejoin his regiment with all speed. So, carrying his heavy sack, he took the road to Clermont and went on to the mountains of Forez.

With the best will in the world he couldn't walk as fast as he wanted to. His sack was terribly heavy, his legs felt like lead, he was weak and his head was swimming. Oh, he'd never catch up with his regiment again. And a cold, sinister little wind was blowing. A pallid twilight fell. He took a path leading off the road into a wood, and then through the wood into a ploughed field where he could rest for a moment. Unknown to him, these deep, impenetrable woods were the hiding place of many deserters. He started to say his rosary. Turning to the Virgin Mary, his customary refuge, he prayed most trustingly that she should not desert him.

In each crisis of his life, one sees Jean under the special protection of the Mother of God. Her love is like a golden thread through the arras of his extraordinary life.

Jean had begun to know and love the writings of St. Louis-Marie Grignion de Montfort, who had declared that devotion to Mary would make the great saints that are to appear at the end of the world. The verbose style of St. Louis-Marie Grignion de Montfort's spiritual writings sets English teeth on edge. However, with patience one can sift out the pearls of wisdom. He says that when the Holy Spirit finds that a soul has drawn close to Mary, His dear and inseparable spouse, He quickens His activity of forming Jesus Christ in it.

Anyway, here was poor Jean shivering with fever, saying his rosary. As he reached the last Gloria Patri, he heard behind him a rustling of dead leaves. He turned, and all of a sudden, as if from nowhere, appeared a strange young man in a peasant blouse. He said to Jean abruptly, "What are you doing here? Come along with me." And he took Jean's sack and began to walk, motioning to Jean to follow him.

"We walked for a long time in the night through the mountain woods," Jean said later. "I was so tired that I found it very difficult to keep up."

The bitter wind blew, the raging winter torrents swept on their way down the gorges. Even today, though less thickly wooded than they were a hundred and fifty years ago, those hills are im-

pressive. At length the two of them reached the Madeleine mountains and passed the village of Les Noës.

After a while they got into conversation. "You don't look like
a soldier," said Guy (for that was the man's name).

"Oh, how true! But I must obey."

"If you will follow me, you can hide in our village which is
surrounded by woods."

"No, I couldn't. My parents have already had enough bother
about all this."

"Oh, don't worry. There are plenty of others who are hiding
in these parts."

Jean did not take a great deal of persuading. Conscription was
too new a thing in the modern world to have any roots in his conscience; he could hardly have felt that he was under any moral
obligation to fight in Napoleon's wars.

They were given refuge for the night in the hut of a maker of
sabots, an extremely poor man but hospitable. He and his wife
gave up their bed to this young man who looked ready to die of
hunger and fatigue. They even gave him clean sheets. Then for
two days Guy and Jean worked together in a sawmill, after which
Jean had to find other work. He went to the mayor, Paul Fayot,
who, strangely enough, had a fellow-feeling for deserters and was
already hiding two in his own barn. But when Jean appeared he
didn't exactly embrace him with delight. He scratched his head
and looked at him. No, he was too nice a lad to turn adrift.

"Look, you can go to my cousin over there, Claudine Fayot.
She's a widow with four children and keeps a farm. I'm sure she'll
be good to you."

That proved to be an understatement. This woman of thirty-
eight, who was to become a second mother to a saint, was one of
the most charitable souls he ever had the good fortune to meet.
She was particularly kind to the poor and would put aside a loaf
for them from each batch of bread coming from her oven. She
advised him to change his name—he became Jérôme Vincent—
told her children that he was a cousin and made quite sure that
they wouldn't chatter outside.

At first Jean hid during the day in the stable (it is still standing), and Mère Fayot would bring him his food in a wooden pail. Only at night-time, when there was no fear of patrolling soldiers on the look-out for deserters, would he risk coming to her house. It was during those winter evenings that Mère Fayot began to realize that a treasure had fallen into her family. He would read the Gospels or the lives of the saints aloud to them or tell them wonderful stories. One of the sons of the house, Jérôme, remembered many years afterwards how, when he wasn't behaving himself during evening prayers, his so-called cousin would give him a light tap with his hat. Jean at first shared a bed in the stable with thirteen-year-old Louis, but he spent so much of the night in prayer that soon another bed had to be put up so that Louis could sleep in peace. Mère Fayot loved Jean so much that she used to rise in the night, to see whether he was resting and was well covered.

In the depths of winter when the earth is frostbound, farm people enter a season of enforced leisure. Now that the snow lay in great drifts outside, Jean, unwilling to remain idle, opened a school for the peasants round about, giving lessons in reading, writing, and catechism. The children of the hamlet of Les Robins, the young people and even grown men came to learn from him, and the children liked the lessons so much that they asked to come again after supper. When the snow melted and farm work began again, the classes were held in the evening.

And all the time he was eaten up with anxiety about his parents, wondering whether rough soldiers would be billetted on them as a punishment for his not having rejoined the army. Also, it hurt him not to be able to go to church. The risk involved was clearly too great, and on Sundays when the others went to Mass he was left in charge of three-year-old Claudine. One winter morning before dawn, however, he did venture to go down the precipitous path to Les Noës to confession and Communion. After a while he began cautiously to go to Mass, and his recollection in prayer was soon observed by many members of the congregation, who were strongly attracted to him.

Winter passed and spring came with all its field work. Jean offered his services on the farm. It was arranged that if anyone in the family caught sight of soldiers in the vicinity a warning whistle would be given, so that Jean could slip into the stable, climb to the loft through an aperture in the rafters and conceal himself in the hay. The exact spot where he hid can still be pointed out, and also the stone platform on which his bed was set.[1]

That strange gift of second sight which he possessed in such an extraordinary degree in later life seems already to have been useful to him then. He would sense when the soldiers were coming and hide in time. Often they came to the stable at night, and he would lie quivering with fear in the hayloft while they searched below.

But one terrible day—it was a scorching summer afternoon—this intuition seems to have failed him. He heard the warning whistle and sped to his place of refuge, but perhaps the soldiers had seen the figure streaking through the fields. Anyway, they were extraordinarily persistent in their search. Completely covered by a great weight of new-mown hay, he was slowly suffocating, almost overcome by the fierce heat of the sun on the roof combined with the pungent odours of the stable, when a soldier drove a bayonet through the hay into his flesh. The pain was agonizing, but he uttered not a sound. He confessed later that he had never suffered so much in all his life, and that he promised God that he would never complain of anything again.

Presently it was found that Mère Fayot had become anaemic from overwork. Jean insisted on lending her a hundred francs, and he was delighted when the doctor ordered her to take the waters at Charbonnières-les-Bains, quite near his parents' village. Such an opportunity was not to be lost, and great was the surprise and delight of Madame Vianney when Mère Fayot appeared at her door with a letter from her son. She wept with joy and the women kissed one another.

"I want you to stay with us and we will look after you," Madame Vianney cried. Jean's father, however, once he was assured of

[1] I have seen all this, and met the descendants of the Fayots.

his son's safety, was not too overwhelmed with delight to inquire where this stranger had come from. He had already been heavily fined in an effort to make him disclose Jean's place of concealment —which, of course, he did not know—and he saw no reason why Jean should not now rejoin his regiment and put an end to this drain upon the family's resources. But Mère Fayot was adamant. "He's worth more than all your possessions," she said.

In mid-September Jean decided to have his theological books sent to him, and he offered to pay Mère Fayot for her hospitality. The books were brought by the widow Bibost, a devoted friend of the Vianneys. She will reappear later in the story.

But he hardly had time to settle down to work at Les Noës, for by mid-October there was joyful news. To celebrate his marriage with Marie Louise, the daughter of the Emperor of Austria, Napoleon had decided to grant a pardon to all deserters. There were many tears shed on that day at the farm. Little Claudine cried most bitterly of all. She kept saying to her mother, "Then we won't have any more cousin."

When they heard that he wanted to be a priest, the whole village of Les Noës contributed something towards it. Mère Fayot insisted on his accepting some napkins she had received long ago as a bridal gift. Two spinisters called the Demoiselles Dadolle, whom Jean had visited, went from house to house, taking up a collection for him. A tailor was sent to measure him for a cassock, and when it was ready he was induced to put it on for an hour just to show it to his friends. A poor old woman brought him thirty francs, the price of her little pig. "You will remember me when you become a priest?" she said.

And so in January 1811, about a year from the day he had come, Jean-Marie left his friends and walked back to Dardilly.

There a great grief awaited him. His mother, who had lived solely for him and who had been able to bear the time of anxiety and exile only because Monsieur Balley had assured her that her son would eventually be a priest, was now in her last illness, although she was only fifty-eight. Jean found her lying in the alcove under the picture of the Virgin Mary. She said to him in a weak voice, "Look, Jean, in the box there. The little oak chest. Bring the parcel. I have something to give to you when you become a priest. Unwrap the handkerchiefs."

Jean in tears found the white alb which she had made for him during his year's absence. It was just right for his height, 1 metre 57—say, 5 foot 2. (It was Monseigneur Trochu who said to me that God likes little saints.) It was long and straight and made of finest lawn. The sleeves were lace-edged and the lower part embroidered. This moving relic of a mother's love can still be seen at Ars.

While François and Marguerite sat by the fire with their father, who looked utterly broken, Jean knelt by the bedside of his dying mother. All that she had meant to him from his babyhood came back to him in a flood. It was her love which had been to him the threshold of the love of God. She had taught him everything he knew about the mysteries of the Faith. Till the end of his days he could never mention her name without tears starting to his eyes. Years afterwards he told Comtesse des Garets that after he had lost his mother he never clung to anything in this world. She died on the 8th of February and was buried in the little churchyard of Dardilly, where her tomb can be found today.

On her deathbed, Jean's mother had begged her husband to let him carry on with his studies for the priesthood, and because Mathieu loved his wife very dearly, he kept his word to her.

6. *COURAGE IS A LONG-TERM VIRTUE*

FROM BABYHOOD JEAN'S MOTHER HAD BEEN THE FIRST PERSON HE
had seen on waking in the morning, and she had always been
there to teach him to open his heart to God. As a child he had wept
if she was not there, and now that child's desolation returned to
him. But then the great love for the souls of men which she had
fostered rose in him like a tide sweeping all before it. He dried
his tears and walked swiftly down hill to Ecully. Monsieur Balley
received him with open arms. He had never ceased to pray for
his return. One of the women parishioners who was not very devout exclaimed when she saw him, "All the better! We will have a
Pater and an Ave less to say every day."

"You must come and lodge with me this time, my boy," said the
Curé.

Jean's face lit up, then he flushed and seemed to hesitate.

"You needn't worry," Monsieur Balley said. "During your recreations, you can help me in the garden. You can help me in the
church too, and when I go visiting the parishioners I'll give you
theology lessons if you come along with me."

We don't know very much about Jean during this time except
that the same kind Mère Bibost who had brought his books to
the farm at Les Robins looked after his clothes, and that he asked
a friend of his to go to Monsieur Ruzand, a bookseller at Lyons,
and buy him an old book called the *History of the Desert Fathers*.
In the autumn of that year Monsieur Balley thought him ready to
take his philosophy at the Seminary of Verrières. He confessed in

later life that he had to suffer "a little" in that place. He was twenty-six, a great deal older than the others, he had no memory at all and he still could not master Latin.

It is very painful for a young man to be the butt and laughing-stock of boys, many of them much his inferiors. It is excellent, of course, to be humble and to learn by humiliations. But always to be mocked, for no reason at all save that those youths had better memories than his, must have been galling. All the while he was profoundly convinced of his own incapacity and stupidity. In later life he used to say laughingly that the man who painted his portrait rightly made him look like a goose. It was Jean himself who played a great part in spreading the legend of his stupidity: what is so moving is that this humble man had an enormous re-spect for intelligent people. He had been born with a great attrac-tion to the higher faculties of the intelligence. If he praised any other priest, he would end his panegyric with: "What I like par-ticularly is that he's so learned."

And here he was. When he was asked a question in Latin he would gape, unable to say a word in answer, and a titter would sweep over the class of a hundred boys. Here was this over-aged student faced with the task of learning the laws of logic when he had already developed a God-given practical intelligence by no means wanting in solidity.

His loneliness was a blessing in disguise, for he turned from the young men who could have been his friends to the Eternal Friend who loves us utterly for ourselves. It was probably at this time, during one of his long visits to the chapel, that he gazed more deeply at his heavenly Mother and his devotion to her became tenderer still. And it was then that in imitation of St. Louis-Marie Grignion de Montfort, he pronounced the vow of servitude in which he gave her his whole life.

A report on his knowledge showed it very weak; but on his character and behaviour and his capacity for work the report was good. The house was very poor and the regime extremely austere, but that suited him entirely.

In July of 1813 he went to spend his last holidays with Monsieur

Balley, and in October he entered the great Seminary of Saint Irénée, an immense and rather palatial building on the ancient Fourvière hill, encircled by beautiful lime trees.

The young gentlemen training for the priesthood there all lived according to the traditions of Messieurs de Saint Sulpice. It is amusing to reflect, when one recalls how little use Jean was to make of this advice, that when Cardinal Fesch came to visit the young gentlemen, he invariably recommended that their ecclesiastical dress and appearance should be beyond reproach. He wanted all his priests to be very clean, very tidy, with everything decently arranged. He even advised them to use powder on their hair and have buckles on their shoes. (When one thinks that for the rest of his life Jean refrained from cleaning his shoes out of a spirit of penance!) The Cardinal even wished his Lyons seminarists to wear long cloaks, just like parish priests, when they went into the town.

This young ascetic of twenty-seven, during his walks and recreations, behaved rather like a Trappist monk. His room-mate was amazed when he would not rush to the window to see a Swiss regiment passing in the street with drums and fifes. Someone else owned that he thought he was a saint. Another thought that he showed great simplicity in his behaviour.

The Roman arena, the place of the martyrdoms of St. Blandina, St. Pothinus and St. Irenaeus, had not then been excavated, but of course the traditions were there, and there was the ancient chapel of Our Lady on the top of the hill of Fourvière. In those days before railways, the Rhône and the Saône were scenes of great activity, for there was much river travel.

On the Saône, workmen loaded boats, and the women sang by the banks as they pounded their linen. And for eight days around the Feast of Corpus Christi, the boats would be crowded with people holding baskets brimming with lavender and rosemary and branches of laurel to strew the streets with aromatic flowers in the path of the sacred Host. In Lyons itself the streets were badly paved. The old houses were so high that the air could not circulate freely in the narrow alleys. The atmosphere was heavy and the odor execrable.

Some of the houses were built on the rock; some, on the tops of very high cliffs, could be reached only by ladder. On the quays were houses so vast that six hundred tenants could lodge in each of them. Coal was brought to the town from the mines nearby on boats.

One of the most fascinating places in Lyons is the eleventh-century Benedictine Abbey of Ainay. In that century, Pope Pascal II consecrated an altar in honour of the Virgin conceived without the stain of original sin. According to ancient tradition, St. Blandina was buried there. There had been an abbey on the site in the fifth century. It is a mysterious, dimly lit basilica, built by monks for monks. The whole Benedictine tradition rises up before us there, with its serenity and stability. Birds and animals from mediaeval bestiaries adorn the capitals. And the Orient has spilt its palm trees and *fleurs de lis* abroad there. Did Jean go in to pray, and gaze on the spectacle of his patron saint being beheaded? It is more probable that young Monsieur Vianney lived in a world of his own. The picturesque, the splendid, the historically interesting or romantic did not impinge on his imagination in any way. He had all the single-mindedness of his great patron, St. John the Baptist. All he could think about was souls, souls, souls to be saved. And for that he prayed and worked. But his work still seemed fruitless. He could not master Latin, and after a while in desperation his masters gave up questioning him in class. After he had been at Saint Irénée for five or six months, the directors, believing he could not succeed, asked him to leave.

Many of his fellow students were very much upset to see him go. It is easy to imagine his anguish of mind as he climbed the hill from Lyons to Ecully with his little satchel under his arm, his head down, defeated. He fell into the arms of the admirable Monsieur Balley, who received him with his usual trust and confidence, believing in him in spite of every appearance of failure. The two of them set to work again at once, and this time Monsieur Balley explained his theology to him in French. Long afterwards Jean told a friend how, when he had been brought close to despair by his difficulties in mastering his studies, he had heard a voice encouraging him to go on. He said: "I did not know what to do. I can see the place in Ecully now. I was just passing by the house of Mère Bibost when I heard these words, as if someone whispered them in my ear: 'Be at peace. You will one day be a priest.'"

Monsieur Balley arranged with Monsieur Groboz that Jean's next examination in theology should take place in the presbytery at Ecully, and that he should be questioned in French. And this time he passed.

On April the 11th, 1814, Napoleon abdicated. His nephew, Cardinal Fesch, took refuge in Rome under the protection of Pius VII, and the Vicar-General, Monsieur Courbon, took over the administration of the diocese in his place. Monsieur Courbon, a simple and good-hearted priest, asked: "Is this young Vianney devout? Does he know how to say his rosary well?"

"Oh yes, he's a model of piety."

"A model of piety! Very well, I shall receive him. The grace of God will do the rest."

And so on July the 2nd, the Feast of the Visitation of Our Lady, Jean received minor orders and the sub-diaconate in the cathedral church of St. Jean.

A priest who walked next to him recounted that when they went in procession from the church to the seminary he was struck by the fervour with which Jean Vianney sang the Benedictus of thanksgiving.

"His face was radiant, and with a sort of intuition I applied to him the verse 'Thou shalt be a prophet of the most high; and I said to myself, 'he has less knowledge than many others, but in his ministry he will do greater things.'"

And so he returned to Monsieur Balley. In May 1815 he was accepted for the diaconate and went back to the seminary; and on the 23d of June, on the eve of the feast of his patron, St. John the Baptist, he was ordained deacon by Monseigneur Simon, Bishop of Grenoble. He had to submit to another examination—again at

Ecully and again in French—and he astonished the examiners by the clarity and the precision of his answers.

One can imagine his joy when he was told that he would be admitted to the priesthood in August. For that he had to walk to Grenoble from Lyons, a distance of a hundred *kilometres* (sixty-odd miles). One can imagine him going beforehand to Dardilly to tell his father and to fetch the alb which his mother had embroidered.

On the way to Grenoble he met Austrian soldiers who swore at him in their guttural tongue. Several times they stopped him and threatened him with their bayonets.

He reached Grenoble on the evening of the 12th of August and was ordained priest in the ancient Church of the Minims on the following morning. He was the only one to be ordained. When it was explained to Monseigneur Simon that he had been disturbed for so little—one young deacon only and he not of the diocese—he looked at Jean, alone and unaccompanied by friend or relation, and replied with a grave smile: "It is not too much trouble to ordain a good priest."

Jean, whom we must now call Monsieur Vianney, heard the bishop's words and repeated them to someone many years later. This was remembered during the beatification enquiry.

"A priest is the charity of Jesus Christ made manifest." In his catechism instructions in later life, whenever Monsieur Vianney spoke of the priesthood, he used to soar into an ecstasy of joy. He said that the priesthood could only be understood in Heaven. "If we could understand it on earth we should die, not of fear but of love." And so at last, at the age of twenty-nine, he had reached his journey's end. Souls! Souls! And now he would be able to garner them into the barns of his heavenly Father.

A great joy awaited him on his return. He was named curate to Monsieur Balley at Ecully. This must have been good news to his father and relations, for he would be near them. Indeed, his sister Marguerite went to hear him preach his first sermons, and though she recognized their lack of formal perfection she marvelled at the fact that he filled the church whenever he preached.

He spent much time in the confessional and in visiting the sick. "This took a great deal of his time, and he would sometimes neglect his meals," it was afterwards said.

He taught the children their catechism with tireless patience. Those who were slow in learning he would teach in his own room.

When he walked he usually kept his eyes on the ground. He conducted himself with a reserve which ruled out the least hint of familiarity. The early thirties can be a time of great temptation for a priest, especially one with a delightful personality. To a priest friend who had persistently asked him how he had obtained deliverance from temptations against the holy virtue of chastity he confided his secret. "In the end he told me that it was as a result of a vow he made during the time when he was curate of Ecully. Each day he recited the *Regina Coeli* once, and six times the prayer 'Blessed be the most Holy and Immaculate Conception of the Blessed Virgin Mary, Mother of God, for ever and ever, amen.' "

The large blue eyes under their lowered lids, when they were revealed for a moment, were the innocent eyes of a child. With regard to Monsieur Vianney's chastity, the testimony of a celebrated graphologist of Geneva who analyzed his handwriting without knowing who he was is extremely interesting. The graphologist reports:

"He has had to fight his passions to triumph over them. . . . But he has been absolutely victorious. What energy he has spent in this struggle! All that has become sublimated for him.

"This handwriting shows an extremely violent nature but also a real saint, one of the most attractive saints possible.

"Since his genius has not been able to expand in the direction of the arts—literature, sculpture, painting, music—it has developed in his love of his neighbour, but a sublimated love."

It has been said that you truly possess only the things you have renounced. He himself was to say: "When one has kept one's innocence, one is borne up by love as a bird is by its wings. . . . Those whose souls are pure are like the eagles and swallows which fly in the air. A Christian whose heart is pure is in this world like a bird which is held by a thread. . . . He is only waiting for the moment when the thread shall be cut to fly away."

Very soon the peasant population of Ecully and Dardilly began to be aware that young M. Vianney, by virtue of his ardent chastity, was able to love them with a great—because a supernatural —love. He had sacrificed the innocent pleasures of earthly friendship in order to give them the burning heart of God.

His penitential ardour was fed by almsgiving carried to the point of heroism. Once when he had been given a new pair of trousers by a kindly friend of Lyons, he bestowed them on a beggar he met on the way home, and returned wearing the beggar's old pants. For his hidden mortifications he asked Claudine Bibost and her daughter, Colombe, to make him a horsehair waistcoat, which he wore next to his skin, probably in imitation of Monsieur Balley. Neither of them drank wine, except, of course, when they entertained their fellow clergy. They lived chiefly on black bread and a few potatoes; the same piece of boiled beef reappeared on their table so often that in the end it had turned black.

They were so poor that they possessed only one umbrella between them. On rainy days, if both of them had to go to Lyons, they went together under the one umbrella.

On one of these rare excursions to Lyons Monsieur Balley, glancing at the rather haggard appearance of his spiritual son, exclaimed: "Today we are going to have a little recreation. Oh yes, you must obey me. I am going to take you to see a very old friend of mine in his country place at Tassin. He is a rich man and a kind one, Monsieur Jaricot. And I want you to meet his young daughter, Pauline. She's eighteen. She was once very frivolous, but she's quite reformed now. She is absolutely devoted to a newly discovered virgin martyr named Philomena. She hasn't yet been canonized, but if she goes on performing as many miraculous cures as Pauline says she does, I wouldn't be surprised if quite soon she became an official saint."

Now, ever since the days when his father had spoken to him about Benedict-Joseph Labre, ever since that hot July day when the hawker had talked of the martyrs of Lyons, young Monsieur

Vianney's imagination had been fired by the idea of martyrdom. Was he not an inhabitant of Lyons, a city glorified by St. Blandina? Christ his Master, who had watched his struggle to attain the virtue of chastity, wished now to give him a companion on his way. Henri Ghéon speaks most beautifully of this. After reminding us how every bond of natural love is transmuted into a mystical relationship, and giving as examples St. Francis of Assisi and St. Clare, St. Teresa and St. John of the Cross, and so on, he says, "The Curé of Ars never knew close friendship, even in the spiritual order, with any woman. Yet his heart was tender enough. From the first day of his priesthood, his family was, so to speak, erased from his life. . . . But in secret God had chosen for him a companion no longer of this world. A little maid of the olden times, who was to be at once his lady, betrothed, sister—and even later his daughter, for whereas he grew old, she remained fixed in the spring of her youth. Soon, speaking to her as a father, he might more easily press her with his entreaties: he need no longer be on his guard with her: he might even scold her, though gently. . . .

"So hand in hand they will go down the centuries, and the world awaits a Giotto to depict their betrothal."[1]

At last Monsieur Balley and Monsieur Vianney reached Tassin, near Lyons, Monsieur Balley, as was the custom in those days, carrying his umbrella, the umbrella, with its handle down. After the usual elaborate exchange of courtly and ecclesiastical greetings, Mademoiselle Pauline was introduced to them. Much to the amusement of her family, she had given up all her frivolities and now wore the plain bonnet of a church worker and very ordinary clothes. She was in the springtime of her love for God, in those days when He was preparing her for her great mission in the world. Her charity would embrace the uttermost ends of the earth, and when, to further the cause she had at heart she died in great poverty and hardship, overwhelmed with the reproaches of the just, she was very near perfection. But on that day all this was in the distant future. Monsieur Balley introduced Monsieur Vian-

[1] *The Secret of the Curé of Ars,* tr. by F. J. Sheed; in *Secrets of the Saints:* Sheed & Ward, London and New York, 1944.

ney: "Mademoiselle Pauline, here is my curate, newly ordained. I know that you would love to tell him about your little Philomena. Perhaps you will tell us the whole story, because I would like to hear it again myself."

Pauline Jaricot gave an appraising and rather amused glance at young Monsieur Vianney. Clothed, or rather draped, in the ample folds of his only cassock, with an enormous three-cornered hat held in place by black cords turning green, wearing enormous shoes innocent of shoe polish, and thin as a rail, he looked, let us say, original. When they were all seated she began:

"I must first remind you that in the year of Waterloo when Napoleon was defeated for good, our Brothers of Saint John of God, who had been driven away to Italy by the Revolution, returned to France. And as they wanted to rebuild their old hospitals, some of the monks made themselves beggars. They went from house to house singing hymns, and when they came to us here, they sang the 'Complaint of Saint Philomena.' I happened to be here that day. I had brought a few of my little dressmaker girls over from Lyons for some recreation. I made the Brothers tell me the story of this Philomena, of whom I had never heard.

"Well, it seems that in the year 1805, a young priest of Mugnano in the Campagna, wishing to convert the peasants who were his parishioners, went to Rome to beg for the relics of a martyr from the Catacombs. After many trials and disappointments, he was given those of Saint Philomena.

"The Emperor Diocletian had ordered that all the accounts of the lives of saints be destroyed, so we know practically nothing about her. Unknown though she was, the little saint started working such miracles in Mugnano that she was very soon known as the Queen of Mugnano."

Then Pauline Jaricot turned to Monsieur Balley and said: "Now you know more about the burial of martyrs in the Catacombs than I do. Will you tell us about them before I go on? Tell us how she was found."

"Of course I will," said Monsieur Balley. "You know of course that several devout women were in the habit of going to the Colosseum by night to collect the bodies of the martyrs for burial. They came with water and sponges to cleanse their wounds, and glass phials for holding a few drops of their blood. They took the bodies out of Rome into the desolate places of the Campagna, where the entrances to the Catacombs were. (The body of Philomena, a martyr of the end of the first century or a little later, was found in the Catacomb of Priscilla, in which the bodies of St. Praxedes and St. Pudentiana were also found.) And then by the flickering light of their little clay lamps, they used to walk down the long subterranean corridors under Rome and place the body in a hollow in a wall. Then they used to kneel down and pray to their sister in Christ and venerate the relics in silence. Those little holes in the wall remind one of dove's nests."

"Oh," exclaimed Monsieur Vianney, whose eyes were alight with enthusiasm, "how I wish I could go to Rome!"

Monsieur Balley smiled and continued. "It was the custom in those days for the early Christians to sprinkle flowers around the tombs, touch them to the martyred body and then to use those same flowers to adorn the altar of sacrifice. Just after the *loculus* (the little chamber containing Philomena's body) was closed, some grave-digger set three tiles in the wall outside the niche. Then, dipping his brush in red lead, he traced these words on the tiles: *"Pax tecum Filumena"*—"Peace to thee, dearly beloved one." And there she slept for long centuries, forgotten, unknown, just as her real name is unknown, for *Filumena* means beloved one. But although the Vandals in the fifth and sixth centuries attacked the Catacombs, they left this grave alone. From the tenth century onwards, the cult of the Catacombs seems to have died out entirely, and many of the relics of the saints were taken out and placed in churches of their own. St. Praxedes herself is in a wonderful mosaic church in which the column of Our Lord's scourging is kept. The entrances to the Catacombs soon became blocked up with earth and fallen trees. The grass grew over them and they disappeared from sight altogether.

"It was around 1578, I believe, that an accident revealed the existence of the Catacombs again. The cemetery of St. Priscilla was discovered. Alas, the wonderful basilica of St. Silvester had disappeared without trace, for the ruins were completely hidden by thorns and intertwining ivy, centuries old. Earth and stones had blocked the galleries, the staircases and the skylights."

At this point Monsieur Balley turned to Pauline Jaricot and said, "Now you tell us how your little saint's grave was found."

"Well," said Pauline, "it was on the morning of May the 24th, 1802. It's strange, isn't it, that it should be in the same year Napoleon opened the churches in France? A grave-digger was surprised when his pickaxe hit against some tiles closing a *loculus*. On the brick of the middle tile he found painted a palm, which was one of the signs of martyrdom. He had received very strict orders from the guardian of the Holy Relics, so he stopped work at once and went to tell them about his discovery. The next day they all went down and uncovered the tomb. By the light of torches they saw the inscription and several signs painted with red lead. The *loculus* was rather a short one, as if it held a young person. They found the little glass flask for holding the martyr's blood, but it was in fragments. Of the blood there remained just black dust adhering to some of the pieces of glass.

"Providence had not brought this saint up to the great churches of Rome to be placed on the altars, but had reserved her for some special destiny. Providence had her hour. I wonder—oh I hope, that it is connected with France!"

Monsieur Vianney whispered: "Oh indeed, I hope so too. How I wish I could have her! Perhaps she would help me save souls."

They were all silent for a time. Their spirits were in those crypts with the martyrs whose blood was the seed of Christ's Church. Then Monsieur Balley turned to Pauline again and said, "Can you read us the hymn of Saint Methodius, the hymn he puts on the lips of Thecla when she gives thanks at the end of the Banquet of Ten Virgins?"

"Oh," said Pauline, "it is very beautiful! And isn't it strange that when virgins were consecrated to Christ, their veils were bands of purple wool twined round the head and not floating? Anyway here is the hymn." She took out her prayer book.

For Thee, divine Bridegroom, I keep myself spotless.
I come to Thee with my lamp lit.
Farewell, pleasures of life, the bitter happiness of
human beings, I want to see Thy beauty for evermore.
For Thee, divine Bridegroom, I keep myself spotless,
I come to Thee with my lamp lit,
Disdaining the hand of a mortal I have fled a house
full of gold.
Welcome me in the mystery and the bliss of Thy love.
For Thee, divine Bridegroom, I kept myself without spot,
I come to Thee with my lamp lit.
Jesus, I have frustrated the wiles of the serpent, I have
braved the fire, I have borne the assaults of the wild
beasts, I wait for Thee to come from Heaven.
For Thee, divine Bridegroom, I keep myself spotless,
I come to Thee with my lamp lit.
Oh Word, enamoured of Thee alone I forgot my native
land and the sweet games of my companions, my
mother and my noble forbears, for, O Christ, Thou
art all in all to me,
For Thee, divine Bridegroom, I keep myself without spot.
I come to Thee with my lamp lit.

Again there was a long silence, and they all noticed that Monsieur Vianney was lost in a day-dream, as if in the company of those consecrated virgins of the early centuries.

At last he said: "And now, Mademoiselle Jaricot, all that remains for you to do is to go to Rome and beg that priest at Mugnano to give you a tiny, tiny relic, and then perhaps to give half of it to me!"

Monsieur Balley smiled affectionately at his spiritual son. "And that will help you in the only aim you have—to save souls. That's so, isn't it?"

Several days later, in the Archbishop's house at Lyons, Monsieur Courbon, the Vicar-General, was holding his sides with laughter. His secretary asked him what was the matter. The Vicar-General said, "Oh, you would be laughing like me, *mon cher confrère*, if only you'd been here half an hour ago. That dear Monsieur Balley of Ecully came to see me to denounce his curate, Monsieur Vianney, because his austerities exceeded the bounds of reason. And a few minutes later, when he's disappeared down one path, up the other path near the lime avenue comes Monsieur Vianney himself, to make an identical complaint against his vicar."

The secretary smiled. "It's high time that Monsieur Vianney had a new cassock," he observed. "The one the people of Les Noës gave him is really falling to pieces. Few of the buttons match. Very soon there'll be more patches than cassock, and it's green instead of black."

"Oh," said Monsieur Courbon. "Haven't you heard the latest about that? Monsieur Balley complained so much that at length Monsieur Vianney decided to get himself a new cassock. And having scraped together a little money—for you know he gives everything away to beggars—he gave the sum into the safekeeping of the sacristan's wife, planning to order a cassock in due time. Alas, a few hours later he received a visit from a great lady—you know, one of those poor aristocrats, impoverished by the unhappy times we live in. She's been so generous in giving alms that she was reduced to the most painful poverty. Monsieur Vianney could hardly bear it. After an interview in which he heard the most heart-rending things about her poverty his only thought was to help her. He ran to the sacristan's wife and asked for his money back. She, though, realizing that her husband, the tailor concerned, would be done out of the order for the cassock, gave him all sorts of good, clear and persuasive reasons for holding on to the money. But Monsieur Vianney was stubborn. 'That's all right, that's all right,' he said in answer to her objections, 'but give me back my money all the same. We'll see what to do afterwards.' Well, you can imagine where the money went to, that very evening. It was given to Madame de X anonymously."

"Yes," said the secretary, "and I've heard what happened to his watch the other day. His father gave him a watch and he sold it to give the money to a beggar. So he's always unpunctual for everything, never gets to meals on time. A rich man of Lyons said he'd give him a watch, but only on loan, so that he couldn't give it away."

"Do you know," said the Vicar-General thoughtfully, "in spite of his deplorable appearance, and the lack of brilliance in his sermons and conversation, people become utterly devoted to him? Monsieur Balley was telling me how old Madame Fayot—the woman who hid him that year at Les Noës—burst in on him when he was entertaining a few fellow priests. She went straight up to him, took him in her arms, and gave him two resounding kisses. He blushed furiously."

In the first weeks of 1817 Monsieur Balley, aged sixty-five, exhausted by his austerities and the hardships he had endured, was laid low with an ulcerated leg. He went to bed and was ill and bedridden from then onwards. Gangrene set in, and on the 17th of December he died, having made his last confession to his spiritual son and received Viaticum and Extreme Unction at his hands.

Monsieur Vianney had inherited from his dear master his instruments of penance, his library, his looking glass and his bed. (The penitential belt all studded with little iron nails is preserved in the museum at Ars.) Throughout his life he never ceased to extol Monsieur Balley's virtues. If anybody wanted him to talk at length and without pause, he had only to mention the name of Monsieur Balley to set him off. He remembered his face so clearly that towards the end of his life he said, "If I were a painter, I could still make his portrait." He kept till the end the little looking glass above his bedroom chimney piece because it had reflected his friend's face.

And now, where was he to go, more completely stripped of human affection, more detached, than ever? Never again would he be the disciple at the feet of a saint, never again know the joy of speaking a common language with a dear friend.

The new vicar came, Monsieur Tripier. It would be interesting to know more than we do know about Monsieur Tripier. He cannot have appreciated the plain living and high thinking of the presbytery. "Why, just like a monastery of Trappists or Carthusians," he must have thought to himself. "Oh no, that won't do for me at all." And then, this very shabby-looking Monsieur Vianney refused to go with him and visit the rich parishioners of Ecully, on the pretext that his cassock was too old. It is quite possible that Monsieur Tripier, in an attack of secret exasperation, asked for another curate.

In any event the Vicar-General, Monsieur Courbon, soon summoned Monsieur Vianney, now thirty-two, to Lyons. He was most reluctant to tell Monsieur Vianney of his new assignment, for the hamlet of Ars was in a region viewed by the Lyons clergy as a kind of Siberia. To be sent anywhere near the Dombes country amounted almost to a disgrace. Ars was not a proper parish, but a dependency of Misérieux, three kilometres away. It was lost in the wilds with no road leading into it; and, owing to the stagnant ponds round about, the air was heavy; a resident would first be reduced to a kind of low fever, then to a permanent state of depression. The income for Ars was very small. The last incumbent, who had been tuberculous, had stayed only three weeks, and then died.

"There is not much love of God in that parish," the Vicar-General said. "You must bring it there. But there is one cheering thing. The lady of the château is a good woman. She will help you."

On the 3rd of February, Monsieur Vianney brought his ministry at Ecully to an end. He went to say good-bye to his father. (He was never to see him again, he died in the following year.) On the anniversary of his mother's death, he paid a farewell visit to her grave. Farewell to his friends and relations, to the farmhouse where he had been born, so full of happy memories. Perhaps a quick glance at Montmerle, bare and bleak in winter, where he had lighted fires as a little shepherd boy. The widow Bibost, always ready to do him some service, offered to come and be his housekeeper. When he hesitated, she said; "But you will need a little help to start with, anyway. Somebody to settle you in. Your brother-in-law, Melin, can lend us an ox cart and drive two oxen.

I don't know what the roads are like. Perhaps just tracks across the mud. What a pity you've got so many books to take."

"Oh, but they're my chief treasure," said Monsieur Vianney, as he lovingly packed the calf and morocco volumes left him by Monsieur Balley, the books he was to pore over and ear-mark so lovingly in the years to come. There were two calf-bound volumes of the Works of St. Gregory; there was St. Bernard; there was a new book on how to direct souls in the confessional. There was *Moral Theology for Decisions in Cases of Conscience; The Duties of Masters and Servants,* by a seventeenth-century priest of Paris; the spiritual works of the Dominican Louis of Grenada and those of Blessed John of Avila; *Holiness and the Duties of the Monastic Life,* and then a book by a Jesuit, entitled *A Practical Method of Conversing with God;* a seventeenth-century *Imitation of Christ,* edited by R. P. Camaret; *Instructions for Ursuline Nuns. . . . Outpourings of the Heart. . . .* by a Benedictine of St. Maur, in five volumes; four volumes of the spiritual works of the late Monseigneur François de Salignac de la Mothe-Fénelon, 1740; three volumes of sermons by la Colombière, eleven volumes of sermons by Monsieur Massillon. (Monsieur Balley had inscribed his name in this.) Then a course of homilies for the use of country priests. (This was Monsieur Vianney's own book and he had marked it with his name.) Then the *Lives of the Saints* by Père François Giry, the only book in which is written "Jean-Marie-Baptiste Vianney, Curé d'Ars." There was a treatise on French spelling in dictionary form; and *Virginie, or the Christian Virgin: A Sicilian History to Serve as a Model for Girls Who Aspire to Perfection.* And finally an enchanting book whose full title is: *The Sacred Bouquet Composed of the Roses of Calvary, Lilies of Bethlehem, Hyacinths of Olivet and Several other Rare and Beautiful Meditations from Palestine.* This was a description of a pilgrimage to the Holy Land, certainly of the seventeenth century. Yes, this young priest who was supposed to be so ignorant certainly loved his books.

Very early on the dull, misty morning of February the 9th

Monsieur Vianney set out. The widow Bibost, practical as always, had packed a basket of provisions, for she knew very well that he would never think of such things. The parishioners who had come to see him off stood watching until the slight retreating figure was lost to sight in the mist. He left the enchanted fields of his birthplace and went to a strange land where suffering awaited him, a tiny hamlet where he was to fulfil his spiritual destiny of saving so many souls in France, and indeed throughout Europe, that the Devil, screaming at him through the mouth of a possessed woman, was to say, "How you make me suffer. . . : If there were three like you in this world my kingdom would be destroyed. . . . Miser of souls. . . ."

PART II

7. *MONSIEUR VIANNEY WALKS TO ARS*

IN THE THIRD CHAPTER OF HIS BOOK ON THE CURÉ OF ARS, JOSEPH Vianey describes the Ars of his own day:

"The scenery around Ars is devoid of character. It is situated where the plateau of the Dombes begins. The chain of wooded hillocks whose graceful outlines are reflected in the listless Saône thins out before you reach Ars on the way from Lyons. A little further on, as you go towards Bourg, begins that region of wide pools bordered by twisted elms, with their flights of wild duck, which an artist has immortalized with melancholy poetry in his masterpieces. The flat horizon, yellow earth, meagre hedges, the double line of alder trees along the little brook, the old castle of the Ars family in a grove of trees. . . . There are several houses of puddled clay around a low-built church. . . ."

Let us try to picture now this landscape on a bleak winter day, and the central figures in it, the new curé and his two companions, walking with the ox cart, the curé a little ahead of the others.

We who are so accustomed to seeing pictures of the Curé of Ars in his old age, with his flowing white hair and the sorrow in his eyes which had come from so many years' experience in the confessional, may find it difficult to reconstruct the features and the personality of the man in his early thirties. At the moment when this biography is going to press a remarkable book has appeared in France, *L'Apôtre de la Confiance en Marie,* by Abbé J. Pagnoux. It contains a charcoal drawing, hitherto unpublished, of the Curé as a rather young priest, done by the painter J. Borel. (The original is

in the possession of the painter's family.) It is captivating beyond
words. To begin with, it is a face of great beauty, with that added
element of "strangeness" produced by spiritual distinction. The
features are well-proportioned and delicate, the lips are controlled,
but with a sensitive, sardonic quirk about them. The eyebrows, like
wings, curving up at the ends, suggest a man of quick perception
and critical discernment. The eyes are veiled in gentle melancholy.
One wants to look, and look again.

He was small, wiry and active, full of nervous energy. His control over his temper and his impetuosity was complete. (Yet it is
said that under stress he would take his large handkerchief out of
his pocket and tug and twist it round and round. It is related that
on one occasion, having controlled his tongue when somebody
insulted him, he broke out in a rash. He was what the French call
so picturesquely *un grand nerveux*.)

We already know what his clothes were like. He never in his life
possessed an overcoat, but would walk long distances through
winter snow in a near-freezing temperature, clad only in his cassock. He warmed himself, he said, by thinking of the fiery furnace
of God's love.

One thing his fellow priests did not know was that his underlinen
was changed often, and that he was scrupulously clean. He mended
his own socks and botched the job out of a spirit of mortification.

Despite the fact that he most often walked with his eyes on the
ground, he was most extraordinarily aware of everything which
went on about him. His hearing remained so acute even in his old
age that the ticking of his watch would have kept him awake at
night had he not muffled it. When he did look about him he was
very keenly observant, not only of the beauties of nature but of all
the habits of creatures. As we have said, his sermons and moral
instructions are enriched by this lore.

As is so frequent with the saints, it was his eyes which were the
most extraordinary of his features. When he spoke of the love of
God, they dilated and sparkled; they were veiled with tears when
he talked about sin. When he looked at anyone his glance was so
searching that he seemed to have summed him up entirely in an

instant. Abbé Monnin says that next to the eyes, "the most re-markable thing in the countenance of the Curé of Ars was the pro-file, the lines of which were bold, harmonious, and well defined. Although the sweetness and serenity of his face betokened the divine peace which dwelt within, its characteristic and familiar expression when at rest was that supernatural melancholy which belongs to the habitual consciousness of the invisible. . . . It was deepened by the continual contact with sin and sorrow, which had impressed many a bitter thought on his soul, and cast their mourn-ful reflection on his face. But when he came forth from that ha-bitual state of recollection to converse with men, it was with a bright and gracious smile, which was ever ready to respond to every look which was turned on him. There was not one of his features which did not seem to smile."

Anyway, here he was, plodding along on that misty February day, doing the twenty miles from Ecully to Ars. He walked alone, ahead of the cart. He was journeying towards the souls for whom, for the first time in his life, he would assume complete responsibil-ity. For this had he struggled all those long years, for this had he gone on that penitential pilgrimage to La Louvesc. He was so lost in his own thoughts that he had almost forgotten the existence of the good widow Bibost. But being of a most grateful and kindly nature, he eventually shrugged himself out of his brown study and turned back to talk with her.

"What have you heard about the Ars people?" she asked.

"Oh, some sad things. For example, a schoolmaster says they are so dense that they are only distinguished from animals by their baptism. However, one doesn't need to be intelligent to be a good Christian. All the same, a great deal of their ignorance is culpable. In summer they are too mean to spare their children from work-ing in the fields to let them go to school. And then if those children break anything on the farm, I've heard that they beat them so hard that sometimes they injure them for life. Yes, cruelty and avarice very often go together. What a pity, in a parish which was once so much devoted to the Sacred Heart! And then, I wouldn't put it past them to cheat in their business dealings at fairs and markets—you know, try to sell some beast without pointing out his bad points. And they pilfer crops from each other's fields. Yet there must be some hope for them. They were devout at one time, and very fond of processions and pilgrimages."

"Did they have a non-juring priest during the troubles?"

"Alas, their priest broke away from Rome and came back to live in Ars itself as a shopkeeper. You can imagine what scandal it caused, and one can hardly blame his parishioners for falling into apathy. How shall I entice their children to come to catechism? I'll have to promise them a little reward if they come early."

The widow Bibost asked whether the church had been pillaged during the Revolution.

"Yes, a band of fanatics came from the neighbouring hamlet and took everything they could lay hands on, even the bell. They turned the church into a club and the *sans-culottes* came and made long speeches there. There are four taverns in the place, and it's full of drunks. The girls think of nothing else but dancing, and all sorts of unseemly things happen during the winter night assemblies."

"Well, you soon set those things right at Ecully," said Mère Bibost. "You will surely do so at Ars, although it may not be easy."

"No, for I no longer have my good Monsieur Balley. But I have his memory. And do you know," he added more cheerfully, "I'm even glad I've got his old looking glass, for every time I use it to shave, I can almost see his reflection in it."

The widow Bibost knew quite well that once she had got Monsieur Vianney started off on Monsieur Balley he would never stop. But she was beginning to be anxious, for she felt they had lost their way. The cart wheels were heavy with mud, and she and the Curé could hardly lift their boots, all clodded up with wet clay.

The fog seemed to be thickening. She began to imagine how pleasant it would be to light a fire the minute she got to the presbytery of Ars. Yes, to warm her hands and feet, and perhaps have a quarter of a glass of red wine. It really was high time they got there. Behind them to the south they had left the valley of the Saône and the Mont d'Or. If it had been clear, they could have

seen in the west the mountains of the Beaujolais. They did not
know that on a hillock now could be seen, on a clear day, the fields
of Misérieux and the trees around the Château de Cibeins in whose
park Monsieur Vianney would take so many meditative strolls
during his first months. To the east was the church spire of
Savigneux, barely visible above the mist, and to the north, but
completely blanketed in fog, were the oak trees surrounding the
château of Ars. A little beyond was the village of Ars itself. The
oxen's breath mingled with the steam of the fog.

"I wonder if we are lost," said the widow Bibost.

Just then Monsieur Vianney descried in a distant field some little
shepherd boys looking after their sheep. He approached them and
asked in French the way to the château of Ars. As they spoke only
patois, they did not immediately understand. But at last a little boy
named Antoine Givre managed to understand and pointed the way.
The Curé said, "My little friend, you have shown me the way to
Ars. I will show you the way to Heaven."

The boy watched him as he went down along the narrow path,
and he saw that when he got into the parish itself he went down
on his knees.

When they had crossed the little Fontblin stream which was the
boundary of the parish, Monsieur Vianney saw all the small
thatched, mud-coloured houses. "How small it is!" he thought to
himself. And then the strange thought flashed through his mind:
"This parish will not be able to hold all those who will come to it
later on."

He knelt and prayed to the guardian angel of the parish.

"I wonder when he is going to get up," thought widow Bibost,
"and, oh dear! his cassock is heavy with mud. I will never get it
clean again."

But she was to be disappointed if she hoped to get him to the
presbytery before nightfall. "You go on," he said. "Somebody is
sure to show you the way. I'm just going to stop at the church."

"But it's very dark," she said, "and I'm sure there isn't a light."

He didn't answer but went into his church. That is, he stumbled
in, for at first there seemed to be no light. He groped his way

around benches and stacks of old books, for he could see a flicker
of light near the high altar. Some kindly person must have left a
night-light for him. He lit the candles on the broken-down altar.
The altar cloth was far from white; it was torn in places, and the
tawdry lace was half ripped off. The candlesticks had not been
cleaned for a long time. Candlewax, cobwebs and dust were everywhere; a bird's nest had fallen in, and there were bird droppings.

On that night of February the 9th this minute twelfth-century
church was as dilapidated and untended as any church in the
whole of France—enough to discourage the most stout-hearted
priest. Monsieur Vianney knelt down on the hard stone, made the
sign of the cross and buried his face in his hands. Souls. Souls. Here
they were, awaiting him, and he would be their servant.

He spent a long time there; indeed time ceased to exist for him.

In the meantime a village woman had good-naturedly lighted a
lantern and brought the key to open the presbytery for the widow
Bibost. The Curé's brother-in-law, Melin, stabled the oxen and,
mounting to the attic, fell into the sleep of exhaustion.

The presbytery was a small, ancient peasant house surrounded
by a little yard and outhouses; beyond, a rather large garden containing a few fruit trees and red currant bushes. At the end of the
yard was a picturesque old well. The widow Bibost had hardly
entered the house when a woman appeared at the door.

"Good evening to you and to the company,"[1] she said as she
crossed the threshold. "May God be praised! I am the widow
Renard from next door. I was told to meet you when you came. You
must have lost your way. Look, here on the left is the kitchen. Here
on the right is the dining-room. Now let's go up this flight of stairs.
On the left is the guest room and on the right is the bedroom.
Quite a good fireplace, you see. And this little staircase leads to the
attic. I'm afraid the dining room's rather damp, but we'll soon fix
that with fires. I live just next door with my daughter, Marianne.
If you need me, you only have to knock on the wall. Now, we must

[1] This country greeting included her guardian angel!

get something nice and warm for your Curé. He's had a long tramp, hasn't he? And you look pretty tired yourself."

"Thank you kindly, my good friend," said the widow Bibost. "What elegant furniture there is here!"

"Oh, that was given by Mademoiselle at the château. She likes to feel that the presbytery is properly furnished."

"Well, you know, our Monsieur Vianney's not used to luxury. I wonder what he's going to say to all this—and all the kitchen implements. I know his habits of old at Ecully. He and Monsieur Balley, the rector, used to live on black bread and water. Hardly ever any meat."

At that moment the said Monsieur Vianney, holding a candle, was stumbling towards the vestry on the right-hand side of the altar, his figure casting weird shadows against the walls. He looked unhappily at the vestments, which were in a very bad state. There were some shabby crimson and white damask banners; the monstrance and ciborium were of some base metal, the censer and the chalice were tin plate; the altar cloths and other linen were scanty and of inferior quality, and all smelt of mildew. The vestry itself, facing north, was very damp and cold.

"We shall have to mend all this as quickly as we can," he murmured to himself. "What a good thing I brought some money. I will furnish the Lord's house with my earnings. Oh yes, I have to buy a new altar, and then I'll walk into Lyons early one morning after Mass and get two little angel heads to put near the tabernacle."

He surveyed the worm-eaten woodwork around the tiny church.

"I could paint it up. That would certainly look more cheerful. Apart from the glory given to God, if my parishioners began to find the house of God attractive, they might come to it more often. And they need a few good pictures and statues of saints."

Meanwhile the few poor pieces of furniture which Monsieur Vianney had brought in the cart from Ecully had been stacked in the dining-room, and the widow Bibost was awaiting his return from church before arranging them. She looked appraisingly around at the furniture lent by Mademoiselle d'Ars.

We have complete lists from two inventories which still exist. Amongst other things there were six chairs with high backs and an armchair covered in velvet pile, an armchair covered in red and green Siamese cotton, a dining table with four leaves. "Hm," she thought to herself, "so he's expected to entertain the neighbouring clergy." There were also two beds with blue and white canopies and quilts and a foot coverlet in gold and yellow taffeta and white piqué and two mattresses covered with new chequered cloth.

She looked out the kitchen window and saw a roosting-perch for hens. "Good, that means he'll have a few eggs. He can't say no to an egg." Then she caught sight of the meat safe with its pulley and six iron hooks for holding the meat inside the cage. She smiled to herself, knowing very well how little meat Monsieur Vianney ever ate. She closed the window and poked up the fire. Then she noticed a shaving-bowl. "Well, he certainly can't throw that away, for he's very careful about proper shaving."

Alas for all the plans of the housekeepers of holy men! Within half an hour of his arrival at his presbytery, the widows Renard and Bibost were utterly discomfited. Most of Mademoiselle d'Ars' loans were heaped up into the empty cart in the outhouse and covered over with sackcloth and dust sheets. They would be returned to her without delay.

Monsieur Balley's four-poster bed with its palliasse of ordinary cloth and its torn coverlet with sea shells on it, the ragged blue curtains, the cheap little cherry-wood table which pilgrims to Ars still see in the presbytery, and the high-backed chairs—all these things the Curé left to a Mademoiselle Ricotier in his will of 1841 in exchange for the sum of ninety francs, probably money which he urgently needed then for his charities. But he reserved the use of these objects for himself until his death.

Of the kitchen utensils, he kept a cast-iron saucepan. "This'll do for boiling my potatoes," he said. (This too can still be seen in the little kitchen.) "And this big frying-pan with the long handle will do for making my pancakes."

As the widow Bibost heard him talking about doing his own cooking she realized that her days as his housekeeper were numbered, and she sighed resignedly.

Monsieur Vianney did not want to warm himself at the fire. Oh no, there was still much to do in church. He went back in the dark. Two men who were just staggering out of a tavern stared at him. "Our new Curé—hic," they said.

Back in his church the new Curé prepared the vestments for the next morning and cleaned the altar. Then he knelt down for a long time and said Matins and Lauds for the Feast of St. Scholastica, the sister of St. Benedict, the nun as innocent as a dove.

He had come into Ars on the Feast of St. Cyril of Alexandria, the defender of the Divine Motherhood of the Virgin Mary. An omen. So many of the great events of his life had taken place under the protection of Our Lady.

It was nearly midnight when he left the altar and went back, lantern in hand, to the presbytery. He was stiff and tired. Widow Bibost was asleep in the first-floor guest room. He looked into the bedroom which was supposed to be his and hung up his favourite picture of St. Francis Regis, but he did not sleep there. Instead he lay down on a pile of faggots in the kitchen and was soon fast asleep.

Before the slow February dawn broke, the cocks were awake in the neighbouring farmyards, crowing on one prolonged note which sounded like the desolate cry of a lost soul. By the time Mère Bibost had stumbled downstairs, the Curé was in the church ringing the cracked bell.

People were astonished when they heard the Mass bell ring after such a long interval, and they said to one another, "*Tiens*, a new Curé has come to us." The congregation was meagre, to say the least—one or two black-cloaked women and perhaps the mayor, Monsieur Mandy, who was to become the priest's great friend and his champion for years.

Monsieur Vianney was completely absorbed in his Mass. If the people in the congregation had hoped to meet him afterwards, they were disappointed, for as soon as he had unvested he came to kneel

by the altar on the bare stone floor. He knelt upright without any
support, his hands joined, gazing at the tabernacle. An hour passed,
two hours, three hours, while he said his thanksgiving, his morning
Office, prayed for the souls of his flock.

In vain did widow Bibost wait for him in the presbytery with a
bowl of coffee which she kept warming up hopefully. He never
came. Melin, knowing his brother-in-law, ate his breakfast and
went for a stroll.

"He must be perishing with cold," widow Bibost thought.

She went up to make his bed and found it all smooth. "Hm, he
made it himself," she thought naively. "I'd better make a fire in
here tonight. It's really raw."

There was a scuffling noise upstairs. "Rats!" she said. "I'll have to
set some traps. They'll keep him awake all night. What a good thing
I came. I'm sure he wouldn't think of all this. The one good thing
about this place is that his predecessor seems to have left plenty
of wood."

In the Château d'Ars, a quarter of an hour's walk away, Mademoiselle Marie-Anne-Colombe Garnier des Garets, who was an
early riser, had finished reciting the hour of Terce with her devoted
old manservant, Saint-Phal, whom the villagers, with becoming
awe for his age and high position in her household, respectfully
called Monsieur de Saint-Phal. She had said morning prayers with
her household and had read to them about St. Scholastica in *The
Lives of the Saints* when she suddenly heard the Mass bell in the
distance.

"Ah," she said joyfully, "that must be our new Curé. What a pity
I didn't know in time to get to Mass."

Then she turned affectionately to Saint-Phal. "But it would have
been a little too chilly for you to go today. We must be careful of
you in the winter."

"Let us hope, Mademoiselle," he said, "that Monsieur le Curé
will call on us this morning. He is quite sure to be overwhelmed
with gratitude for the loans you have made to the presbytery."

"Yes," she said. "You had better tell them in the kitchen to put aside a crock of meat broth for him. And perhaps he'd like a turkey. His housekeeper could roast it on the turn-spit I've lent him."

Soon all the château servants, who lived like monks and nuns in a well-regulated convent, were at their several tasks. Mademoiselle d'Ars was an excellent housewife. She kept scrupulous accounts, and it is owing to them that we know what she gave the Curé and how she helped the needy. Even as far as Villefranche the poor were the recipients of her charity. She spent very little on herself—all her clothes were out-of-date and she had no horse and carriage. She had to walk everywhere, but this she did cheerfully and with great *panache* in the manner of old ladies of a hundred and fifty years past, careless of wind, snow and mud.

Mademoiselle d'Ars came of a sturdy generation, having been educated at Saint-Cyr, the boarding-school for poor young ladies of aristocratic lineage established by Madame de Maintenon in the reign of Louis XIV. "The object of Saint-Cyr," wrote the king's confessor, the Jesuit La Chaise, "is not to multiply convents, which increase rapidly enough of their own accord, but to give the state well-educated women; there are plenty of good nuns, and not a sufficient number of good mothers of families. The young ladies will be educated more suitably by persons living in the world." In the beginning the educational program had been broad enough to include the acting by the pupils of Racine's plays, but this cultivation in young girls of a taste for the theatre had brought criticism from both Jesuits and Jansenists, with the result that in 1692 Madame de Maintenon transformed Saint-Cyr into a monastic boarding-school subject to the Order of St. Augustine. Nevertheless the essential principles were retained, and in the eighteenth century Saint-Cyr afforded its pupils a comprehensive education as well as a sound spiritual training.

Mademoiselle d'Ars and her mother had survived the Revolution without being molested in any way. Indeed priests in hiding were able to say Mass in the little oratory of the château garden. Her mother had now been dead for seven years. Her brother, the Vicomte, lived with his wife in the Faubourg Saint-Germain in

Paris. Every year they came to Ars to visit during the fine weather. They had no children and were not in line to inherit the place.

Mademoiselle d'Ars now picked up some coarse cloth and thick thread: she was making a pair of breeches for a poor man. She was an excellent needlewoman and could do delicate work, but as she thought that hard labour was a Christian's salvation she selected the roughest work for herself. After two or three hours, a servant came in to tend the fire and bring her a box of her favourite books, for she had her set time for study and recreation as well as for work. At Saint-Cyr, where she had stayed until 1774, when she had reached the age of twenty, she had acquired the habit of reading good books—Bossuet, Fénelon and St. Francis de Sales.

A small oil painting still hanging in the château shows Mademoiselle d'Ars seated, a ruched bonnet on her head, a shawl over her shoulders. On the large, round, black marble table beside her is a crucifix mounted on velvet, at her feet purrs the homely, necessary cat. She looks plain but kind.[1] Thus we can picture her as she sat on the day of the Curé's first visit.

Round about her were family portraits: her mother as a girl with roses in her hair, holding a mandolin; her naval brother in full battle-dress (he had been killed in an engagement with the English). He had been a page to Queen Marie Leczinska, and his face was jolly and rubicund in the best eighteenth-century manner. Alongside his, a perfectly enchanting small portrait in oils of an ancestress at the court of Louis Seize, her decolleté gown showing to advantage the long, lovely line of her white neck, a rose in her powdered hair.

On the other side of the chimney piece was a picture of Madame de Maintenon. Mademoiselle d'Ars loved having it there, for it brought back memories of happy years at Saint-Cyr.

She recalled the visits of Louis Quinze to the school—his elegance, his bored blue eyes half hooded by the drooping lids. Little girls, however carefully guarded, always seem to know everything. She heard whispering about a Madame de Pompadour and a Ma-

[1] I have seen her table. Monsieur Vianney leaned on it during his flying visits. He never sat down.

dame du Barry, though of course she never saw either lady. But she could remember visits from Louis XVI's small sisters, Madame Clothilde, who really was such a little saint, and Madame Elizabeth, very headstrong; and also from Louis XV's spinster daughters, Mesdames de France, who occasionally came to hear Vespers and to partake of some delicate refreshment with the Mother Superior. The eldest daughter, Madame Adelaide, was very fond of children. She remembered her in a red velvet dress, and with only two front teeth left.

Mademoiselle d'Ars recalled the thrilling time when the young Austrian Dauphine, Marie-Antoinette, rode over on a donkey, much to the dismay of the Duchess who was supposed to supervise her manners. She was very pretty and had a beautiful complexion, but seemed bored and restless. No, the school of Saint-Cyr with its severity and old traditions would not have suited the Dauphine.

One April day when Mademoiselle d'Ars was only ten, she heard the housemaids whispering among themselves that the Pompadour had died and that her body, covered by a thin sheet, had been carried out on a wheelbarrow, for there was a stern rule that no corpse was to be kept in the palace of Versailles.

She had seen the new Petit Trianon for which the architect, Gabriel, had drawn plans in 1762. In 1768—that is, four years after the death of the Pompadour—Queen Marie Leczinska died, almost forgotten in her palace of Versailles. A shockingly short time after that, the King had taken an unspeakable street woman, Madame Du Barry, as a mistress. (How unlike Louis Quartorze, the co-founder of Saint-Cyr, whose mistresses had all been aristocratic! She could almost imagine Madame de Maintenon turning in her grave.) And then had come the terrible May of 1774, when Mademoiselle d'Ars was twenty and left Saint-Cyr for good. Louis XV died of smallpox, and scarcely had the announcement been made when the palace was emptied. All fled for fear of contagion. Oh yes, she had lived through exciting times. And now she was here at Ars and would be here always. She never went to Paris.

She was completely content. The system of education at Saint-Cyr had been precisely suitable for girls who were to live quiet and useful lives in remote country châteaux. And at the age of sixty-four, Mademoiselle d'Ars was to be rewarded for her virtue by becoming for fourteen years the friend of a saint. A lovely omen hints that she too had attained to holiness. Every year on his feast day of St. John the Baptist she used to give Monsieur Vianney a bunch of madonna lilies, and once, when he had forgotten them and left them out in the sun for a week, they still remained fresh. "'Mademoiselle d'Ars must certainly be a saint for her flowers to live in this way," said the Curé.

On that first afternoon, Mademoiselle d'Ars, having finished her reading for the day, put away her books, took out her well-bound apothecary's notebook and began to copy a recipe for curing scrofula out of an old herbal. Outside, the February day was fading into dun, ashen twilight. Just at that time Monsieur Vianney, having despatched his meal standing up in the kitchen, put on his great tricorne and left the presbytery. He crossed the village square under the walnut trees, glanced at the graves huddling close up to the little church, then turned to the right at the end of the village street and walked towards the château to pay his first call.

A sullen boy driving an emaciated cow with a goad looked up at him with indifference and did not greet him. The Curé smiled at the boy and blessed him. The clock struck the hour, and he paused to bless it, just as he'd seen his mother do in the middle of all her farm and household tasks.

He looked up at the Château d'Ars in the distance. In the eleventh century it had been a feudal manor with towers, ditches and crenellated battlements. These had been dismantled, and it was now, as Monseigneur Trochu says, "nothing more than a vast country house standing in peaceful melancholy, forgetful of all the hunts and joyful clamours of long ago."

Monseigneur Trochu has also said, in his book, *Autour du Curé d'Ars:* "He grew to love this ancient dwelling place for the austerity of its stones, for the solitude and peace of its great oak trees. In time of sorrow he would be among the first to come to it with consolation."

The Fontblin brook, swollen by the winter rains, separated the village from the château. At length the Curé caught a glimpse of the big house behind a row of poplar trees and in the shadow of a grove of hornbeams. When he got closer he saw the faded pink bricks clearly.

And now the untidy, shabby little Curé was presenting his compliments to the lively, courteous Mademoiselle d'Ars, who was also small. He did not notice what other people found so charming —that she was very distinguished; that her manners of the *ancien régime*, although of an older fashion, were easy and graceful; that she had a charming flexibility of mind; that when she talked of the past she could be like a living chronicle, her conversation bearing comparison with the most interesting memoirs. Oh no, those were only externals and the Curé of Ars really was not much interested in them. Those large piercing blue eyes looked straight into the soul of his parishioner, and after the first quarter of an hour of conversation he realized two things about her, which nobody else had thought important. The first was that she had been unloved and misunderstood by both her mother and her school mistresses at Saint-Cyr (their letters to her were frigid and conventional). The other was that her own warm heart, although it had taken refuge in works of charity, had never found room to expand in her life of prayer. Her poor soul had been frozen in the chill breath of Jansenism which was blighting the spiritual life of France at the end of the eighteenth century. She went to Communion very rarely. He persuaded her to go more often.

To him she was a soul to be saved, one of those to whom his whole life was dedicated, and for whom he had prepared himself so devotedly. He noticed many things about her that he valued; her soul was tranquil, joyful, she was outwardly happy. Whenever they spoke of anything alarming, she would say, "Oh, *mon Dieu!*" Grey hairs might peep from under her white bonnet, but age had only mellowed her disposition; she had an indulgent and understanding heart for the frailties of others.

"Ah, Monsieur le Curé," she said, "if you only knew how hard I have tried to teach the catechism to the children here, but it's nearly impossible. They are so very ignorant. For example, what do you think one of the little boys answered the other day when I asked him who were the three persons of the blessed Trinity? He said: 'Mary, Jesus and Joseph.' "

Monsieur Vianney laughed. "Well," he said, "from All Saints Day until the time of First Communions I will teach catechism to the children at six o'clock in the morning."

"Oh, I will come too then, and I will learn my catechism with you. I'm afraid those children are culpably ignorant," she added, "and unworthy of receiving Holy Communion."

"Oh, you must not be so severe," he said. "The moment I see the first elements of understanding and good-will pierce the cloud of their ignorance, I will let them come to the classes preparing them for Holy Communion."

Monsieur Vianney's glance travelled up to the portrait of the ancestress with the decolleté evening dress. "You would think she was going to the guillotine," he said. And he looked away.

Mademoiselle d'Ars decided to have the portrait removed to an attic as soon as he left.

To change the topic (for she was blushing furiously) she said, "Monsieur le Curé, I know every family in the neighbourhood, particularly the poor ones. I know their genealogies and the names and ages of their children. Do come to me if you want to know the names of your parishioners. I hope they will give you the welcome you deserve. They're not bad people, you know. I mean, they're not anti-clerical—" and she laughed uncomfortably. "I suppose they have plenty of excuses for not being very pious, shall I say. But there are one or two excellent families in the neighbourhood. For example, there is the farm of the Lassagnes. Madame Lassagne is a devout woman with many children, and I'm sure she'd back you up anywhere. And Monsieur Mandy, the mayor, an excellent man, would be a good friend to you."

"I wonder if he'd help me to eradicate the dancing on feast days? It takes place quite near the church."

"The dancing?" she said, surprised. "Isn't it quite harmless? I give little dances myself here with the neighbours when my young relations come to stay in the summer."

"Ah," he said, smiling, "it may be all right for you, for you dance,
I suppose—what do you call them?—gavottes and minuets, but
these poor peasants, they dance *bourrées*. Your dancing may all be
in perfect decorum. But theirs is rough and coarse and can lead
to sin. Ah, mademoiselle, help me in this! In order to set an example
to these poor souls who are jigging to their ruin, give up minuets
in the château. They set such a bad example to the peasants."

She hesitated a moment as she thought of the innocuousness of
her old brother the Vicomte, for example, prancing on his old-
fashioned red heels. But already she loved and respected her Curé,
and she said: "Of course, Monsieur le Curé, just as you wish."

(Her friend Madame Christine de Cibeins said rather haughtily
of the Curé: "He only knew about dancing from the disorders it
caused in the country.")

He said, "I was brought up on a book by Messire Joseph Lambert, on the manner of instructing country people. He always
speaks very strongly about dancing being an occasion of sin. He
even quotes from St. John Chrysostom and explains that the Devil
is always present at dances, for his ministers and slaves take their
recreation from them." Then he thought of his own patron and
said, "St. John the Baptist beheaded for Salome's pleasure by
wicked Herod—his head was the price of a dance. I think I will put
that up on a notice board if ever I have the privilege of building a
chapel for him. I remember Messire Joseph Lambert said that
the shameless dancing-woman who asked for the head of John
the Baptist must make us hate all dances."

At this point Monsieur de Saint-Phal came in with a tray on
which was a steaming infusion of lime-flower tea, a large bowl
containing lumps of sugar, and a little silver plate of delicately
flavoured macaroons. All of these Monsieur Vianney refused with
the greatest courtesy and firmness. Then he suddenly remembered
one of the chief reasons for his visit.

"Mademoiselle, I have to thank you with all my heart for your
kindness in supplying me with so many kitchen utensils and so
much good furniture. I ask your permission most humbly to return
them in the morning before my brother-in-law goes back to Ecully.
You see—" and he laughed apologetically—"I did bring a few

things of my own and I won't need many kitchen implements."

"What does your housekeeper have to say to that?"

"Oh, my dear old friend the widow Bibost. Well, she's come for a day or two to settle me in, but I don't think she will stay very long. You see, I prefer to manage for myself. I love my privacy and solitude, and I have such a small appetite and such a very queasy stomach that I would much prefer to choose my own times for eating, and indeed to prepare my own food."

"Oh," she implored, "you must be careful to eat enough. You don't want to lose your health."

"Oh, I am very strong, mademoiselle. I am as strong as a horse, and two hours sleep always restores me. And now, my dear mademoiselle, I give you my blessing. I will pray for you at the altar every day and I will rejoice if I can be the means of bringing you oftener to Holy Communion. But I leave you now, as I want to start on my parochial visits. . . ."

A few days later Mademoiselle d'Ars, sitting very upright at her desk in front of her quills, ink, sealing wax, candle, and her sand-pot for blotting, began a letter all about the new Curé to her brother the Vicomte, in Paris. She bubbled with enthusiasm. She said: "We are the spoilt children of Providence. I have never known a priest as devout as our new Curé. He never leaves the church. At the altar he is a seraph. In the pulpit he is not an orator like Monsieur Berger, but he is completely filled by the spirit of God . . . He eats practically nothing. Pray that God may uphold him and keep him for us a long time. . . ."

Mademoiselle d'Ars was to experience many alarms about the health of her beloved Curé. Indeed, there came a time when he had damaged his health to such an extent that she was able to persuade him to see a doctor of her choice, Monsieur Timécourt. This apothecary very painstakingly wrote out a most careful new diet sheet. It is almost laughable to think what a waste of time that was. And the only thing that Mademoiselle d'Ars could make the Curé accept was . . . a packet of tea.

8. *MONSIEUR VIANNEY STARTS SAVING HIS FLOCK*

WHILE MONSIEUR VIANNEY WAS PAYING HIS FIRST CALL ON MADEmoiselle d'Ars, the widow Bibost was getting ready to return to Ecully, with many tears shed into her large red handkerchief and many blowings of her nose. She bade good-bye to Madame Renard and her daughter Marianne and commended her dear Curé to their care.

"I would have stayed on had I thought I could be of any use to him. But he will not eat and he will not look after himself. I'm wasting my time," she wailed. "Oh, saints are very difficult to look after. And then, of course, I myself might starve into the bargain, and I'm not made of the stuff of martyrs."

"Never mind, *ma bonne,*" murmured Madame Renard. "We will do our best. I will come every day with a supply of good white bread and some pancakes. When he realizes all the trouble and expense I've been to, he'll have to eat them."

"I shouldn't be too sure," said the widow Bibost.

"And I will do the laundering of his shirts and nightshifts."

"But he doesn't always wear a nightshift. I suspect that he'll sleep in his clothes up in that attice with the rats. As for his sheets—oh dear, it is all too painful and complicated. I wonder what his family would say. I shall have to tell his sister, Marguerite, and his brother, François. Perhaps if they came to visit him quite soon they could make him see reason. Mercy! If his mother were alive, she wouldn't like it—although, to be sure, she agreed with him in everything.

But it was always like that at Ecully. That's what has come of living with Monsieur Balley. He was a saint too. He set Monsieur Vianney the bad example of missing meals."

When the Curé had settled in to the presbytery, well-intentioned Madame Renard had many shocks. Her appetizing loaf of white bread was at once given by Monsieur Vianney to a beggar who came to the door. She burst into tears when she saw it. It was only the first of such incidents. Once she asked him if he would fancy a pie if she made one. He said he would love it. She expended her best efforts in making the pie and again he gave it away at once. His excuse, when she complained of this, was that he thought he could do what he wanted with his own things.

Madame Renard was forbidden to be in and out of the presbytery at any hour. Monsieur Vianney specified the day and the hour when she might come; otherwise the door was uncompromisingly locked. He safeguarded his privacy completely. He knew what villages could be for small talk.

Anyway he wanted to be alone to start his life of penance for the souls of his parishioners. And then, it was delightful not to be tied down to definite meal times. Indeed he chose the time of the midday meal to visit his parishioners, for he knew that he would always find them at home then.

At first he wasn't received with very great enthusiasm, but when they saw how charming and amusing he was, and how, being a peasant himself, he understood all about their lives and labours and enquired so intelligently about their crops and cattle, they accepted him, and after a while they even welcomed him. He did not stay long in any place. He refused to accept any food or drink offered to him, but used to stand by the hearth and chat for a short time, asking the names and ages of all the children, perhaps glancing at the mantelshelf to see if there was a crucifix, perhaps saying grace at the end of a meal. Anyway, bringing God in somehow. After a while the farmers began to say among themselves: "We have a poor church, but we have a holy Curé."[1]

Opposite the church is still to be seen today, quite unspoiled, the

[1] These are the mayor's words, and he was echoing the people of Ars.

farmyard and the great doorway of the Cinier family. Cinier was a
farmer with twelve children. You got into his house by a flight of
outdoor stone steps. A little Cinier boy was to remember to the end
of his life how one day the Curé, seeing a plate of steaming potatoes
on the table, picked one up. He said, "It looks very good," and then
returned it to its dish. This was his form of mortification. He was
simply longing to eat that potato!

He did his own cooking when he remembered. Indeed, throughout that first Holy Week of 1818 he had only two meals. He offered
his fasts—terrible and inimitable—for the souls of his flock. He
would cook a week's supply of boiled potatoes in the large iron
saucepan which we can still see in the kitchen; then throughout the
week he would help himself to one or two at midday. Towards the
end of the week they would go downy with mould, but he would
peel them with his fingers and eat them standing up. Occasionally,
as a great luxury, he would cook an egg on hot ashes, or he would
make some of the local pancakes called *matefaims* (hunger-
slayers) in his long-handled frying pan. They consisted of flour, salt
and water, and were, of course, extremely heavy. Speaking of those
early days he used to say: "How happy I was in those times when
I was alone! When I needed food I made three pancakes. While
I was eating the first one, I would bake the second; when I was
baking the third, I was eating the second. I would be eating the
third while I was tidying away my frying pan and putting my fire
out; I would drink a large glass of water, and that was enough for
several days. . . !"

One day widow Renard, who had been allowed to pasture her
cow in his neglected little garden, found him eating sorrel. But the
sorrel-eating didn't last long.

The Gospels say that the demon of impurity can only be driven
out by fasting and prayer. The Curé took Our Lord at His word.
He wanted his flock to be chaste. He knew that taking the discipline was not so effective as doing without food, drink and sleep;
the Devil was more frightened of that. The Curé said some years
later that during those early days he could obtain from God

everything that he wanted. And he said that those days of mortification were also times of extraordinary graces.

A little frightened by widow Bibost's tearful accounts, his sister Marguerite hastened to Ars accompanied by a friend. (They prudently provided themselves with a loaf of bread.) Her brother received her very cordially but had nothing better to offer them than potatoes which were already going green. His elder brother, François, was treated even worse than that—he was obliged to go and dig up the potatoes in the garden and cook them himself.

The Lenten weeks went by; the church still seemed almost as empty as before, and the congregation just as sleepy as ever when he preached. Easter came and he was even more discouraged to see how few kept the precept of the yearly Communion. When the weather improved, he would go for long walks in the country round about, and in the intervals of saying his rosary and his Office, he would talk to himself and pray for the souls of his dear flock. Oh, he saw their sins quite clearly. They would work on Sundays and feast days, because they loved money. They would keep their children away from church and catechism through the same avarice. They blasphemed the holy name of God. So many men spent all their earnings at the taverns and left their families to starve.

Then there were the junketings to celebrate weddings, and these were not as innocent as we might imagine. They were not just charming rural festivities of the *ancien régime*; with their coarseness, drunkenness, over-eating and lasciviousness they were more like pagan Bacchanalia. (Some things of this sort still go on; in the Dordogne district of France, for example, where the bride and bridegroom, after going to bed at the end of the day's festivities, are awakened from their first sleep by all the wedding guests, who come to sprawl on their bed, make them drink champagne and then, horror of horrors, take their photographs.) The Curé deplored the night-long dancing in the village square under the walnut trees. He would see the couples leave the square and go off to the hedgerows. And he knew quite well that bastards would appear in due course.

The other evil was the gatherings at night. In order to econ-
omize lamp oil several families composed of both old and young
people would meet in a barn and sing songs together—some of
them rather brawling, drunken songs; then, under cover of the
semi-darkness, things would be done which would have put
pagans to shame. But some of the mothers of families, returning
home very late at night, would see that their Curé was still in
church, and they would go in to confession. After a while he suggested to them that they should read aloud to one another at these
late night gatherings and sing some of the old laments like "The
Wandering Jew":

> Sur le mont du Calvaire
> Jésus portait sa croix:
> Il me dit, Débonnaire,
> Passant devant chez moi:
> Veux tu bien, mon ami,
> Que je repose ici?

Monsieur Vianney had already gained experience in dealing
with those night assemblies during his time in hiding at Les Noës.
At Ars, he would gently suggest that they should start the evening by reciting the rosary—and what about some holy songs, like
a hymn to the Passion or the "Lament of Geneviève de Brabant"?
And before they parted for the night, they should all say their
prayers together. (In the autumn, he collected his people at the
presbytery to crack nuts for sale, to provide lamp oil for the
church.)

As he walked in the woods around Ars, he would sometimes look
up at the birds, for they raised his mind to God. A little shepherdess, Catherine Lassagne, used to watch him disappear into the
woods with his breviary and rosary: "He took pleasure in going
off to pray in the woods. There, alone with God, he gazed at His
glories, making use of everything, even of bird-songs, to rise to
Him."

He always returned to his sorrowful thoughts about the souls
of his sinners. One day when the Mayor, Monsieur Mandy, was

crossing the wood called the Bois de la Papesse—full of vipers, incidentally—he caught a glimpse of Monsieur Vianney on his knees. He was sobbing and saying over and over again, "My God, convert my parish. My God, convert my parish."

Monsieur Mandy, unobserved by the Curé, went away, delicately. Like Agag.

The Curé loved in particular the ancient trees of the woods surrounding the Château de Cibeins, which was across the Fontblin brook. And there, thinking himself alone, he would often kneel down to say the Gloria Patri of his Office, whatever the weather. But he was seen by Madame Christine de Cibeins, the one who had been rather disdainful when he persuaded Mademoiselle d'Ars to give up dances in her château.

Quite soon people began to exchange impressions as to what they had seen or heard about him. For example, there was a man living near the church who saw him going in with his candle and was rather curious to see what he was going to do in church so early in the morning. He peeped through the door and saw him at his prayers. He went back to his house saying, "This man is not like other men!"

These weeks of that first spring and early summer, before the Curé's time was completely taken up by work in his confessional, were to be the last in which he would enjoy the beauties of nature, although to the very end memories of lovely country sights and sounds returned to enrich his catechism lessons. In fact, Comtesse des Garets said of him years later: "Our old St. Francis of Assisi is more poetic than ever."

One day he said in one of his sermons: "I was coming back from Savigneux. The little birds were singing in the wood. I began to cry. Poor little things, I thought. God created you to sing, and you sing... Man was made to love God, and he does not love Him!"

Yes, in the springtime he slipped into poetry.

"Good desires are the breath of the Holy Spirit, which passes over our souls and renews all within them, like the warm wind which melts the ice and brings back the spring."

"A soul indwelt by the Holy Spirit gives forth a delicious fragrance like that of the vine in flower."

"In the soul united to God, it is always springtime."

"The Holy Spirit rests in a pure soul as on a bed of roses."

"The pure soul is a beautiful rose, and the Three Divine Persons come down from heaven to breathe in its perfume."

One can see that he had tended the vine. There are so many similes and lessons taken from his father's vineyard. "There is a delightful sweetness in prayer which is like the juice trickling down from a ripe grape."

"Put a fine bunch of grapes in the wine press and delicious juice will come from it. Our soul under the pressure of the Cross will give forth a juice which nourishes and fortifies it."

But whereas people of the older generation who had known good teaching in the pre-revolutionary years, and beggars who were overwhelmed by his kindnesses might listen to his exhortations, the young people were hard to win. And that was because the young men were enraged with him for stopping the dancing. He did it in his own deft way. He would go to the hired fiddler and say, "What are they giving you to play for their dance?" and he would give him a little more than he had been promised, to go away without playing. So when the dance began, no fiddler. He refused to give absolution to girls who confessed that they had been present at a dance, even without dancing. He said that a ballroom was attended by the Devil; the dancers left their guardian angels at the door and there were as many devils as dancers.

Gradually some of the more decent girls, threatened by their parents, stayed away, and only a few maid-servants would turn up. In the confessional he was always very strict with girls. He would not give them absolution unless they promised to give up the occasion of sin, which of course was quite in accordance with the teaching of the Church. The young men were furious.

It was these youths who persecuted poor Monsieur Vianney so cruelly during those first years and made his life so complete a hell that he would have rejoiced to leave Ars altogether. They would shout at him from the street in the mornings when he appeared at his front door. And he would see that they had covered the door with filth, or had written disgusting insults on placards. Or at night they would rouse him from his short hours of sleep by catcalls and whistles.

To one father taking his daughter to a dance—"just to look on," he explained—the Curé said, "Ah yes, but if her feet don't dance, her heart will." He knew how frail young people could be.

Soon those lecherous youths began a slandering campaign. They egged on an immoral girl to stand under his window and cry out that he was the father of her bastard. (Slander is one of the distinguishing marks of the lecher. He must smear others with his own filth.) They said his pallor was due to secret excesses.

And all this Monsieur Vianney bore in silence, grieved silence like that of his Master before Pilate. He disdained to vindicate himself from the pulpit, or even in private conversation. He knew that eventually the Lord would clear his name. At length rumours of these slanders reached the bishop, and he sent a priest to enquire into it all.

Monsieur Vianney's personal appearance did not do much to reassure his clerical colleagues in the neighbourhood. In fact there was a luncheon at which a priest refused to sit next to him because he said his hat was dirty. And this was said to a man of great sensitiveness, with a boiling temper to keep under!

The owners of the four taverns, when they served wine to those wild youths, would join them in their vituperations. But soon it seemed as if any tavern-keeper settling in Ars was doomed to failure. Eventually they all went bankrupt, and when new ones took their place, they too had to leave. Gradually, moved by the Curé's sermons, the drunkards became fewer and fewer, and as a result, paupers became scarcer too. How well the homilies of Messire Lambert had described the evils of country taverns, thought Monsieur Vianney.

It would have been too easy if he had become a great saint without undergoing temptation to despair. That is the direst crucible for the soul. Both St. Bernadette and St. Margaret-Mary, to mention only two, knew it from bitter experience. His consolations must have ceased for a time. Perhaps his fasting had worn down his physical resistance to the breaking point. He was so humble that he knew himself to be less than nothing; he lacked those resources of natural vitality and ambition which fortify an ordinary man, and therefore was at the mercy of his low opinion of himself. He once asked God to show him his own nothingness, and the sight was so "awe-full" that he quickly took back so rash a prayer.

He began to despair of his own salvation, and he almost despaired of being able to save the souls of his parishioners. In those early days there was a touch of Jansenism in his outlook. (This was to melt away during the mellower years of middle age.) It seemed to him that sins of impurity were beyond complete redemption even by Christ's blood (which of course is totally against Christian teaching). He said, "The soul which has committed sins against purity is like a rag which has been dipped in oil. However much you wash it, it is never quite free of the smell and the taint of oil." Whereas Scripture teaches us that the Blood of the Lamb can make any soul whiter than snow.

One can see that he could only have given way to such bad theology through despair.

To live on great heights, either of mystical experience or of idealism, isolates a man from his neighbours. Although towards the end of his life he was surrounded by devoted friends, there were very, very few indeed—in fact hardly any—who could understand the joys and griefs of his mystical experience. Sin to him was not just an act which when repented could be forgotten; it was a rejection of God's love. He would look up with tears in his eyes and say: "Oh children, how much we ought to love God." And he knew that the sinner was constantly rejecting that love.

In the interval between attacks of despair, he was now having more than fleeting glimpses of God so lovable, so loving. He could not bear to think of that unutterable tenderness being affronted by the smallest neglect or hurt. The remorse he experienced bears some comparison to the grief we should feel if, after the death of a parent greatly misunderstood, we came upon some private diary or correspondence which revealed him as an exquisite and deeply-loving person, and knew we had sent him to his grave unloved and misunderstood. (But of course the analogy breaks down because we can, to our dying day, always turn to the Divine Lover in repentance.)

He stormed and wept in the pulpit. He strained his poor voice until it cracked. He employed all the arts of oratory and mime to bring these poor souls back to God. And if, as was sometimes their unpleasant practice, the parishioners began leaving before the sermon, he would have recourse to a trick, for he too was a wily peasant. For example, preaching about restitution of stolen goods: "My brethren, I am going to preach against thieves. Any among you who feel guilty would do well to go out, because I have some hard truths to tell." Of course no one dared to leave.

Though he preached on morality, he could never keep away for long from the love of God which was his favourite topic.

"Our Lord who takes pleasure in doing the will of those who love him. . . ."

". . .Oh my God, how you love those who love you! How afraid you are that they should suffer! . . . ."

But in those early preachings there was a great deal about Hell and the Last Judgment. One can imagine how dramatic he was with his gestures, his tone of voice, and his use of imaginary dialogues. Here is the young girl on her deathbed: "Where is that seducer who has robbed me of Heaven? No, no, come forward, there is no more escape now. . . You are damned! No hope for you; yes, you are lost; everything is lost since you have lost your soul and your God. . ."

Can not one imagine the fright of some of the guilty girls in the back seats? And there were terrible passages too about sacrilegious Communions, which must have made many tremble.

"I want to fulfil my Easter duties, you say, I want to make my Communion. You want to make your Communion? But, unhappy one, where will you put your God? Will it be in your eyes, which you have soiled by so many impure and adulterous glances? You want to make your Communion? But where, then, will you put your God? Is it in your hands which you have soiled by so many sinful touches? You want to make your Communion, but where will you put your God? In your mouth? Ah, great God! A mouth which you have so often profaned by impure kisses. You wish to make your Communion, but where, then, do you hope to place your God? In your heart? O horror, O abomination! A heart which is all darkened and blackened by sin, like a brand which has been rolling in the fire."

Sometimes the sermons of this young priest would reduce these sensual peasants to tears. They would listen to his reproaches and sarcasms and then discuss them on their farms and in the fields and even in the taverns. And often young men who had come from the neighbouring hamlets to scoff and jeer remained to weep.

A little seven-year-old boy, one of the mayor's sons, testified that even when he was a very small child he could listen to the Curé preaching with pleasure, that he understood him quite well and time did not drag during the sermon. What a good testimonial that is.

The Curé used to say, as if to excuse himself for having kept them too long, "When I am with you, my brethren, I am not bored."

He knew that religious instruction was one of the things necessary to the eternal salvation of his flock, but there was a means more powerful than the pulpit. We can see some evidence of his terrible mortifications on the rough-cast walls of his bedroom; the wall behind the curtain of his bed is splotched with blood, as if in the midst of taking the discipline he had leaned his bleeding shoulder against it, half-swooning, or had braced himself with a blood-stained hand against the wall as he rose. His instruments of penance never lasted much more than a fortnight. When Madame Renard was allowed to clean his bedroom, she used to find chains, keys, nails and little bits of iron, struck from the discipline by the violence of his blows, all over the floor when she swept. A woman who came to stay with her was filled with fear and pity when she heard the Curé giving himself the discipline for two hours on end.

A man who saw the Curé in March of the year he died has written: "I am still struck by the terrible resemblance which he had to a picture of Our Lord Scourged hanging on the wall. . . By dint of imitating his Master, the Curé of Ars had come to look like him."

And Catherine Lassagne, who sometimes washed his linen, used to say it filled one with pity to see the left shoulder of his shirts all torn and stained with blood. But he had told God that he was prepared to suffer torment for a hundred years if only he could save the souls of his flock. For them too he offered up the pains endured from sleeping on the damp ground. He had to stop it after a time because of the facial neuralgia it caused. He had this neuralgia for fifteen years. He had in sober fact offered his body as a sacrificial victim for all the sinners under his care.

After a while, swept into his wake through the sheer force of his example, the people of Ars began to listen and obey him. They could not fail to see that he was utterly devoid of avarice or ambition. In little ways they began to try and live up to what he expected of them.

It would have been quite understandable, quite natural, if he had sought a little relaxation in the devoted friendship of Madame Claudine Renard and of a certain good Mademoiselle Pignaut who had left Lyons and come to live at Ars because she admired him so much. But he kept them at a distance, taught them supernatural detachment. Occasionally these two would reproach him for never asking them to a meal. Abbé Monnin tells us what he did about this: "On an evening when Monsieur le Curé had renewed his supply of bread for the poor and his basket was full, he went to find his neighbour. 'Claudine,' he said to her, in a tone of voice which was more lighthearted than usual, 'you must visit me soon with your daughter and Mademoiselle Pignaut. I want all three of you to come.' The women were delighted and looked forward impatiently to the hour of the rendezvous, when they would find out what Monsieur le Curé wanted of them. 'What I want of you?' he said to them when they came in. 'Can't you guess? I want you to have supper with me! Aren't you pleased?

We shall eat the bread of the poor, the friends of Our Lord, and we shall drink the good water of the good God. So much for the body. And then we shall read the lives of the saints, so penitent and so mortified. That will be for the soul. Come along, let's set to work.'

"The good Curé had spread his table and arranged the feast in this way. In the middle was a basket filled with the bread of the poor. On the right, the *Lives of the Saints* in a large folio volume. On the left, a pail of water with a wooden cup. When she saw this careful arrangement, Claudine Renard, who was in the secret, exchanged a glance with Monsieur le Curé and smiled. The two others were a little startled. Without seeming to notice their embarrassment, Monsieur Vianney gravely blessed the table and offered to each a crust of bread. 'I did not dare refuse,' said Marianne Renard, when she told this story. 'I got to the end of my portion of bread, and my mother did too, but Mademoiselle Pignaut, with the best will in the world, could not swallow hers. All the time this visit lasted, she was on tenterhooks—never before in her life had she attended such a feast. She never mentioned getting herself invited a second time.' "

This mortification of his was all the more admirable because, as he once let slip, he loved really good new bread. One day when he saw it coming out of the oven at his orphanage, he said, "Some day I shall really have to be greedy and eat as much as I want."

Poor widow Renard! She always had recourse to tears when the Curé defeated her, and that was often. He discarded the feather tick and mattress of his bed, then the bedspread, so that only the palliasse remained. This miserable palliasse was not sufficiently filled with straw to make it comfortable, but for him it was too luxurious: he used to take handfuls of straw out and throw them into the fire. Catherine Lassagne tells how she and his other occasional housekeeper, Claudine Renard, tried secretly to put a few handfuls of straw into the depleted palliasse, only to find the ashes in the fireplace. Finally he put a board on top of it. He would have thought it a sin to lie in bed if he were awake, because it meant yielding too much to what he called his corpse (*mon cadavre*), his old Adam. He saw a direct connection between sloth and sins against purity. He said that the Devil despises us for sexual sins, since the fiends do not themselves commit them, being spirits. Here is an extract from one of his sermons on the subject:

"There are some souls so utterly dead and corrupt that they grovel in their pollution without perceiving it, and without having any power to free themselves from it. Everything leads them to evil; everything, even the most holy thing, reminds them of evil; they have these abominations continually before their eyes, like an unclean animal which delights to wallow in filth. Such souls are abhorrent to the eyes of God and His holy angels."

He never relaxed his vigilance, never gave himself a moment's respite from his self-denial. There was something mischievous in his determination to refuse any treats. One day a good housekeeper (of whom we shall hear more later) said to him, "Would you like some pancakes?" "Yes, I would," he replied with an eagerness which should have made her suspicious. She sifted her flour, beat her eggs, called in Mademoiselle Pignaut for advice. While she was doing this in the kitchen the Curé cast many a sidelong glance at her from blue eyes in which there was a hint of mockery. When all was finished the steaming, appetizing dish was put before him with due solemnity. He joined his hands, lifted his eyes to heaven as if he were about to say grace; and while they were praying with their eyes modestly downcast, he gave a quick glance round, seized the dish, sprinted down stairs with it and gave it to a poor man! Most disheartening for all of them.

Sometimes the village people who met him would see him trying to hide something in his cassock. It was some dainty tidbit he had been given and was determined not to eat. He was very much upset when the people to whom he wanted to give it were away from home. When this happened he would hide it and go to look for someone else who would like it. Often, by the time he returned, a cat or dog had cleaned the dish.

There was an old blind woman who begged by the church door: she was very dear to him, and often as she was spinning flax, he would go up to her on tiptoe and put something in her apron without uttering a word. When she felt it with her hand, she would say, thinking it came from one of her good women neighbours, *"Grand merci, ma mie, grand merci"*—"Thank you a thousand times, my love, thank you a thousand times." This always sent the Curé off into gales of laughter. He used to pay her rent too and looked after her in many other ways.

Occasionally somebody used to try to bribe him to eat better, but only once did this strategy succeed: a friend promised him the sum of ten francs if he would eat some chicken. When he was at the end of his tether he used to say to himself with gentle mockery: "Come along. Hold yourself up straight." He was imitating the village drunk, who used to talk to himself in that way when he could no longer walk straight.

When he was upbraided later on about his mortifications, he used to call them his "youthful follies." Once in a sermon on sanctity he said: "To become a saint one must be mad, one must have lost one's head."

9. THE DEVIL IS ANGRY: 1824

MONSIEUR VIANNEY KNEW THAT IF HE COULD MAKE SURE OF THE Christian education of the parish children, the battle was won. He did not in the least approve of the mixed school in the mayor's house, where a farm hand gave lessons to dilatory pupils in winter when they were not needed in the fields. In 1823 he was praying about this and thinking whom he could get to teach in a school for little girls, when one day, kneeling in the church (which he had hardly left all that day and half the night before) he made a mental review of all those among his young parishioners who led good lives. With his marvellous gift of intuition he knew that he had found just the right pair of girls when he saw in his mind's eye their simple and candid faces. One was Benoîte Lardet, aged twenty, and the other Catherine Lassagne, aged seventeen—the same little shepherdess who had caught a glimpse of him praying in the woods, and who herself loved the contemplative hours she spent by the Fontblin stream. Both girls consented.

There was much to be done before the school could be started. The two teachers had to be sent away for training and a house had to be bought. By November 1824 all was ready, and the school was opened on Thursday, the eleventh.

In the meantime, it was in that very year, 1824, that diabolical infestations began in Monsieur Vianney's presbytery. They were to continue for the next thirty-five years of his life. So while Benoîte and Catherine were preparing to found La Providence, the most remarkable little school and orphanage that has ever been recorded in history, let us pause upon this awful new trouble of the Curé's.

The Devil chose this time because he knew the immense good that La Providence would do. It would play a great part in the conversion of Ars, and after that the example of Ars would help to convert the thousands and thousands of pilgrims from all over Christendom who came every year to the confessional of the Curé.

Monseigneur Trochu has pointed out the parallel between this terrible trial of Monsieur Vianney's and the afflictions of Job.

The Prince of Darkness, wandering up and down the country roads of France, had come upon this simple country priest. True, he had not lacked afflictions up to then—the filthy slanders of the young men in his parish, the insults screamed at him by the village harlot, the suspicions of his colleagues. But he had not yet, in Gerard Manley Hopkins' words, been touched in his "bower of bone," "turned for an exquisite smart." He had had terrible attacks of despair, and the sins of men against so loving a God grieved him beyond measure. But he had also had consolations. In those early days he had much time for prayer, and prayer was an utter joy to him. And then when the day's prayer and work were over, he still had two or three hours' sleep in quiet, in privacy, in the little bedroom of his presbytery. A room of one's own!—the only luxury we crave; just a little solitude at the end of the day, an hour or two in which to restore one's strength. And that was the very thing which was now taken from him.

By disturbing his sleep, the Devil hoped to weary the poor priest to such an extent that in desperation he would abandon all, and in so doing would cause La Providence to collapse. Loving Our Lord as he did, the Curé had, as we have seen, a tendency to despair of himself, and it is precisely on this point that the Devil tempted him. During an illness in that first winter of 1824 he heard a voice repeating to him: "Now is the time to fall into Hell."

Imagine him. It is near midnight. He is sleeping his usual uneasy sleep, having done various penances. The hamlet is utterly quiet. The dogs are chained up, the cats are asleep. No scratching or clucking of hens in the farm. It is winter. We must remember that Monsieur Vianney had unusually acute hearing, even to the day of his death. He wakes with a start. What is that coming across the floor, coming nearer, nearer, climbing up the curtains of his four-poster? Oh, it's a rat. It starts to nibble at the curtains. The Curé puts his hands to his ears. No, he still hears it. Very tired, aching in every limb, he sits up. He shakes the curtains. Strange, no rat falls down. Yet the scrabbling noise is now heard on the tiled floor.

The room is pitch dark, there is no moon. He falls again into unquiet slumber. But no sooner has he fallen into the sleep of exhaustion than he is wakened again. Again the same gnawing sound. "Oh," says he to himself, "I shall have to take a pitchfork to bed tomorrow night."

He does so. He notices that there are no marks of nibbling on his bed curtains, but he is so busy he has no time to give this much thought. Yet that second night, he goes to bed with a feeling of unease, as if there were a presence lurking in ambush for him, waiting for him. Something is lying in wait. "Nonsense," he says to himself, "so many weird ideas go flitting through my head. Perhaps I am overtired tonight. I must take no notice."

All this drama takes place in the bedroom on the first floor. That historic little bedroom has remained just as it was. The floor is made up of red tiles and some are missing. As you go in at the door the chimney piece is on the left, and on it the looking glass left by Monsieur Balley. Opposite the door is the bed with its cotton curtains, its palliasse on the plank. On the left of the bed are his two chests and over them the pictures of the bishop and the saints, including St. Francis Regis. Opposite the chest is the window. Between the bed and the window is a bookcase containing, among other works, the *Lives of the Saints*. (He read a chapter every night before he went to bed. His housekeeper, who put away the book every morning, saw that it had been taken out every night.) In the middle of the room is the poor little table of cherry wood with his soup bowl, his watch, his spectacles on it, and a chair in front of it, though he very rarely sits down. He even eats his meals standing.

That night he says the Compline prayers with special fervour, shuddering at the words: "Our adversary the Devil as a roaring lion goeth about seeking whom he may devour." He thinks of Michael the Archangel, "who defends us in the day of battle against Satan and other wicked spirits who wander through the world for the ruin of souls." He looks round the bedroom uneasily as he prepares to get into bed.

He doesn't blow out his candle for a time. What long shadows in the room! He looks at the pictures of his saints. Yes, they comfort him, particularly Our Lady. He is visited by one of his periodic attacks of despair. "Oh my God," he groans, "make me suffer anything you want, but give me the grace not to fall into Hell." And then he thinks he is abandoned by God for ever, totally. And at such moments he wants to flee away from Ars, leave everything, leave everybody, find some solitary place where he can weep over his life.

At length he blows out his candle. The room is plunged into Stygian darkness, but still he cannot sleep. He turns to thinking of the pictures of the saints with which he has adorned the church, so near to the presbytery. Yes, there is St. Sixtus, the patron of the church. There is St. Michael the Archangel, there is a picture of Benedict-Joseph Labre. He begins to shiver a little—an attack of marsh fever perhaps. With a great effort he turns his mind again to the pictures of the saints. Yes, there is St. John the Baptist, St. Laurence, St. Francis of Assisi, St. Catherine of Sienna, the Archangel Gabriel, the Archangel Raphael with young Tobias. Then there is the picture of Our Lord's face, surrounded by the instruments of the Passion.

He begins to plan a chapel in which he will place a statue of Christ crowned with thorns. (Comtesse des Garets said that big statues enchanted him and he would weep in front of his Ecce Homo.)

He is just falling asleep when he awakes with a start in the silence of the night. Somebody is thumping on his front door and there are voices crying out in the courtyard. Could it be thieves, perhaps, who have heard of the riches given to his church? He lights his candle. He goes down, opens the door. Nothing. He feels very much afraid.

The following day, as evening draws near, he feels even more afraid, and begins to dread the night all alone. Why hadn't he kept good old widow Bibost as his housekeeper? So he puts his pride in his pocket and goes to André Verchère, the village carter, a stout-thewed man of twenty-eight. He says hesitantly:

"I've been hearing noises these past few nights. I don't know if it's thieves. Would you come and sleep in the presbytery?"

"Very willingly, Monsieur le Curé. I will go and load my gun."

André Verchère gave the following testimony: "At night-time I went to the presbytery. I warmed myself. I talked to Monsieur le Curé until ten o'clock. 'Let's go to bed,' he said at last. He gave me my room and went into the one next door. I did not go to sleep. Towards one o'clock I heard the latch of the hall door which gave onto the courtyard being shaken violently, and at the same time, against the same door, the sound of a club being struck, and in the house itself a thunderous noise like the rumblings of several carriages.

"I took my gun and leapt towards the window, and opened it. I looked out and saw nothing. The house shook for about a quarter of an hour. My legs did the same, and I felt the after-effects of it for a week. As soon as the noise began, Monsieur le Curé had lighted a lamp. He came to me.

" 'Did you hear?' he asked me.

" 'You can see I heard, since I'm up and I've got my gun.' The presbytery was shaking as if there had been an earthquake.

" 'So you're frightened?' asked Monsieur le Curé again.

" 'No,' I said, 'I'm not frightened, but I feel that my legs are giving way. The presbytery's going to crumble.'

" 'What do you think it is?'

" 'I think it's the Devil.'

"When the noise had ceased we went to bed again. Monsieur le Curé came back the following night to beg me to go back with him. I answered him, 'Monsieur le Curé, I've had enough as it is.'"

Monsieur Vianney made a great joke of the affair at La Providence the next day. He mimicked the faint-hearted André and laughed heartily at his fear.

Other young men came and heard various strange sounds, and one night, some of them saw a tongue of fire streaking towards the presbytery. And still Monsieur Vianney, who, according to his physicians, was the most imperturbable, calm and level-headed of men, would not own that it was the Devil.

And then one snowy night he was convinced.

He wakes up with a start. There are terrible cries in his yard. (He told Catherine Lassagne afterwards that it was like an army of Austrians or Cossacks, speaking confusedly in a language which he did not understand. You will recall that he had met Austrians on his way to his ordination at Grenoble. Their speech seemed to him very guttural.) He rises, lights his candle, and goes downstairs. In fear and trembling he opens the door. The sounds have ceased. The snow lies untouched in the yard. There is not a single footmark. And then he knows. It is horrible but it is the truth: the Devil and his angels are there.

He was later to say to his bishop, Monseigneur Devie, a man of great tact and understanding, beloved by his clergy: "I concluded that it was the Demon because I was frightened. *Le bon Dieu* does not frighten."

And he continued to be terrified for a long time. One can just picture him motionless on his plank, his eyes starting out of his head. He might joke about it the next day, but at the time it was horrible enough.

Ah, God! the door handle moves, the door opens and he realizes with horror that the Devil is near him. "I did not ask him to come in, but he came all the same."

Abbé Monnin quotes the scholar Görres when he says that vexatious pranks and malice are natural to the kingdom of evil spirits. "Their manifestations are peculiar, very noisy and malicious. It is as if they enjoyed peering from time to time through the comic masks they assume and seeing poor mortals strutting in their foolish gravity and taking a pride in their vain civilization which does not believe but does tremble. They come down to tease and mock them. But it is obvious that they fear all those who will not yield to them. Irony goes with a cunning, malign spirit. The comic sense of these spirits is anarchical, hateful. And in the midst of their pleasantries, more than once we have seen a flash, a gleam, from the strange light of the fire which devours them."

Satan is sometimes almost laughably puerile with the good Curé. Some nights he snuffles like an ox, and the Curé imitates his noisy breathing. At other times he howls like a wolf, or barks like a dog; and again and again he cries out stridently, "Come out, Vianney, come out," or "Vianney, Vianney, *mangeur de truffes*,[1] we are going to get you." The Curé used to say "*Le grappin* has a very ugly voice." He called him the "grappin" or grapnel, a good name because it does make us think of the Devil getting his claws like iron grappling hooks into people's ribs—a thing he does in nightmares. And the poor trembling Curé with teeth chattering, the end of his long nose showing above his sheet, manages to answer back: "I'm not afraid of you."

In his play *Dialogue des Carmélites*, which is about the conquest of fear, Georges Bernanos has declared with so much truth that fear is God's daughter, and is an integral part of man. It is the thing over which we have least control. We can bear temptation, illness, spiritual disgust, great loneliness, great grief, but when it comes to fear, control may escape us.

If some of Monsieur Vianney's fellow priests come to his room to talk to him before bedtime, he is watching the hands of the clock as they move relentlessly on, dreading the time when his visitors will have to leave. He is very much afraid.

"Vianney, Vianney, we've got you!" But far more terrible even than the voices is the presence itself. The Devil is breathing against the Curé's face, so heavily it seems as if he would snuffle him up.

---

[1] Potatoes were called *truffes* in that region, and we know that the Curé lived almost exclusively at that time on potatoes. So it was "Vianney, Vianney, eater of potatoes."

There is the touch of a hand against the Curé's cheek. Sometimes there is the sound of gravel being spewed on to the floor.

Once the Curé, near the end of his strength, exclaimed: "I'm going over to La Providence to tell them about your nasty tricks. They'll despise you as you deserve." And that was the end of his persecution for that night.

Then there is the morning about which he told Catherine: "You like strange news. Well, I'm bringing you something quite fresh. Just you listen to what happened to me this morning. I had something on my table. You know what it was? [It was his discipline.] It began to crawl like a snake. That frightened me a little. You know there was a cord at the end. I took that cord and it became as stiff as a piece of wood. I put it back on my table and it began to move. It did this three times."

Then there was a night when he awakened with a start and felt himself lifted up into the air. "Little by little I was rising above my bed. I quickly made the sign of the Cross to protect myself, and the Grappin left me."

Occasionally Satan imitated a death rattle, or stifled moans or sighs. And then one night came a sensual temptation: the Devil took the form of a very soft, very comfortable little pillow in which the poor Curé's head sank voluptuously, as if in cotton wool. And at the same time Satan moaned in a plaintive way. The Curé confessed later that this time he was very frightened. It seemed to him that this new kind of snare was imperilling his soul. He invoked the help of Heaven and the illusion left him.

What is so very extraordinary about the whole story is that the Curé, as we have seen, is not the only one to hear the sounds. One night a policeman came very late to make his confession. He was outside the presbytery when all of a sudden he heard a strong, shrill, strident voice inside, crying out distinctly, "Vianney, Vianney, come along." He was so frozen with horror that he went away for a while. The clock struck one. Then the Curé appeared with his lantern in his hand. Monsieur Vianney tried to reassure him, but he was shaking for a long time afterwards. (The Curé only laughed about it.)

La Providence was not without its infestations, either. All night long could be heard strange footsteps on the stairs and in the dormitories. In the morning no one could discover who it had been.

St. Louis-Marie Grignion de Montfort in his *Treatise on True Devotion to the Blessed Virgin* says that the Evil One fears the Blessed Virgin Mary more than God or all the saints. So it is not surprising that sometimes Monsieur Vianney would come down in the morning and find his old picture of the Annunciation at the turn of the stairs covered with filth. In the end he had to remove it from that place.

And always there is noise overhead in the attic—the sound, perhaps, of a great flock of sheep; it is impossible to sleep with the toc-toc of their hooves, like hailstones on a hard road. One night when he is more exhausted by this than by anything else, he says: "My God, very willingly I offer you the sacrifice of several hours of my sleep for the conversion of sinners." The toc-toc instantly stops and he is able to sleep.

Monsieur Vianney noticed that on the days after the worst nights some very great sinner would come to confession after practically a lifetime out of the Church. Or there would come to his confessional a man whose influence for good or evil in his social milieu was very great. The Devil damaged his own cause, and he was thus most useful. The Curé used to say with a laugh, "Ah, a big fish is coming into the net today."

But as Jean de Fabrègues said in his book *L'Apôtre du siècle désespéré*, "This almost ceaseless duel only served to raise the spiritual temperature of the one attacked. The struggle against temptation is one of the soul's constant needs, especially if it is engaged in the apostolate, as was Monsieur Vianney."

The temptation to despair then turned into a blessing and blossomed into a supreme humility.

But we now get to the core of the matter. How is it that a being so pure, so spiritual as Monsieur Vianney, could be troubled by this kind of roughness, coarseness, uproar? I think myself that the Devil camouflaged his traps. He had a deep-laid plot under this seeming foolishness. He wanted Monsieur Vianney to leave Ars for good, to drop the souls committed to his care. He knew quite well that in the end he would not be able to make him leave simply from fatigue. But fatigue could help to undermine his confidence in his own love of God. If only the Devil could convince Monsieur Vianney, who was already so humble, that he did not love God sufficiently in the way God wished him to; that he did not serve Him as God wished him to; if he could, therefore, induce him to flee to some solitary place to weep over his sins, then he would have won the victory. To quote Jean de Fabrègues again: "The saint who is living on the heights of love and self-renunciation is tempted in the very centre of this love. . . . Bernanos has understood this very well. Despair is at the heart of Monsieur Vianney's temptation, and it is in this particularly that he was tempted by the diabolical power."

How nearly successful Satan was! There is a distinct connection between his infestations and the Curé's three flights from Ars, of which we shall have more to say later on.

Satan tried first, as we know, to make his life impossible through excess of fatigue and anxiety. We all know that exhaustion engenders despair. His life in the confessional was enough of itself to do this, when he looked into those sinful souls drowned in their woes. His nights were short according to the clock, but long in anguish. For many nights on end he was at the limit of his endurance and flight would have been the victory of despair. St. Ignatius Loyola has said that to unmask Satan is to conquer him. It took the Curé a long time before he unmasked the Devil behind his temptation to flee from Ars. The subtleties of the Devil are greater than those of our intelligence. An angel's intelligence, even that of a fallen one, is exceedingly great. And then Satan is the father of lies. When his power does not work, the Devil tries deceit. He deceives us about ourselves: he worked on Monsieur Vianney's tremendous humility and was able to convince him that he was really unworthy of his task, unworthy of the trust God reposed in him. Nothing was left but to go away and weep for the sins of his poor life.

But the Divine Lover did not abandon his beloved of Ars on those terrible nights. True, the master of nothingness had tried to keep Monsieur Vianney off the path to Divine Union, but one day the Curé let slip that he was consoled on those occasions. At the end of his life, Monsieur Toccanier, his curate, who was very skilful at trapping him into betraying supernatural secrets and who knew that he was visited by the Devil, said to him one day with a sort of detached air: "You pray also at night?"

"Oh yes, my friend, when I wake up. . . I am old now. I have not long to live. One must profit by every moment."

"You lie on a hard bed and you do not sleep very much."

"Oh, one is not always lying on a hard bed." ("*O, on n'est pas toujours couché sur la dure.*") There was an uneasy silence, and then the Curé understood that he'd said more than he'd meant to.

A young man who later became a priest was spending his holidays with Jean Pertinand, the school teacher. He was leaning out of his window on the first floor at midnight when he saw a great light above the presbytery, and he concluded that something extraordinary was happening inside.

And indeed extraordinary things were happening, though the Curé never told anyone about them except when a word would slip out by accident, or a flash of revelation in a smile or a glance. Indeed, his little bedroom was hallowed. It was the Holy of Holies to him. He said to someone: "If you only knew what had happened on such and such a tile of the floor." He saw Our Lady, he saw the saints, especially his patron saint and St. Philomena, and he spoke with them in a familiar way, as a man speaks to his friends.

And, as each morning he saw Our Lord at Mass, actually saw Him with his eyes, he could gain courage during those terrible nights at the thought of the joy awaiting him at dawn.

The Evil One often betrayed his plots through the mouths of people possessed by the Devil who came to be healed in his church. A possessed woman once exclaimed, the evil spirit speaking through her: "Ah, black toad, how you make me suffer! You keep saying you want to go away. Why don't you go?"

And, as we have already said, another possessed woman cried out: "How you make me suffer. . ! If there were three like you in this world, my kingdom would be destroyed."

Abbé Monnin quotes Görres on the connection between physical illness and the mystic state: ". . . in the mystic state, each of the powers [of the soul] is freed from the corporal element which is its organ. The soul dominates it instead of being subject to it. Each organ in its turn is transported into a higher region. It gets close to the soul. It acquires by this closeness a more fragile, more nervous, more delicate, more ethereal nature. There results from this an ailing disposition, because here below man is unable to rise to a higher clime without paying for that privilege by suffering or by death."

The Curé had much to suffer from terrible stomach pains and practically continual headaches. Catherine Lassagne has told us that often when she wanted to speak to him he would point to his brow, with an expression of unutterable suffering. Usually when God wants to use one of his servants for great apostolic labours in saving souls He gives him the necessary health. Also, Père Poulain says that when God has lifted up a soul to high contemplation He usually frees it from attacks by the Devil. In both these respects God made an exception of the Curé, for he suffered from acute physical ailments and from diabolical obsession. It is extraordinary, considering all things, that he could be so active and could remain so sane. His doctor said: "I do not worry any more about the health of the Curé of Ars. It depends on another than myself, and when I can do no more, this other one can still do something. At the moment when it seems that he's going to slip from us, new strength seems to rise up in him all of a sudden, as if by magic."

Dr. J. B. Saunier, who was his physician for seventeen years, left a note, quoted by Monseigneur Trochu, on the perfect physical and mental balance of his patient. He speaks of "The serenity of ideas, the delicacy of perceptions, the sureness of judgment and

insight or penetration, the complete self-possession, the mainte-
nance of miraculous health almost without a break in the midst of
the incessant hard work which absorbed his life."

Another physician, Dr. Michel of Coligny, said that he could
not believe the Curé was ever the victim of any illusion or hallucination. "As to the attacks of the Demon of which I have heard
some talk, if Monsieur Vianney says that they took place, I must
believe that they did."

One of the greatest proofs of his sanity is that he even ceased
to be afraid of the Devil. When Abbé Toccanier asked him in
later life if he were not very frightened by these diabolic manifestations, he replied: "One gets used to everything, my friend.
The Grappin and I, we are *quasi camarades*—almost pals."

And of course it was most convenient to have the arrival of
great sinners announced beforehand by a diabolical attack of particular virulence the night before!

The Devil was always thinking up new ways of annoying the
Curé. For instance, with regard to nocturnal sounds, it is interesting to note that he would sometimes imitate the pounding of a
hammer driving nails into the floor. I know of two people, sane
and truthful, who in a great Elizabethan manor in the north of
England, both in separate rooms in a haunted corridor, heard
that very same sound late at night, and could give no natural explanation to it. Their hostess, who apparently had not heard it,
since she had fallen asleep earlier, looked very uneasy when it
was mentioned and quickly changed the subject of conversation.
At Ars the Devil would drum on the table, the chimney piece, the
water jug, and he would even—this is entertaining—imitate a
nightingale singing away in the chimney.

When the Curé's sister, Marguerite, came to stay with him, she
had various frights of this kind, but her brother reassured her.
"Oh my child," he said, "you shouldn't have been frightened. It's
the Grappin. He can do nothing against you. I'm the one he torments. Sometimes he takes me by the feet and drags me about in
my room. It is because I convert souls to God."

He always found rising from bed at one o'clock in the morning a great hardship; habit never made it easier. He would stumble downstairs to go to church, his face deathly pale. People would ask him what was the matter and he would say it was the Grappin.

The Curé's parishioners believed in all these diabolic manifestations of course; they had seen and heard too much to have any doubts. But the clergy round about were sceptical. As Abbé Monnin says, "They sought in the immoderate fasts and vigils of the holy man for natural and physiological causes of these diabolical manifestations. . . . 'If the Curé of Ars,' they said, 'would live like other people, if he would take his proper amount of sleep and nourishment like them, this effervescence of the imagination would be quieted, his brain would no longer be peopled with spectres, and all this infernal phantasmagoria would vanish.'"

During the winter of 1826, when these prejudices against Monsieur Vianney were at their height, he preached for three weeks in the neighbouring parish of Saint-Trivier-sur-Moignans. Abbé Monnin obtained an eye-witness account of certain occurrences which took place there.

"One evening his critics took a higher tone; the discussion waxed warm on their side, and the raillery grew more bitter and less restrained. It was agreed that all this infernal mysticism was nothing in the world but reverie, delusion, and hallucination, and the poor curé was openly treated as a visionary and a maniac."

Monsieur Vianney made no reply. He went to bed, joyful at having been humiliated. The clerics wished each other good-night and went to their respective bed-chambers.

Suddenly at midnight they were all awakened by a terrible din.

"The presbytery seemed to be all upside down, doors slamming, windows shaking and rattling. There was a tremor in the walls, and ominous crackings made them fear that the whole place was coming down. In an instant everybody was up." (Can one not imagine Messieurs les Curés in their nightshifts and nightcaps, holding their candles?) "They began to remember that the Curé of Ars had said, 'You must not be surprised if by chance you hear noises tonight.' They rushed to his room. He was sleeping quietly. 'Get up,' they cried, 'the presbytery is falling down!' 'Oh, I know very well

what that is,' he replied smiling. 'Go back to bed, there's nothing
to fear.' They were reassured and the noise ceased.

"An hour after that, when everything had relapsed into silence,
there was the faint tinkle of a door-bell. Abbé Vianney got up and
opened the door to a man who had walked many miles to come to
confession. The Curé went to the church immediately and stayed
there till Mass, hearing many confessions."

The reputation of the Curé of Ars as a confessor had been spread
by the missions which he gave in the neighbouring villages, and
that is why the Devil was so angry. What happened when he went
to Saint Trivier to preach the jubilee is an example of the efforts
the Devil made to keep him from going out on these missions. The
Curé left on foot before dawn, alone. He was saying his rosary.

"The air around him was full of sinister scintillations. It seemed
to be ablaze, and on either side of the road it was as if the bushes
were on fire. Foreseeing the fruits that Monsieur Vianney would
produce in souls, Satan, clothed in the burning fluid which con-
sumes him, was following him step by step, seeking to frighten
him."

Fire is the Devil's native element. It broke out in the Curé's
beloved presbytery late in February, two years before his death.
Again we have Abbé Monnin's account of the scene which he himself witnessed:

"There was an enormous crowd at Ars for the Forty Hours Devotion. As I set out very early to go to the church, I was met on the
threshold by such a powerful and revolting smell of burning that
it nearly knocked me over. I crossed the square quickly. After
Mass, catechism and some confessions, at about seven o'clock,
when I had finished all this, I found the whole village crowding
around the presbytery. I should have thought that something tragic
had happened, had it not been obvious, as I looked at the crowd,
that the general impression was one of gaiety: they were laughing,
joking, questioning one another from one end of the square to the
other, and the words 'bed' and 'Grappin' were all that I could pick
up in this commotion.

" 'What's the matter?' I asked, going up to a group.

" 'What, don't you know that last night the Devil set fire to Monsieur le Curé's bed? Look, look!'

"Indeed, through the half-open door of the courtyard I saw several men coming out, taking away half-burnt debris. I went in to Monsieur Vianney's bedroom, where I found everything in disorder and the remains of a barely extinguished fire. The bed, the tester, the curtains and everything around; several pictures whose only value lay in the fact that the servant of God was devoted to them, some old paintings on glass which he loved so much. Several days before, he had told us that they were the only things in this world to which he was still a little attached. He had not consented to sell them because he wanted to leave them as a legacy to the missionaries. Everything had been burnt. The fire had stopped only in front of the shrine of St. Philomena. . . ."

After Mass Abbé Monnin went to see the Curé, who was autographing some pictures. He interrupted himself all of a sudden.

"I can still see him with his quill raised, his gentle, deep glance fixed on me. 'For a long time,' he told me, 'I've been asking God for this grace, and He has at last granted it to me. . . . I think that this time I'm about the poorest person in the parish. They all have a bed, and I, thanks be to God, have none!' "

Having borne so triumphantly with this diabolical obsession, it is not surprising that he could deal with cases of diabolical possession.

In his book *The Graces of Interior Prayer*, Père Poulain, S. J., explains clearly the difference between obsession and possession. "A person is possessed by the Devil when, at particular moments, the Devil makes him lose consciousness and seems to take the place of the soul in his body; making use, apparently at least, of his eyes to see, of his ears to hear, of his mouth to speak . . . it is the Devil who suffers as though from a burn if any object that has been blessed is brought into contact with the skin. In a word, the Devil seems to be incarnate in a man.

"We say that the person is obsessed when the Devil does not make him lose consciousness. . . . The word obsession in Latin implies the siege of a stronghold. In possession the place is captured; . . . the Devil can never enter without our consent. . . .

". . . with possessed persons, the Devil acts upon the body from within, while with the obsessed it is from without . . . the angelic spirit is independent of space, it is only its operation upon matter that is localized. . . ." Père Poulain goes on to say that possession does not befall those who are striving earnestly after perfection. "God does not permit diabolical persecution except in order to enable these souls to acquire great merit. But for this the use of their reason and their liberty are necessary, and these are often diminished or suspended in the case of diabolical possession.

". . . It is exceedingly rare for possession to occur in the case of souls called to contemplation and close union with God. It is rather a punishment than a purifying trial."[1]

A most extraordinary dialogue between the Curé and a possessed woman from the neighbourhood of Puy-en-Velay took place in the afternoon of January the 23rd, 1840, in the chapel of St. John the Baptist, in the presence of eight witnesses. They were crowding around the confessional and could not help hearing the loud harsh voice of the possessed woman.

The possessed woman speaks: "I am immortal."

The Curé speaks: "So you alone will not die?"

The possessed woman: "I've only committed one sin in my life, and I bestow this beautiful fruit on all who want it. Lift your hand, absolve me. You lift it sometimes for me."

The Curé, in Latin, *"Tu quis es?"* ("Who art thou?")

The possessed woman, answering in the same tongue, said: *"Magister Caput"* and went on in French, but in diabolical French: "Nasty black toad, how you make me suffer! We wage war against each other. . . . But whatever victory you gain, it sometimes happens that you work for me. You think your crowd outside is prepared, but it isn't. Why do you examine your penitents' consciences? To what good purpose so many enquiries? Isn't the examination I get them to make sufficient?"

[1] London, Kegan Paul, 1950.

The Curé: "You say you get them to examine their consciences? But they pray to God before examining themselves."

The possessed woman: "Oh yes, yes, in an artificial manner. But I tell you it is I who make the examination. I'm oftener in your chapel than you think. My body goes, but my spirit remains. I'm very glad when they chatter in here. Not all those who come here are saved. You're a miser."

The Curé: "It is difficult for me to be a miser. I've got little, and that little I give willingly."

The possessed woman: "I'm not speaking of that kind of avarice but of another. You are a miser of souls. You wrest away as many souls from me as you can, but I try to get them back. You're a liar too! For a long time you've been saying you want to go away, and yet you always stay. . . . You wanted to go to Lyons." (That again was true. He was torn between these two longings—retiring to Fourvière or to a Trappist monastery.) "Why don't you go?"

The Curé: "What else have you got against me?"

Then came a long dialogue, when the possessed woman referred to the bishop, Monseigneur Devie, as "*ta robe violette*" ("your purple robe") and called the Blessed Virgin Mary a disgusting, unprintable name. She said that but for the Virgin the Curé would already be far away. Then she added: "I have a lot of your parishioners on my list."

The Curé: "What do you say of so-and-so?" (He mentioned the name of a priest of great virtue.)

The possessed woman: "I don't like him." (These words were pronounced with concentrated rage and much gnashing of teeth.)

The Curé: "And so-and-so?"

The possessed woman: "Oh, he's splendid, that fellow. He lets us do what we want. There are some black toads who do not make me suffer as much as you. I serve their Mass, they say it for me."

The Curé: "Do you serve mine?"

The possessed woman: "You get on my nerves. Ah, if only the . . . . . . [Virgin Mary] did not protect you! Why do you get up so early? You disobey the purple robe who's ordered you to take care of yourself. Then, why do you preach so simply? You sound like an ignoramus. Why don't you preach in the grand manner, as they do in towns? Ah, how pleased I am with those majestic sermons that upset nobody! At your catechism instructions, some sleep, but there are others for whom your simple language goes straight to the heart."

The Curé: "What do you think of dancing?"

The possessed woman: "I surround a dance the way a wall surrounds a garden."

The testimonies of possessed people could sometimes be very consoling to the poor Curé, as for example when the Devil, speaking through the mouth of a woman schoolteacher, in December 1857, was heard to say "Yes" to him when he asked the evil spirit if it wanted to go away.

"And why?"

"Because I'm with a man I don't like."

Monsieur Vianney ironically took this up and said: "Then you don't like me?"

And the evil spirit replied by a shrill and strident "No!"

The square outside the church must have been the scene of strange events sometimes. For example, there was an old woman from the neighbourhood of Clermont-Ferrand who had been possessed for forty years. She was taken to Ars and made to drink a few drops of holy water. In a fury, she started biting at the church walls. When Monsieur Vianney appeared and found her with her mouth bleeding, he blessed her and instantly she became perfectly calm.

The saint used to say he owed his protection from the Devil to the great statue of Michael the Archangel at the entrance of his church.

One day a possessed woman was overheard saying to the Curé, "You've taken more than eighty thousand souls from me." Before being brought to Ars, she had said to her attendants: "What a filthy place your Ars is. How bad it smells. Everybody stinks. But the Rotonde!" (a well-known amusement centre in one of the ill-famed quarters of Lyons). "It smells lovely there—roses, jasmine and carnations." And then, addressing those around her: "Ah, if the damned could come to Ars, they would profit by it more than all of you."

And now to conclude. Père Poulain in his twenty-fourth chapter, "On the Trials Sent to Contemplatives," tells how to deal with demons.

"A soul can derive advantage from obsessions. She conceives an ever-growing horror of him who thus torments her for all he suggests. She throws herself all the more vehemently into God's arms, says St. John Chrysostom, like a child taking refuge with its mother when it finds itself threatened by something horrible. He advises us to show contempt for the demons . . . but we should attribute the victory to the divine protection, not to ourselves. If the arch-enemy were entirely in control, we could not resist him. . . . I would add that many temptations vanish if we attach no importance to them." He quotes Blessed Angela of Foligno, who endured trials of this sort, as saying that sometimes God allows a person to be twisted and trampled on and trodden underfoot before He permits the storms of temptation to leave him; He behaves in this manner chiefly towards His true children.

Tauler, the great Dominican spiritual writer, said: "When our heavenly Father has decided to adorn a soul by exalted gifts and sublimely transform it, it is His custom to cleanse it, not gently but in a sea of bitterness; to plunge it, to drown it as He did the prophet Jonas."

So with Monsieur Vianney: he emerged with his common sense and his humour unimpaired. Sometimes even a little cheered and amused. His own temptation to despair, his spiritual trials, his longing for solitude, the grief he felt at the vile sins pouring into his confessional—all these were much harder to bear than the silly tricks of the Grappin.

As we have already noted, St. Louis-Marie Grignion de Montfort says that Satan fears Our Lady more than God. "First because he suffers infinitely more in his pride from being conquered and punished by a small and humble handmaid of God, her humility humiliates him more than the power of God; and secondly because God has given Mary such power over evil spirits that, as they themselves have often unwittingly admitted through the mouth of the possessed, they fear one of her sighs as more powerful than the prayers of all the saints, and dread one of her threats more than all their other torments. . . .

"But Mary's mastery of Hell will shine forth especially in the latter times, when Satan will lie in wait for her heel, that is for her humble slaves and her children whom she will rouse up to war against him. In the eyes of the world they will be little and poor, they will be lowly in the eyes of all, downtrodden and persecuted . . . but, like the heel, they will crush Satan's head and bring victory to Jesus Christ."

10. *IN WHICH MONSIEUR VIANNEY'S ORPHANS LIVE ON DIVINE PROVIDENCE*

AS WE HAVE SEEN, THE DIABOLICAL ATTACKS BEGAN IN THE YEAR THAT Monsieur Vianney opened his school for little girls. It seems strange that so humble and poor a house should have aroused the Devil's ire, but it is easier to understand this when we recall the saying of St. Francis de Sales: "The basis of renown is goodness." Here were to be housed and fed (later when it had become an orphanage) anywhere from sixty to eighty girls, who would afterwards live in the countryside and excel as trained farm servants and mothers of Christian families. It was in that house that the Curé would give his eleven o'clock catechism instructions, which were so often listened to by strangers outside in the street. In the end, the concourse of strangers grew so great that he had to move his famous catechism class to the church itself. For once the Devil foresaw the future.

To found his school, Monsieur Vianney chose, as we have said, Catherine Lassagne, aged seventeen, and Benoîte Lardet, aged twenty. Catherine, as we know, had already fallen under his spell at the age of twelve. Here is how Monseigneur Trochu describes their first meeting in his enchanting little pamphlet on Catherine Lassagne:

"Catherine Lassagne, so slender under her black cape and in her ruched bonnet . . . Monsieur le Curé had known her quite early on. The first meeting went back to the Sunday of the patronal feast, the 'St. Sixte,' around August the 6th, 1818. Catherine, the daughter of farm labourers established in the Tonneau hamlet a quarter of a mile from the church, was then twelve years old, having been born on the 8th of May 1806, just twenty years—a curious little detail—to the day after the saintly Curé Vianney.

"On that Sunday the yearly Ars festival was going on. The dances, which had hardly ceased all the preceding night, were going to begin again in the square at the hour of Vespers. However, several young village girls, better brought-up or more strictly supervised, had come to church for Vespers. After the ceremony was over, they remained near the confessional, waiting for Monsieur le Curé. Behind them was a mother lost in her prayers and surrounded by her children. This woman, Claudine Lassagne, wanted to go on praying.

"Monsieur le Curé heard the confessions of each of the young people. Then he addressed himself to the little group.

" 'Children,' he said in a fatherly manner. 'Instead of going to the square, where there is nothing good to see, come to my garden for some recreation. And then, as it's a feast day, you can have some red currants.'

"Next to Claudine Lassagne was her daughter, Catherine, who was just twelve years of age.

" 'Mamma,' she whispered, 'please give me permission to go to Monsieur le Curé's garden with the girls.'

" 'But my poor little one, he has not invited you.'

" 'Oh, he won't mind.'

"So Catherine followed the others. In their wake, she slipped into the little courtyard of the presbytery. She went past the outhouses with them and came into the garden. Nobody stopped her, and without being asked, the little girl attacked the red currants with the others.

"Through the hedge Monsieur le Curé could see the couples dancing in the square. Abbé Vianney's young friends laughed pityingly at the fiddler scraping away, but Catherine had something else on her mind. From time to time she would turn towards the entrance as if she were frightened of being caught.

" 'You needn't be frightened,' whispered one of her companions kindly. 'Monsieur le Curé, from what they say, never comes into his garden.'

"However, by exception, he appeared. Under his arm was a large folio volume with a tawny binding.

" 'Oh, children,' he said to all this little group. 'Here in the peace of God, are you not happier than those who are dancing in the square?'

" 'Oh, to be sure, Monsieur le Curé.'

" 'Ah, well then, children, as there is hardly anything left now of my red currants, come and I will give you another feast by reading to you some beautiful pages from the history of my good saints.'

"And as he said this, he pointed to his big book.

"As the girls went towards the courtyard of the presbytery, Abbé Vianney suddenly noticed the little girl who appeared to be hiding behind the others.

" 'What is your name, my child?' he asked kindly.

" 'Catherine Lassagne, Monsieur le Curé.'

" 'That's splendid,' replied Monsieur Vianney. 'Children, to give pleasure to your little friend Catherine, we're going to read the story of her holy patroness.'

"Catherine blushed with pleasure.

"The listeners went into the kitchen, the room on the left on the ground floor. They sat down, some of them on chairs round the large hearth. Monsieur le Curé, who had remained standing near the window, opened the second volume of the *Lives of the Saints* . . . by 'Reverend Father François Giry, sometime Provincial of the Order of Minims.' He read aloud the story of St. Catherine the Virgin Martyr who converted the Empress Faustina and was killed by the cruel Emperor Maximinus. Catherine Lassagne, greatly honoured by the choice of reading, listened open-mouthed, enchanted."

One must date from that August Sunday of 1818 the respectful, powerful, unfailing attachment which she vowed to her pastor.

Catherine came of a family of nine children. Her mother was a good Christian who was delighted that this Curé had come to

Ars. In spite of the great amount of work she had to do, she went
to Mass every day; she loved to pray at length, and her daughter
Marie used to yank her dress and say: "Mother, do let's go home."
In Lent all the Lassagne children gave up their four o'clock bread
and butter. Every night they all said prayers together, and Madame Lassagne would bend over Catherine before she went to sleep
and say to her: "My little Catherine, have you said your 'Visitez?' "
("Visit, we beseech Thee, O Lord, this dwelling. Drive far from
it all the snares of the Devil. May Thy holy angels dwell in it, to
keep us in peace.") In later life Catherine was to say this prayer
not for herself but with great intensity and fervour for her Curé
in his hours of direst need.

She was a shepherdess for her parents. In a field quite near the
Fontblin brook, she, like so many other shepherd lads and lasses,
would say her rosary, and she learned to pray without realizing
it. (After she had become a schoolmistress, she often sighed: "Oh
my beloved solitude near the brook; what happy moments I spent
there!") When the Curé asked her to train as a teacher, she could
so easily have said that her health was too bad, but instead she
eagerly agreed. In January 1823 he sent her and Benoîte to the
nuns of Fareins and paid for their upkeep. They learnt the catechism, cooking, laundering, ironing and general housekeeping.

At last in March 1824, the Givre family agreed to sell him a house
for 2,400 francs, "*pour tenir un collège*" (to hold a school). This
house was to the west of the church. In this way the Curé used up
the whole of his meagre inheritance; he had no money left to pay
the notary. And then he found domestic help—a girl of twenty-
six, Jeanne-Marie Chanay, used to hard work. She would cook,
knead and bake bread, tend the oven, wash the linen in the Fontblin, sew, and in her spare time supervise the children and teach
them their alphabet.

These three girls wore no special religious habit, were bound
by no vows and, above all, earned no money. They were to give
up long years of their lives to the work, just for the love of God.

This charming little house is still standing, just as it was. In
those days the large, ground-floor room was the one in which the

pupils ate and did their lessons. Then on the first floor were the two rooms where the school-mistresses slept. Above them were attics; eventually they were turned into dormitories for orphans.

According to the nuns who succeeded Catherine and the others in 1849, the building had been neglected. There was much need of sweeping and scrubbing. The damp walls had begun to crumble, and masons had to be called in. But of course the good nuns were more used to keeping their floors shining, and all the chairs well polished and everything spick and span and orderly, than these three girls: they were not so thoroughly trained, and they had far more work on their hands than they could get through properly. (Teaching pupils, taking in vagrant orphans, all the tasks con-nected with keeping the house going.) These three very rightly put Christian charity above dusting, and they were sometimes criticized for this by the ungrateful housewives of Ars.

It must not be imagined, however, that Catherine took to the training of the saintly Curé as a duck to water. In the years be-tween twelve and seventeen she even prayed to God to send him away from Ars, because his direction seemed unbearable to her. From the very first moment of his appearance, no more vanity! Her mother, who had always spent quite a long time titivating her before church, now got her ready in two minutes. Her mother had certainly taken in the sermons against vanity: "There are some mothers who think of nothing but their daughters' appear-ance. They do all they can to make them shine in the eyes of the world. They load them with vanities, perhaps even to the point of getting into debt. When they watch them go out in the morn-ing, they are too anxious to see if they are wearing their bonnet straight to ask them if they have given their heart to God."

On his midday visits to the farm, when the Curé spoke to the assembled family as they were eating their meal, the Lassagnes were always delighted to see him; but one can imagine the half-frightened, half-admiring glances of Catherine from the end of the table. This reverential fear remained throughout her life, so that one can never say there was really friendship between the two. Catherine herself said: "I hardly dared to look at him or speak to him. I served him, I believe, wholly for the love of God and without natural affection. When I brought him anything, I always expected to be sent away again."

In fact, in this work which she did solely for the love of God, Catherine was to find many crosses up to the very day of her death. When her first companion, Benoîte Lardet, died the death of a saint, she was replaced by Marie Filliat, a dressmaker from Misérieux. Marie was imperious and contrary: she was so great a cross to Catherine that she probably helped, one might say in the archaic idiom of the time, to "embroider her mystical robe for the banquet of the Lamb."

Thursday the 11th of November, 1824, the opening day for the school, was the feast of St. Martin. Catherine and Benoîte had come to sleep there the day before, and Jeanne-Marie Chanay had been there since the Tuesday. All three were under the blissful illusion that their Curé had seen to everything. But he, lost in adoration before the Blessed Sacrament, had forgotten, as Monseigneur Trochu says, his own dinner and that of his school teachers. It must be remembered that he loved St. Francis of Assisi and Lady Poverty.

After a long hard morning's housework the three girls were very hungry. There were only a few small pieces of stale cheese in the house. Catherine and Benoîte were going back to their parents when all of a sudden the inspiration came to them to rely on God to provide for them. "Let us stay here," said those three sparrows of Providence. Just then Madame Lassagne and Madame Lardet appeared at the door with some food. Catherine confessed afterwards that never had a meal been eaten with such pleasure and gaiety.

The next day the little girls came to the school for the first time and were welcomed by the gently smiling Catherine. These were the children a schoolmaster before Monsieur Vianney's time had described as "practically indistinguishable from animals, except by baptism, because of their stupidity and their incapacity." They flooded in, because they were received free of charge. When Catherine had asked the Curé how much she should charge them he said, "Nothing." However, when in 1825 sixteen children came from neighbouring parishes prudent Catherine informed the parents that if they wanted their daughters to have a bed and sheets, they would do well to bring them, and provisions would be accepted most gratefully. All consented.

In the meantime, as if this great educational venture were not enough, the Curé was wandering about the roads and thinking of something greater still. He was always meeting poor beggar girls in rags, covered with vermin, who had either lost their parents or been sent away from their homes because the poverty there was too great. They begged for food at the farms, and in their vagrant condition fell prey to terrible moral and physical dangers. Many of them were in a pitiable, even brutish, state, sleeping in barns and hedgerows. We with our Welfare State cannot imagine what pauperism could be in nineteenth-century France. Before the Revolution, these pitiable vagrants would have been cared for by the many religious orders, but now. . . .

One can imagine the Curé—who so often took off his shoes and socks to give to beggars and picked his way home, trying to hide his bare feet under his cassock—doing all he could to help these girls. One day in December 1826, he confided a great secret to Catherine: he had made plans to widen the scope of her school so as to find room for these forsaken girls.

In January 1827, during a Sunday sermon, he asked his parishioners to make a novena to Our Lady to find out God's will about this project. Catherine and her companions, overworked though they were, felt their hearts bursting with motherly love for the vagrants. At the end of the novena Monsieur Vianney called in masons and carpenters to build an annexe. He himself was the architect, he traced the plans. He also lent his labour to the building. This house—La Providence—is made of stones which the saint himself carried. He even put the tiles on the roof. The whole house is a relic.

By word of mouth it soon became known on the highways and in the hedgerows that there was a refuge at Ars. Girls began to stream in, at first looking sullen, obstinate, and very frightened. But they thawed a little when Catherine knelt down, took them in her arms, and held them against her, speaking to them in her gentle, soothing voice. Then she would wash them, cut their hair and rid them of vermin. In the evening, after a good meal, she would pray aloud for those poor children who did not know their Pater or their Ave, tuck them up in bed, sing to them, and soon the sorrows of many days were drowned in sleep.

Quite soon La Providence was full. In September 1827, just five months after the opening day, the pupils whose parents were in easy circumstances ceased to sleep at the school and the whole place was given over to the orphans. From 1830 to 1848 there were about sixty orphans, and in some years between seventy and eighty. There were no terms or holiday seasons, class went on the whole year round. Thursday each week was a whole holiday. The girls of the parish were not separated from the orphans; and the Devil, jealous of the good he saw in that house, used this to stir up strife.

The more snobbish village women—and is there not snobbery in every class of society?—began to slander those poor girls and complain that they were an unbearably heavy burden. The older girls seemed to attract all the unkindness and evil gossip. "Isn't it a shame," the Ars housewives said, "to see big girls who could so well work for their living mumbling prayers from morning till night?" They began to begrudge them even the simple education they received. Of what use, said they, would that be if they were to become poor servants or cooks? When the richer school children left, taking their beds and sheets with them, there was nothing left for the orphans in the attic but straw.

It seems that the noise in the ground-floor classroom was simply deafening. The pupils were divided into two classes, they all learnt spelling aloud, and occasionally one of the mistresses would strike a girl. But Catherine never did. The other two mistresses had piercing voices when they were vexed.

Catherine, who taught the older girls, hardly ever scolded. But though she never got cross, she was the only one to have complete authority. She was loved like a mother, and none of her pupils would ever use a quill which Catherine hadn't sharpened herself. In fact Catherine was the prey of her adopted daughters.

They all went to Mass every morning. When the classes ended

at eleven o'clock, they recited the touching Litany of Providence, one of whose invocations was: "O Providence, who dost feed the hungry."

And then at eleven o'clock, Monsieur le Curé came in person for the catechism class which in the end was to attract thousands of listeners from all over France. Still wearing his surplice and stole, he would go to the end of the room and sit on the edge of the table.

Occasionally the hens from the yard would fly in through the window and then fly out again with great flapping, flutterings and cluckings. Monseigneur Trochu says: "In the walnut trees of the square birds were singing. On the stony road, heavy carts jerked their way down the incline, carrying faggots, hay or wheat, according to the season. Flocks would be returning from the fields: sheep, cows, piglets—these latter rolling about in the mud. Or one could hear the blacksmith at his anvil."

Monsieur Vianney would make use of all these familiar things to illustrate his little sermons. When, after his fame had grown, pilgrims stood in the street listening through the open window, or peeped through the half-open door in the corridor, the members of his audience were as still as lizards.

After the Angelus, which they all recited together at midday, Monsieur Vianney would go to the kitchen. He had eaten nothing since the day before and had been up since midnight. On the hearth waiting for him was one of those little stone pots which one can still see in his room. It contained some hot milk, and on occasion, when the cook had a piece of chocolate, she would allow it to melt in the milk. Then he would take one or two mouthfuls of bread from the immense round loaf on the kitchen table. After he'd said his grace he rested for a short while before going back to church.

In the meantime, Jeanne-Marie Chanay, looking very majestic, would bring in the steaming soup-tureen to the pupils, and Catherine would fill the plates. The poor dears had hardly anything more to eat than potatoes and a little bacon given in charity. The des Garets and the de Cibeins had put themselves down for a certain number of sacks of potatoes.

After this meal and a recreation period, they worked till five o'clock. This was the moment when the Curé—that is, before he had become a prisoner of his confessional—took a little recreation too. He returned to La Providence and talked with the children and their mistresses for a little while. It was mainly through observing him during that short interval that Catherine was able to compose her *Petit Mémoire* on the saint—a document, which, unhappily, is still unpublished but which gives such an admirable and faithful portrait of the saint. Abbé Monnin said: "Amongst the children, this holy priest, who never grew old, would blossom out with all the qualities of Christian childlikeness. A mingling of candour and naïve grace gave an inexpressible charm to his conversation and transformed his life into that spiritual childhood to which Our Lord has promised Heaven."

He must have been at his most captivating in those moments in late afternoon, gently teasing, occasionally giving way to his slightly caustic wit. And though his manner was reserved, his loving kindness towards these poor orphans could be seen in his eyes. He had a special compassion for orphans and widows, and created a particular atmosphere of affection when he was with them. It was easier for these disinherited girls to believe in the infinite depths of God's love when they saw how the Curé of Ars behaved towards them. With his charming smile, he would encourage them to speak to him quite openly. At meals he would give them lessons in table manners. For his orphans' garden he had planted vines; he interlaced the branches to make a tunnel. This soon became an oratory, for he put a statue of Mary Immaculate in it. The girls decked it with flowers, and in the evening they all went there to recite the litanies of Our Lady and sing hymns in her honour.

He taught these motherless girls how to fly to Our Lady as to a new mother.

"People often compare the Blessed Virgin to a mother, but she is far better than the best of mothers. For the best of mothers sometimes punishes the child who has grieved her. She even beats it. She thinks she's doing the right thing. But the Blessed Virgin does not do things in that way. She is so kind that she always treats us with love and never punishes us."

There was nothing the children would not do for the Curé. There was one tiny girl who adored her doll—it was an ugly doll but she was so much attached to it that she carried it everywhere, even to church. One day in the kitchen, Monsieur Vianney asked her to sacrifice it and suggested that she throw it into the fire. At first, the poor child looked appalled. But all of a sudden she made up her mind and resolutely threw her idol into the flames. It was heroic.

"Oh, the poor child!" the modern reader will exclaim. "Surely nothing could be more innocent than the love of a little girl for her doll." We must realize that of necessity the Curé breathed the atmosphere of his times, still infected with Jansenism. The marvel is not that he may have made a mistake but that so few instances of this kind have been recorded. It may well have been that the doll had in fact become for the child what Monsieur Vianney suspected: an idol. In any event, where human wisdom fails, we are in God's hands: we cannot suppose that He would not reward a hundredfold the sacrifice by a little child of the thing she held most dear.

Monsieur Vianney used to bring back to Catherine any girl he found wandering about the fields and hedgerows. He would say imperiously: "You must keep this child. God has sent her to you."

"But Monsieur le Curé, there is no bed."

"No bed? There's yours."

Once he even brought them a newborn baby.

The girls were trained in practical work. They learned to knit, sew, wash and iron. The school inspector realized that they were not acquiring much book knowledge, but he knew that their virtue would compensate for any deficiencies in their education and that they would eventually make excellent mothers. Many of these poor girls, some of whom had lost their innocence, were transported into another world by Monsieur Vianney's catechism lessons. Without being asked, they all wanted to make general confessions. They wept most sincerely for their sins and promised to become fervent Christians. How they basked in the wonderful

family spirit of that house! Monseigneur Trochu has described it.
He says La Providence was, "a poor family ruled by a vigilant
mother, where the love of God preserved understanding, affection
and happiness."

When any of the benefactors of La Providence wanted to send
their protegées somewhere else where they could be better instructed or better fed, the Curé would say: "No, I beg you, do not
take them from the orphanage. Leave them with Catherine Lassagne, otherwise you will hurt me."

And then these girls, despised by the more fortunate villagers,
began to feel that they were having a share in the Curé's work
for the conversion of France. He put such trust in their prayers
that he would often tell them about his work. He would ask them
to do penance to expiate such-and-such terrible scandal or sin,
or to pray for certain unnamed sinners. Each child would take
her turn for an hour's adoration before the Blessed Sacrament
exposed, for Monsieur Vianney had founded the Adoration Répa-
ratrice in his parish. He had by then restored his church, and one
can imagine how impressed these children would be by the beauty
of the altar with candles burning on it all day, and the flowers
which they themselves were asked to arrange. To them, used to
such fearful squalor, the church of Ars was a first glimpse of the
Paradise of the Father's house. How quickly they passed those
enchanted hours before the Blessed Sacrament exposed on the
high altar under the copper dome (surmounted by that tuft of
plumes so greatly admired by the people of the countryside). And
how beautiful was the gilded copper tabernacle on the white marble altar, and round about, all the statues of the saints!

The orphans, rescued from Satan, prayed gladly for poor sinners. When they went for walks on the banks of the Fontblin, the
Magdalens used to run ahead of Catherine, and when they were
out of sight in the Cibeins woods they would beat their forearms
with stinging nettles and offer the pain for the Curé's sinners!
Catherine complained of this to Monsieur Vianney, but he simply smiled, for he knew exactly how they felt. The quiet ascetic
and the ragged girls were at one in the great work of redeeming
by love their fellow Christians outside the fold.

These hungry girls all kept the fasts of the Church. Catherine could say with truth that during Lent not one of them would help herself to a piece of the cook's crusty golden bread or dip her forefinger into the honey. Their reputation for mortification grew so great in the village that an old miser named Lacôte, who owned a large vineyard in Ars, would engage no one but the orphans of La Providence to pick his grapes. (And as an extra precaution he would employ them only during the September Ember days, for he knew that then not a single grape would be taken.)

In September 1830 Catherine had a great grief. She lost Benoîte Lardet, who had always been a devout young girl of exquisite delicacy. As she wept at her bedside, Benoîte said to her "You are very kind to weep. Do you really wish me to stay in this world? I can't get used to it." And when the doctor told her she would not recover, Benoîte cried out, "Joy! Joy! I am going to see God."

With the radiance of such a deathbed to remember, it is not surprising that the orphans whom death claimed rejoiced when their turn came to follow their mistress to Heaven. There was one who had trembled at the thought of death, but when her hour had come, she said: "I suffer indeed in my body, but I am so joyful in my heart. I did not think it would be so sweet to die." She died singing.

When these girls were old enough to leave the orphanage, the Curé found places for them in good Christian households. Some entered religion, and he helped them to choose the right congregation and provided the means for them to enter it. When one of them married, he managed to provide a small marriage portion for her, a few little things for her trousseau. The families they founded, their children and grandchildren, testified to the great vigilance and firmness with which they maintained Christian traditions in their homes—prayer in common, keeping the Sabbath, going to the sacraments and keeping away from taverns or dances. All this they had learned from Catherine, the foster-mother who could always guess all their troubles.

We shall see afterwards what happened to Catherine and what great reward was hers for sacrificing her youth to such hard labour. Her photograph shows her very thoughtful and rather sad, for indeed she had sounded the abyss of human misery, but there was a depth of innocence in her eyes. Hers was the great task of restoring to bodily and spiritual health poor beggar girls who had been victims of the lust and greed of men. Catherine had the sweetness and detachment of the saints. In this photograph she is enveloped in a great shawl, holding a book in her long hands; she is wearing a ruched white peasant bonnet and a large apron.

No doubt the Curé had Catherine in mind when he said: "I have known some beautiful souls in this world who never did their own will, but were quite dead to themselves. That is what makes saints." And later he called her the most beautiful flower of his garden.

He must have been thinking of her and the orphans when he said, "You see, I have often thought that the life of a poor servant who has no will but that of her master can be as pleasing to God as that of a nun who lives by her rule, if she knows how to use this renunciation profitably."

Into La Providence, as we have seen, the Curé had sunk all the money he had inherited from his father, which François one day brought to him from Dardilly. Hoping that his parishioners would help him by gifts in kind, he had gone round the village begging, and brought back, sad to relate, only one sack of potatoes. So he decided not to ask them again. He would go to the owners of châteaux. He even made the journey to Lyons on foot and begged from Pauline Jaricot's father. Sometimes he would appeal to rich penitents whom he knew to be generous.

Monsieur de Cibeins had promised the wood for warming La Providence, and every year Catherine was sent off to remind him.

The store of wheat for the orphanage was kept in the presbytery attic, in that corner which is furthest away from the Curé's bedroom. (In some of the cracks in the floor one can still find grains of wheat.) In 1829 the supply failed altogether. There had perhaps been a bad harvest and the Curé dared not go to the châtelains again. In desperation he thought he might have to send some of the orphans away. Then, recalling how St. Francis Regis had helped him when he was a young man, he begged him to perform a miracle. He swept the remaining few grains of wheat into the middle of the attic, and in that tiny heap he hid a little relic of the saint. He and the orphans prayed, then they waited. After a while he said to the cook, Jeanne-Marie Chanay, "Sweep up the rest of the wheat in the attic." She went up obediently. She tried to push the door open. She pushed again and got it a little way open. And through the crack a flood of golden wheat began to pour out. She ran down to the Curé.

"You only wanted to test my obedience," she said. "Your attic is full."

"How's that, full?"

"Yes, it's overflowing. Come and see for yourself."

They went up together. When they managed to force the door open they found that the cone-shaped load of wheat covered the entire floor of the attic and rose to the ceiling. In fact, they were amazed that the worm-eaten boards had not collapsed under the weight.

They noticed that this new wheat was a different colour from the old.

Some time later, in 1830, there was another miracle. Jeanne-Marie Chanay tells us: "We were in a sorry state because of our children. Catherine and I thought that if Monsieur le Curé asked God, the flour we had left would yield a batch of bread. We went to tell him of our plight. He said: 'You must knead it.'

"I set to work, not without some anxiety. At first I put very little water and very little flour in the kneading trough, but I saw that my dough was still far too thick. I added water, then some more flour, still without using up my little supply. Then the kneading trough became as full of dough as on the days when we put a large sackful into it. We made ten great loaves, each weighing from twenty to twenty-two pounds, and we filled the oven just as usual, to the great astonishment of all who saw it.

"We told Monsieur le Curé what had happened and he said, 'God is very good! He looks after His poor.'"

Marie Filliat and Jeanne both told Abbé Monnin about a third miracle. One day they had gone down to the cellar and found that the wine had leaked from the cask and there was hardly any left. They ran to Monsieur le Curé. He remained calm. "Nothing to worry about. He who allowed the wine to leak can quite well make it come back." They both went down to the cellar again, and saw that the wine had all gone. They tried to collect a little and put it back in the wine barrel. And then to their amazement they found that the wine barrel was completely full. They started laughing. Sixty litres of wine had suddenly appeared from nowhere. They had the surprise of their lives when they put their fingers in the bung-hole and brought them away wet. But the delightful thing about it all is that this wine, like the wine of the wedding feast at Cana, was found to be excellent and of far better quality than the usual wine at La Providence.

Then Catherine Lassagne in her *Petit Mémoire* tells us of a fourth miracle, which is hardly ever mentioned in the biographies of the saint. (Monseigneur Trochu says of this work: "She writes like the evangelists, who had watched Our Lord doing His miracles, with integrity and simplicity recording details taken from life. There is no literary arrangement, there are no descriptions, no exclamations.")

"Monsieur le Curé sometimes took pleasure in coming to serve his children at meal times, but this was rare. One day, holding a dish of pumpkin in my hands, I was worried that there would not be enough for everybody; I was quite upset. Monsieur le Curé appeared just as I was about to serve the children, took my dish and served them lavishly. Anxious because of the large helpings he was doling out, I went up to him and said in a whisper, 'Monsieur le Curé, there won't be enough to go round!' He didn't reply but continued his task. I don't remember if there was any over, but the children were plentifully served."

The time was drawing near when the whole world would be flocking to Ars and the moments the Curé could spend at La Providence would become very short indeed. In fact sometimes he even had no time to drink his milk there, but went to fetch it and then carried the pot back in his cupped hands across the square, greatly to the surprise of some of the pilgrims. Important as the orphanage had been, there was work of still greater importance for the saint, with so many sinners from all over Christendom to convert. His happy hours at La Providence were numbered.

11. *ARS TRANSFORMED*

AFTER HE HAD BEEN CURÉ OF ARS FOR NINE YEARS MONSIEUR VIAN-
ney was able to exclaim from the pulpit, "Ars is no longer Ars!"
Little by little the parish had been completely transformed, with
the exception of one thing, the dancing: this he was unable totally
to eradicate for twenty-five years.

There is a mysterious something in human beings which loves
and appreciates saints and is drawn to imitating them. And as we
have seen, it had not taken the parishioners of Ars long to recognize Monsieur Vianney's holiness. They knew the penitential life
he lived for their sakes, and in gratitude set about the reformation
of their own lives.

He sacrificed, he preached, but in addition, like a good shepherd mindful of the wolf, he was always on the watch. For example, one July Sunday after Vespers he left the church—a most
unusual thing for him—and went walking on the high road. He
met a man bringing in his harvest. This peasant, caught in the act
of profaning the day, was so much ashamed that he tried to hide
behind his cart. The Curé said to him sadly, "Oh, my friend, you're
very much surprised to find me here. But God sees you always. It
is He that you have to fear."

He always seemed to be on the spot when needed. For example,
in certain regions of the Rhône and the Ain, when a husband has
been publicly beaten by his wife, a burlesque procession is organized by the villagers in which a large stuffed doll representing
the husband is promenaded on a donkey, while somebody acting

the part of the wife beats it with her broom. Everybody joins in singing a suitable complaint. One Sunday this procession was just starting when all of a sudden Monsieur Vianney came out of his presbytery. He simply crossed the space between the presbytery and the church, and in two moments everybody had fled. "They flew off like a flock of pigeons," he recounted afterwards with much amusement.

As for the dances, he still continued to refuse absolution to girls who had been to them, even if they had gone only as spectators. Thus, long months would go by during which these girls were denied the sacraments. He maintained that, according to moral theologians, they had put themselves into an occasion of sin. ("Whosoever puts himself freely into an occasion of sin, cannot be absolved if he refuses to renounce this occasion, for he is not then in the requisite disposition.")

His natural gift for mimicry and sense of the ridiculous helped him in the pulpit. He knew how to poke gentle fun at the bespectacled old men who went to these dances, or others who wore ribbons in their hats. "I thought they wanted to put themselves up for sale," he said. As for those who went on carting their crops on Sundays, he said, with terrible imagery, that they were carting their souls into Hell.

Parents were frightened when he included them in his condemnations. He said that they were to blame if the girls got into trouble. Gradually, as a result, the girls began to be more carefully supervised. When they came back from school, instead of being allowed to gad about the fields or streets, they were trained to knit or take care of the household. And if they had to go out, they were always questioned on their return. Occasionally girls who sneaked out to a ball were given a sound beating when they returned.

When, at long last, all four tavern-keepers had to pack up and leave Ars for lack of customers, no more drunkards were seen zigzagging across the square or disturbing the peace of the night with their brawlings, hiccoughings and belchings.

Gradually the children became scrupulously honest. No more

petty pilfering was noticed from the fields, markets or open shops. When he was an old man, Benoît Trève told the story of how he had filched a pear from a shopkeeper and was just preparing to eat it at home when his mother caught him and made him confess his crime. She tied his hands behind his back and whipped him all the way back to the shop. There he had to return the pear and beg pardon.

At four o'clock on summer mornings children could be seen hurrying to church, for the Curé had promised that the first comer would be given a holy picture. Those who didn't behave received a little tap on the cheek with the Curé's catechism manual. Mère Verchère, who when she was a child used to attend catechism on Sunday afternoons and fall asleep, loved to tell, in later life, about how the Curé would wake her up with a gentle pat. She felt rather proud of it!

In the end the bishop declared that the children of Ars were the best instructed in the whole countryside. It was not that Monsieur Vianney taught them so much but that his teaching was clear and vivid. They could really grasp it, and the truths of faith made a deep impression on them. The deepest impression of all, however, was made by the Curé himself, and he was the greatest cause of their conversion. An old man, Père Drémieux, recounted how when all the children had assembled for catechism on the benches of the old choir under the bell turret, they would wait for the Curé, who was still at his prayers: "He prayed, he prayed . . . and then from time to time he would raise his eyes towards heaven and laugh. . . . I believe that that man was seeing something."

Monsieur Vianney tried in vain to abolish crinolines amongst his parishioners, because when the pilgrimage to Ars began in earnest, most of the women who came to the parish were wearing them. They must have filled the narrow aisle of the church and caused much inconvenience. The Curé did not press the point. He simply found the garments ridiculous. He said: "The Emperor has done some fine things, but he's forgotten one. He should have enlarged all doors to let the crinolines pass."

Anyway the pilgrims, crinolined or otherwise, admired the

women and young girls of Ars, for they were as dignified and as modestly dressed as nuns. They had even given up a specially complicated hair style peculiar to Ars. Perhaps the Curé objected to it not so much because it was a form of vanity as because it might take too long to do every morning before Mass. There is a most entertaining anecdote of how he tried to cure young Jeanne Lardet of a quite innocent vanity. She was strutting about wearing a pretty new collar. The Curé, when he saw her, laughed and said: "Would you like to sell me your collar? I'd give you five sous for it."

"Why, what for, Monsieur le Curé?"

"I would put it on my cat."

One cannot help regretting this strictness about clothes when one thinks of the farmers' wives' velvet Sunday dresses, poppy-red, garnet-red, puce-coloured, or clear violet with silver lace trimmings; their pretty aprons, the jewels on their breasts, the original hats of the locality, and the long cloth cloaks, green, brown or black, fastened at the neck by velvet ribbons or even by jewelled or enamelled chains. However, love for picturesque costume was fully satisfied when the great Ars pilgrimage began, for then all the regional costumes of France were represented.

The Curé wanted all his parishioners to be saints, and it is impossible to achieve much contemplative prayer if one has a large wardrobe to look after. And the women, strange to relate, after such unpromising beginnings, did become saintly. When the Curé passed the new churchyard in 1855 and thought of all these old parishioners whose deathbeds he had attended, and whom he had known intimately, he said: "This is a reliquary."

He was able to say that he thought all were saved.

The transformation of Ars was most obvious on Sunday. No more hay carts rumbled out, and the blacksmith's anvil was silent; men had put away their tools and given the whole day to God in peace and happiness. The villagers went to Mass and Vespers, and in between times paid calls on one another; the younger men played at bowls or skittles, the old men sat on their doorsteps. Old Fleury Trève, father of fifteen children, always recited his rosary.

Even on week days the men came to pray in church before and after work. The story of old Père Chaffangeon has been told so often that it hardly bears repeating, except that it is so wonderful. Whether he was going to his work or returning from it, he never passed the church door without going in. He would leave his pick-axe or his spade at the door, and sometimes he would stay for hours sitting or kneeling before the tabernacle. One day a neighbour who had missed him from the fields went to the church to search for him. "What have you been doing there for such a long time?" he asked him. The old man replied, "I am looking at God, and God is look-ing at me."

The Curé never related this story without tears in his eyes.

Jean Pertinand, the schoolmaster, said he never went into the church without finding somebody there adoring God.

According to Mademoiselle Marthe des Garets, several women of the parish whom the Curé had inflamed with the fire of his own charity died like saints. Monsieur Brac de la Perrière, who wrote the recollections of his pilgrimage to Ars, said, "What struck us from the very first was the calm and the peace of the place. In this country region, one seemed to breathe an air which was softer than elsewhere . . . The inhabitants greeted us in a kindly fashion. They were eager to show us the way. Christian hospitality and brotherly love seemed to be a part of everybody's mode of life. We noticed that the houses were ornamented with statues of the Virgin and pictures of the saints."

The Curé had waged such a fierce war against blasphemy and swearing that after a while no one ever heard the peasants swear-ing, but instead, heartfelt phrases like: "How good God is!" or "May God be blessed!" The field workers never sang bawdy songs now but encouraged one another to work by cheerful, innocent ones. Mademoiselle Alix de Belvey said: "I have walked around the fields at harvest time, and I have never heard a single swear-word. I mentioned this admiringly to a peasant, and he said to me, 'Oh, we're no better than others, but we would be too ashamed to commit such faults, living, as we do, so near a saint.'"

Again, Monsieur Brac de la Perrière noticed on the very first

evening he came to the village that three men who were leading
a pair of horses dragging a big tree near the Fontblin refrained
from uttering a single oath when one of the horses had a serious
fall. They didn't lose their tempers and they didn't strike the poor
beast. He had never seen such self-control in the country before.

And thus, having been faithful in small things, both the Curé
and the parish of some two hundred souls were prepared to play
their part in the redemption of some eighty thousand souls who
would be converted by coming to Ars. The charity that had begun
at home was now ready to burst into flame and radiate far and
wide.

We must mention in passing a few of the parishioners of Ars—
unimportant people, living and dying in obscurity and soon forgotten in their graves in the little churchyard; their lives take on
significance when they are caught up in the great destiny of Ars.
There was Marthe Miard who kept a religious articles shop near
the church. (The Curé advised her to alter one of her bonnets
because he thought it too fussy. One day when he met her wearing a brightly coloured muslin dress, instead of saying "Good-day,
my child," he bowed low and said: *"Bonjour, Mademoiselle."*)
She reported: "He pointed out to me that in my shop I had statues
of the Virgin Mary and so many pious objects that I had only to
look at them to know what to say in my prayers."

And then there was that devoted Mademoiselle Antoinette
Pignaut who had left an easy life in her Lyons flat to come and
live in poverty with Mère Renard. She formed part of that inner
court around Our Lord which it had been the Curé's desire from
the beginning to form. The Curé led her up the stony path to holiness. He mortified her and made her learn renunciation in great
and little things, even going so far as to forbid her to come to his
catechism instructions. He wanted the devout women in Ars to
be detached and spiritual. One can't help liking this Mademoiselle
Pignaut, who came to live in Madame Renard's tiny house in order
to spend the rest of her days as a contemplative. She had put
aside enough for bare necessities only. Whenever the Curé was
in great need he would come to her and say, "Come, come. I need

five francs. Give them to me quickly." And of course he wanted
it to give alms.

Lest she should become attached to the church for the beauty
of its externals, he would make her—on Holy Thursday, for
example—go and kneel in a place where she could not see the
altar with its shining monstrance surrounded by candles and lights.
And she learnt never to crave for the Curé's hospitality after he
had invited her to that famous banquet of dried crusts.

Among the men there was André Verchère, the Ars carter—the
one who had had such a terrible fright from the diabolical manifestations the night he had mounted guard at the presbytery. He said
of the Curé: "I look on him as one of the greatest saints that God
has given to his Church." A vine-grower of the Mâconnais said:
"I have seen God in a man." When old Perè Chaffangeon died at
the age of seventy-five, he sang in his death agony, "I am going to
see her, my beloved Mother."

And the Curé liked Soeur Lacon, a sort of lay nun without a
habit. She was another who kept a shop for holy objects in Ars.
She was a cripple, with one leg shorter than the other, and walked
with the more difficulty because she had rheumatism. She was
one of those who used to make him tasty tidbits, which he would
give to beggars—and then laugh incorrigibly at her complaints.

Then there were his physicians, in particular Dr. Saunier, who
was very much devoted to him—as indeed they all were. His
grand-daughter has drawn us a charming little picture about the
way he showed his affection for his patient:

"Dear, good Saint Vianney, he had some hard moments. One
day at twilight, Grandfather was returning from visiting a patient
when he noticed in a field quite far off a black and white figure.
Bon-Papa reined in his horse and went over to what he thought
was a poor lost sheep. What a surprise! It was his good Curé
seated on a stone, sad, discouraged. . . . Grandfather kindly but
firmly forced him to get into the carriage and brought him back
to his church."

And last but not least, there were the Comte and Comtesse des
Garets. They came to live at the Château d'Ars after the death of

old Mademoiselle Colombe des Garets. They had a family of
twelve children. Even when the Curé's astounding daily activity
was at its height, he always found time to baptize the new baby.
When the Curé met the Comtesse with her daughters in the street,
he would say: "Make saints of them." The Comte, who became
Mayor of Ars, was devoted to him and looked after him during
the illness he had in May 1843. He also did all he could to prevent
him from leaving Ars. It was he who brought Père Lacordaire to
church to hear the Curé preach. He and his wife were among the
most valuable of the witnesses at the canonization enquiry. A
whole series of begging letters which the Curé wrote to the Comte
is preserved, and we know that the Comte always tried to respond.

But his chief friend was Vicomte François des Garets, Mademoiselle Colombe's brother, the one who had no children and lived
most of the year in the Faubourg Saint-Germain in Paris. His sister used to write to him so enthusiastically about the new Curé
that he decided to give up his charities at Saint Sulpice and con-
centrate on his country parish church of Ars. We have all his
letters, rather pompous but so affectionate and entertaining. It was
largely through him that the church was restored and beautifully
furnished.

We know how the Curé, at the very beginning, bought a new
high altar with his own money. He liked, as he said in his homely
vocabulary, to improve "God's household arrangements"—"*le
ménage du Bon Dieu.*" He would go to Lyons to visit the work-
shops of embroideresses and goldsmiths. The shopkeepers used to
say, with some astonishment: "From somewhere round about,
there is a little curé, very thin, badly dressed, who looks as if he
hadn't got a sou to bless himself with, but he must have the best
of everything for his church." One day in 1825, when Mademoiselle
d'Ars took him with her to Lyons to buy some Mass vestments, he
kept repeating, when he was shown something new: "Not beautiful
enough. We must have something more beautiful than that."

Vicomte François felt a deep spiritual affinity for the Curé; he
found just the right friend for himself when he came to Ars. In
Paris he used to go to Mass every morning at St. Sulpice. In the

afternoon he would visit the poor, for he belonged to the Society of St. Vincent de Paul. He would write to his sister asking her to dole out his old woollen clothes to the servants, for he said he did not like waste. He had poor health and bad eyesight, but in spite of a cough and continual headaches he still tried to keep the Lenten fast. One can imagine how he was drawn towards this curé his sister called an angel, and about whose health she was so anxious. The attraction between them was evident. At Ars they were often seen kneeling together in prayer, and they would have long talks in the sacristy. And this in spite of a great difference in age, for the Vicomte was sixty-one when he first met the Curé— aged thirty-three—in the spring of 1819. When he left for Paris again, he told Colombe to be a watchful sister to Monsieur Vianney. He said that complaints from all sides had reached his ears: "He gives away so much that he lives on bread and cheese." Would she please, he begged, see to it that the Curé had at least one *pot-au-feu* a week for *himself*.

When he returned to Paris, his sister began to tell him in her letters what a grief it was for Monsieur Vianney that the vestments, like the tabernacle and the candelabra, were so old and shabby, such an unfortunate contrast to the new altar. So the Vicomte made up his mind to see to it. He wrote that "this village sanctuary would never be as sumptuous or as magnificent as he wished." On the 5th of May, 1823, he joyfully announces the arrival of the first gifts: three fine banners embroidered with silver, and so costly that he made a condition that they were to be housed in the presbytery on the first floor. In 1826, it is a vestment in cloth of gold for the principal feasts of Our Lady, and in March 1827 a third vestment of black velvet with red braid for Good Friday. He promised a canopy for May 1824, and begged the Curé to measure the entrance of his church very exactly, to make sure that the canopy could get through. In spite of this, it proved too wide, and one suspects that Monsieur Vianney cheated about the measurements because he wanted a wider door. The canopy was in red velvet with a gold-lettered text. "Nothing beautiful enough for God," the Vicomte used to say. And he spent happy days in Paris in consultation with his embroideress, his painter and his cabinet maker.

Of course the Curé was in the seventh heaven. It was a joy to watch and hear him when the great wooden cases arrived; the eager parishioners would go as far as Lyons to fetch them. Speaking of the banners, the Mayor's registers tell us that never had such banners been seen in the neighbourhood. When they were preparing to unpack the cases in the village square, the Curé would invite as many people as possible to come and admire the contents with him. He would say to an old woman: "Come, good mother, and see something really beautiful before you die." And all the while he was removing the treasures from their wrappings he used to laugh and cry in turn, just like a child. With his hands joined, he would sing the praises of his great friend, the Vicomte.

The Curé took the banner of the Immaculate Conception with him on a pilgrimage to Fourvière, accompanied by all his parishioners, and there he prayed particularly for the Vicomte. He was glad the sun shone, for the Vicomte had forbidden him to take the banners out when there was a threat of rain. All the Vicomte's letters are delightful, full of exquisite politeness and tact, for he was a gentleman of the old school.

Although of course the Vicomte had all the detachment which befits a Christian and was well aware that God looks not at the gift but at the heart of the giver, he was human enough to want to know the impression his gifts had made on Monsieur Vianney. He wrote to his sister: "I ask you to communicate to me quite frankly what Monsieur our Curé thinks of all these gifts. For if he is fully satisfied, *my joy will be perfect.*"

And so in about ten years from the day when Monsieur Vianney first came to Ars the old church was entirely restored. In 1823 had been added the chapel of St. John the Baptist for which Monsieur Vianney paid himself, and of which he said: "Brethren, if you knew what things have happened in this chapel, you would not dare to come into it . . . . I tell you no more." Catherine, who records this, tells us that "he repeated this several times, as if his mind were completely full of it." Perhaps the Baptist had shown him in a vision the great crowds of penitents flocking to the confessional in that chapel, and the conversions that would occur there. In 1824 a porcelain-faced clock was put in the bell turret so that the peasants could bless the hour each time it struck.

There is such a contrast between the old vestry inventory and the new one. After the advent of the Curé there were no fewer than eight chasubles, twelve albs and twelve amices, so that when Monseigneur Devie made his official visitation in 1838, he wrote in the register: "Everything is so beautiful and so rich that all one can do is to admire." For the celebration of the first Mass of the Immaculate Conception on December the 8th, 1854, a most glorious chasuble was designed for the Curé by the future architect of Fourvière—blue velvet with gold arabesques and a marvellous picture of Our Lady. The Curé could never stop admiring it; it is still there today, its beauty wonderfully preserved. He was radiant the first day he wore it. It is not surprising that the parishioners now behaved most decorously in church. Baronne de Belvey recounts that at the three-hour Mass on Sundays there was a procession and a sermon. "The church was full and a remarkable spirit of prayerfulness reigned."

On certain days, for example on Maundy Thursday, the pilgrims were particularly impressed by the devoutness of the parishioners surrounding the altar of repose. The choir was draped with banners, a thousand candles were lit, and the whole parish was in adoration before the altar. In the evening they all kept the Holy Hour, and the Curé on his knees, without sitting down for a moment, would pray through the whole of Thursday night, well into Good Friday morning. But at Corpus Christi, it was even more impressive, and now there was the added note of joy. The Curé would ask all the young girls to wear white for the procession, and even the orphans somehow or other found white dresses. The Curé, his heart overflowing, would walk through the streets and even go as far as the château, encouraging the workmen who were preparing the altars on the route, and helping them.

A pilgrim, writing in a rather pompous style like Chateaubriand's, has given us a most enthusiastic description of what he saw at Ars on the feast of Corpus Christi. He tells us of guns being fired, bells ringing, enormous crowds, roads blocked with stamping horses, flags flying on château and bell turret. He grows poetical about the pomp unfurled before his eyes: the immense procession of pilgrims, the gilded monstrance, the brocade copes glittering in the sunlight and the old man, "the revered Curé of this place," lost in clouds of incense. He describes two thousand heads bowing at the benediction of the Blessed Sacrament, the alleluias, the bouquets of flowers on the trees along the way to the château with its iron gate intertwined with madonna lilies, the rose petals scattered on the sandy avenue, the antique tapestries draped round the keep. And then the procession winding between rows of lemon trees, the hosannahs echoing from the chapel, reaching the crowd and then resounding in the depths of the valley.

It was on this occasion that Comte des Garets saw Monsieur Vianney trembling with joy—*il tressaillit d'allégresse*—as he thanked the Jesuits, who had supplied instrumental music for the festivities as a surprise. All this took place in the year before his death, when he was seventy-two. He had grown so frail that he was hardly able to support the weight of the monstrance, and he returned to the vestry drenched in sweat. Frère Athanase[1] asked him if he were not tired. "How could I be tired?" he said. "He whom I carried, carried me too."

---

[1] In March 1849, through the efforts of Monsieur Vianney, the Brothers of the Holy Family of Belley took over the running of the Ars school. Frère Athanase and Frère Jérôme, of whom we shall have more to say later on, were two of these Brothers.

12. *THE SAINT IN HIS PULPIT*

THE CURÉ HAD SAID: "I BELIEVE ONE WHO DOES NOT HEAR THE WORD of God as he should will not save his soul."

Though his flock were only simple peasants, and he saw all their faults very clearly, he took as much trouble about preparing his sermons to them as if they were university audiences. The tact with which he treated them was exquisite, for the Curé's courtesy was born of charity. This kind of treatment was a new experience for them, and after a short time they stopped yawning and scratching their heads and chatting with their neighbours; they listened, took it all in, made a real effort to amend their lives.

On Sundays and feast days, the Curé would preach in a high pulpit which he reached by climbing many wooden steps; but the eleven o'clock catechism instruction (after the class was moved from La Providence to the church) was always given in a smaller, lower, wooden pulpit which is also still there today, on the right-hand side as you go in. It had a wooden foot-rest; the saint used to lean back and look at his children clustering around him. They were so close to him that they were able to steal his catechism books for relics. What a thunderclap he must have been to the country people who, afterwards, in farm, tavern and field, would discuss his flaming reproaches! Never before had they been preached to in this way.

When he first came to Ars he used to write out all his sermons beforehand. He worked standing up, in the cold, damp little sacristy where the sun could penetrate for only one hour each day

145

through a narrow slit of a window. He would lean on the credence table and fill thirty to forty sheets with his *"écriture fine et serrée,"* sometimes working for seven hours at a stretch, often far into the night, especially as the dreaded Sunday drew near. When fatigue overcame him, he would kneel down, lean his head against the credence and fall asleep for a few moments. Then he would pray before the tabernacle to restore his strength before going back to work. Finally, he set himself the arduous task of learning his sermons off by heart: for one with such a poor memory, this was really heroic. Very often in the pulpit his memory would fail him, and then, much humbled, he had to stop short and come down again. After a while, though, when he had asked his parishioners to pray for him, he improved.

Towards the end of his life, many of his admiring friends were only too ready to buy those hand-written sermons of his, and he would use the money for his good works. That is why we haven't got a complete set of sermons.

Towards the year 1830 when he was overwhelmed with work, he had no time at all in which to prepare his sermons, so he asked his parishioners to pray to the Holy Ghost: thenceforward he preached from the fullness of his heart without notes or preparation. And thus the wonderful preacher was born. He was like the good husbandman of the Gospels who could go to his treasure chest and take out things both new and old: he never suffered from paucity of material. He knew God, for he lived ever in His presence, and he knew human beings because he heard confessions for sixteen or more hours a day, and that for thirty-five years without a stop.

As his parishioners left the church after his sermons, they were convinced that he had been seeing—really seeing—the things he spoke of. Abbé Monnin says: "There was such an extraordinary brilliance, such a marvellous power in his voice, his gestures, his looks and his transfigured face, that it was impossible to remain cold as you listened." He preached with his whole being. Monseigneur Trochu says that before he began to preach his eyes would travel over the audience; sometimes his glance would be arrested and would remain fixed, searching, it seemed, to the depths of a soul he had suddenly caught sight of.

His voice was high, strident and even a little falsetto—perhaps for these very reasons the more arresting. (Mademoiselle d'Ars used to ask him why he shouted so when he was preaching.) It seemed to rivet the attention of his congregation. One listener said that the more animated he became in his preaching, the higher his voice went, and it vibrated frighteningly. Another noted that when he had hardly strength to speak at all, if he began to speak of detachment from the world or the joys of Heaven, his voice would gain volume. It could take on a wonderful sweetness to express thoughts of love. The tone in which he uttered the name of Jesus was music to the ear.

In the early days he was full of energetic gestures in the pulpit. One of his parishioners, August Trève, told long afterwards how "He would clap his hands; he looked as if he were going to fly into the air." And the Comtesse des Garets said, "When Monsieur Vianney was preaching on Heaven, he seemed to be already winging his way there."

He was not above acting in order to capture the attention of a sleepy audience. For example, he would clench his fist and shake it to imitate the Devil.

His sensitive, nervous, impetuous temperament had full play in his preaching. Occasionally he would bang his catechism against the pulpit to emphasize certain points. The truths which rang out, the love sounding in his words, went straight to the hearts of his audience. It seemed as if he felt too much to be able to say all he wanted to.

Even in old age he was agile, his movements quick and lively. His whole physical being had become so elevated by grace as to suggest the spiritual body of which St. Paul speaks. As he came towards the church, breaking through the crowds, what did they see? A small man whose cassock was much too large for him: he seemed to be lost in its folds. Though in the last years of his life his step was heavy, it was still quick—the step of a man who counts the hours, and though exhausted is in haste to return to God's

service. Abbé Monnin says that in the last years his head fell
slightly forward towards his breast, from the habit of recollection.
His white hair, thick and rather long, was like an aureole around
his head. His features still had the suggestion of harshness one
sees in the weatherbeaten face of the countryman, a harshness tem-
pered and subdued by spirituality.

The contrast between the deep blue eyes and the white hair must
have been arresting, for a man who had been a small boy in the
parish at that time remembered it in his own old age—in that
congregation, as we have seen, even the children listened. A certain
Abbé Dufour said: "I remember that one Sunday evening the Curé
of Ars, completely carried away by his subject, suddenly fell silent.
A ray of the setting sun touched his face, showing him to Monsieur
Toccanier and me so glowing with heavenly fire that we asked one
another: 'Is this a man or an angel?'"

Extraordinary to think that in the space of thirty years he must
have climbed those pulpit stairs more than twelve thousand times!
And yet the flame of his enthusiasm burnt high, even in old age. He
had the joyful youth of the children of God.

We must not get the idea into our heads (through neglecting to
read his sermons and taking at second hand the opinion of super-
ficial biographers) that the Curé could only say: "How good God
is!" and then burst into tears, and that that was the whole content
of his preaching; we should take the trouble to get the four volumes of his sermons edited by Dom Delaroche and printed in Paris
in 1925 by Beauchesne. Out-of-date sermons mouldering away on
the dusty shelves of forgotten rectories can be terribly tedious, but
these keep one awake at three o'clock in the morning. One cannot
put them down. They are intensely dramatic and can grip power-
fully. Here are a few specimens. First the sermon he preached on
the Feast of the Presentation—Candlemas Day:

"Have you meditated on the love which consumed the heart of
the holy old man Simeon during his ecstasy? For, assuredly, he was
in ecstasy when he held the Infant Jesus in his arms. He had asked
God that he might behold the Redeemer of Israel, and God had
promised to grant his prayer. Fifty years did he spend in this ex-

pectation, burning with desire for its fulfillment. When Mary and
Joseph came into the Temple, God said to him: 'He is here.' Then
taking the Infant Jesus in his arms and pressing Him to his heart,
which overflowed with love and kindled at the touch of the Holy
Child, the good old man exclaimed: 'Now, O Lord, let me die!'
Then he gave back Jesus to His Mother; he was only suffered to
keep Him for one moment. But we, my brethren, did we know it,
are far happier than Simeon. We may keep Him always if we will.
He comes not only into our arms, but into our heart.

"O man, how happy you are, but how little you understand your
happiness! If you understood it, you could not live . . . Oh, no,
truly, you could not live [the Curé's voice broke with weeping],
you would die of love! That God gives Himself to you. . . . You
can take Him with you if you will . . . to wherever you will."

He was at his best when he was speaking about the joys of
Heaven. "Man was created for Heaven. The Devil has broken the
ladder which leads him to it. Our Lord by His Passion has fashioned a new one for us. He has opened the door. The Blessed
Virgin is at the top of the ladder. She holds it with her hands and
cries out to us: 'Come, come!' Oh lovely invitation! How lovely is
man's destiny! To see God, to love Him, bless Him, gaze on Him
for all eternity. . . .

"In Heaven our hearts will be so lost, so drowned in the joy of
loving God, that we shall be occupied no longer either with ourselves or with others, but only with God."

And what eloquence there is in his improvisations!—for example,
his description of the sinner on his deathbed.

"Alas, it is time to die, and there is no confession, no conversion,
no coming to the truth! Come near, my friend. Do you see the hardened old sinner who has despised everything, mocked everything?
Do you see the young libertine? Only a fortnight ago he made the
taverns echo with his most infamous songs. . . . Alas, what a
change! The time has come to die and to be damned. Do you see
the glittering eyes, the sign that death is at the door? He sees
everybody around him in a state of great agitation. They look at
him with tears in their eyes. 'Do you know me?' they say to him. He

can but open horror-struck eyes, and his look fills all who are around him with fear. They look at him, trembling, and hanging their heads. Go forth, leave him to die without God as he has lived.

". . . Do you see the demons surrounding him, filling him with despair? Do you see his frightful convulsions? No, no, my brethren, all hope is lost. This soul is about to leave the body. O my God, where will this poor soul go? Alas, Hell alone is its dwelling place.

"He has four minutes of life remaining to him, to show him the full extent of his misery. The end draws near. . . . The onlookers and the priest kneel down to see if God will have pity on that poor soul.

"Oh horror! Oh abomination! To Hell, to Hell, since his place there is prepared."

Thus he describes the sinner who will not repent.

Here is the description of Mary Magdalen, repentant: "And then, unable to contain herself any longer, she rises, she tramples all her fineries and vanities underfoot, she runs, or rather she is drawn on by the ardour with which her heart is already inflamed. Unmindful of all human respect, she comes into the banquet room looking broken. Her hair, once so well tended and curled, is now all dishevelled. Her eyes are downcast and full of tears. She looks ashamed, her face is flushed. She throws herself at the Saviour's feet as He is seated at table. . . . Oh no, no, my brethren, no longer Magdalen the sinner, but a repentant Magdalen and a faithful lover of the Saviour."

And then Heaven again: "O beautiful heaven! O lovely dwelling place! When shall we see thee? O my God, how long will You leave us to languish in a strange land, in exile? Ah, if you see Him whom my heart loves, tell Him that I languish for love, that I can no longer live, that I die hourly. Oh, who will give me the wings of a dove, to leave this exile and fly to the breast of my beloved? O happy city whence all griefs are banished, and where we swim in torrents of eternal love!"

There is one point of similarity between his preaching and that of Christ in the Gospels. Preaching about His Kingdom, by the side of lakes and mountains, Jesus was often inspired by nature, by the

customs of the Galileans, by the scenes of daily life. No abstractions
in His lessons. Just parables and imagery which simple country
folk would find easy to understand. Birds, flowers, shepherds,
fishermen, ripening harvest—all these come thronging into the
Gospels. The vine and its branches, oxen, the stones of whited
sepulchres, a falling tower, a camel going through a gate—all
these familiar things. Christ taught by parables. The Curé did so
too. As we have already seen, his artlessness, his lack of sophistica-
tion, infuriated the Devil, as he was informed through the mouth
of a possessed woman.

The Curé's word was a living one. An old man told Monseigneur
Convert, "All his preaching was by comparisons." Here are examples of his images, drawn from the great book of Nature which
he had read from childhood.

"We should imitate the shepherds in the fields in winter—life is
truly a long winter!—they make a fire, but from time to time to
keep it lighted, they run about gathering wood from all sides. If,
like the shepherds, we knew how to keep the fire of God's love
alight by prayers and good works, it would never go out."

"Crosses transformed into the flames of love are like a bundle of
briers which are thrown into the fire and consumed to ashes. The
briers are hard but the ashes are soft."

He preaches to the married on the duty of having children:
"Must little birds serve you as examples? Look at the little creatures, how they rejoice to see their generation multiply. During the
day, they are occupied in finding them food, and at night they
cover them with their wings to protect them from the inclement
air. If a greedy hand takes their little ones away you hear them
weep after their own fashion. They seem to be unable to leave
their nests, always hoping to find their children again. I am not
talking to pagans but to Christians. How shameful that animals
should be more faithful to fulfil the designs of Providence than the
children of God, the fathers and mothers God has chosen for the
peopling of Heaven!"

Many other comparisons are drawn from birds:
"The Holy Spirit has told us that the Lord brings his people out

of Egypt and, leading it to the Promised Land, compares Himself to 'an eagle who flies around his little ones to encourage them to fly, and takes them and carries them on his wings.' Here precisely, my brethren, is what Jesus Christ does for us. He stretches forth His wings, inciting us by His lessons and His examples to detach ourselves from this world, that we may be raised up to Heaven by Him."

To conclude, here are two examples of his vivid imagery:

"The damned fall into Hell fast as the snow flakes on a winter's day."

"A poor creature, directly it is on a slanderer's tongue, is like a grain of wheat under a millstone. It is torn, crushed and entirely destroyed."

There was no preacher his equal for inspiring horror in his audience. Abbé Monnin tells us that once, taking the Last Judgment as the subject of his instruction, he stopped suddenly at the words of the terrible sentence "Go ye cursed ones" and burst into tears. Moaning and sobbing he could only repeat: "Cursed by God, do you understand, my brethren? Accursed by a God who knows only how to bless! Accursed by a God who knows only how to love and how to forgive! Accursed, accursed, without remission! Accursed for ever! How terrible a calamity!" His repetitions, because he meant them so totally, could be most moving. Abbé Monnin tells us that one day when he was preaching about the Apostles in ecstasy on Mount Thabor, he went on to speak of the soul's gladness when it rejoices in Our Lord's humanity in Heaven. The Curé, transported in ecstasy, cried out, "*We shall see Him! We shall see Him!* Oh, my brethren, have you thought of it? We shall see Him for ever and ever. We shall see Him *as He is* . . . face to face!" and for fully a quarter of an hour he never stopped weeping and repeating "*We shall see Him! We shall see Him!*"

The members of his flock were dumbfounded. As there is joy in his picture of Heaven there is horror in his picture of the damned. "Ah, unhappy sinner, you place your God below the scum of your furies, beneath the sordid passion of your avarice. Unhappy man, you place Him under the gall of your anger, under the rage of

your envy, under the smoke of your ambition. Ah, what am I saying? You place Him, as though you would drown Him, in the broth
of your impure and infamous depravities."

He speaks of St. John the Baptist's head brought to Herod on a
platter: "But what horror! When the head appeared in the hall, the
eyes and the mouth, even though closed, seemed to reproach him
with his crime and to threaten him with most terrible punishment.
At the sight, Herod trembled and grew pale."

Again there is horror in his choice of a quotation from a letter St.
Jerome had written about temptations:

"I am in this desert to which I have condemned myself in order
to avoid Hell. I am amidst sombre rocks where I have no other
company but scorpions and wild beasts. Yet in spite of all the
horrors with which I am surrounded . . . my spirit still burns
with my body's impure fire, that body which is corrupted before
I am; the Devil still dares to offer me his pleasures to taste."

And though some of his descriptions of Hell are full of horror—
enough to send chills down one's spine—he tries to indicate that
Hell is still more terrible because man has fallen from so great a
height, because man has separated himself from so loving a God.
In the sermon on the Hell of Christians, he says: "Oh my God, can
one conceive anything more fearful? A Christian in Hell! A bap-
tized person found among demons! A member of Jesus Christ in
the flames! Devoured by infernal spirits! A child of God between
Lucifer's teeth!"

But it would be a mistake to think that Hell and its corroding
miseries dominated his homilies. The Curé of Ars had only to
turn his head a little to see the tabernacle: and then his face would
light up with love: we see it so in Cabuchet's statue, which breathes
adoration, joy, and rapt, smiling wonder. It is as if we could hear
him cry out—as, of course, he did: "O my God, how You love those
who love You! How fearful You are lest they should suffer! Ah my
God, how good You are!"

He quotes the loveliest passages from the lives of the saints, to
show Our Lord's overwhelming tenderness—to St. Teresa of Avila,
for example: "When men no longer want Me, I will come and hide

in thy heart." This passage he always quoted with tears. Or again:
"I am waiting for the Day of Judgment, to make known to men how
much thou hast loved Me." On the feast of the Sacred Heart: "Our
Lord places us on His heart. Ah, if we could remain there always!"
—Then, joining his hands and raising his tear-filled eyes to heaven,
he would cry out—"O Heart of Jesus, Heart of Love, flower of love,
Heart which is all that stayed whole in Our Lord's most holy body.
. . . If we do not love the Heart of Jesus, what then shall we love?
There is only love in that Heart."

In his sermon on temptation, he says: "For Our Lord is there
quite close to us, looking on us with kindness, smiling at us and
saying: 'So you do love me?' " This passage is almost autobiographical in its tenderness. Abbé Vianney speaks lovingly too of the
Blessed Virgin Mary: "When our hands have touched spices, they
give fragrance to all they handle; let us make our prayers pass
through the hands of the Blessed Virgin—she will make them
fragrant." Or again, when he speaks at great length of her life, in
a sermon for the Feast of the Assumption:

"The angels, we are told, intoned a canticle of gladness in the
humble dwelling-place where the holy body rested, and it was
filled with such a perfume that it seemed as if all the fragrance of
Heaven had fallen into it."

Then he quotes St. Bernard about the burial of Our Lady: "The
angels themselves made their own procession, preceding and following the body of their sovereign Lady with canticles of joy. All
present heard the song of those angels, and everywhere, in every
place through which this holy body passed, it distilled a delicious
odour. . . ."

The Curé, speaking of her Assumption, paraphrases the Canticle
of Canticles. "Who is she," cries the Holy Spirit, "rising up from
the desert of this life, overflowing with delights and love, leaning
on the arm of her beloved?"

He was eloquent too when speaking about the saints. In one of
his instructions he said: "Heaven was infused into the souls of the
saints. It was an outpouring of Heaven in which they bathed and
were drowned. Just as the disciples on Mount Thabor who saw no

man but Jesus only, so contemplative souls also on the Mount Thabor of their hearts, see only Our Lord. They are as two friends who never tire of each other."

In those days, before artificial pleasures came to blunt men's sensibilities, in that happy age when they drew their instructions and diversions from the life of their village, the country people found Monsieur Vianney's catechism instructions a source of great wonder. They heard anecdotes about the saints entirely new to them. They found out things they had never heard of before. As a boy at Dardilly and as a young man at Les Noës, Jean-Marie Vianney had read the lives of the saints far into the night, and when he became Curé of Ars he continued to read a little every night before going to bed. Every morning when she went to clean his room his housekeeper put back into the bookcase the *Lives of the Saints,* by Père Giry, as we have seen, and the *Lives of the Saints* by Ribadeneira.

However tired he was he would always read about the saint whose feast fell on the morrow. And so, during his sleepless and devil-ridden nights, by the light of his flickering candle, he would gaze at the pictures of saints on his walls and think tenderly of them as his friends. Of course he had his favourites, the ones to whom he referred more often in his instructions. He loved particularly to speak of St. Clare, because of her love of the Cross and of poverty. He loved Pope St. Gregory (who sent St. Augustine to Britain) particularly because he was so good to the poor. And he loved to tell again and again the story of how, when this pope was feeding twelve poor people at his table, he saw a thirteenth, who turned out to be an angel.

The thought of St. Benedict-Joseph Labre haunted him constantly, not only in the making of his homilies but in his trampings up and down the country roads near Ars. Often he would search out a beggar again to give him more alms, fearing that he had not given him enough. Who knows, perhaps he thought that any day he might meet a second St. Benedict-Joseph Labre in the person of one of these beggars? But he always taught his congregations that when we give alms to a beggar, we feed and clothe Christ. He said: "There are some who say to the poor when they look healthy: 'You're an idler. You could very well do some work. You're young, you've got strong arms.' You do not know whether it may be God's good pleasure that this poor man should go and beg for his bread. You expose yourself to murmuring against God's will.

"Look at blessed Benedict-Joseph Labre. Everyone turned him away. They called him an idler, children threw stones at him. That saint knew that he was doing God's will. He never answered a word. One day he sought out his confessor, who said to him, "My friend, I think you would do better to go out and work. You are the occasion of offence to God. The world says that it is only idleness that makes you beg.' Benedict-Joseph Labre replied very humbly, 'Mon Père, it is the will of God that I beg.' "

In that passage it is evident that Monsieur Vianney was recalling his own difficult experience when he walked from Lyons to La Louvesc to pray at the tomb of St. Francis Regis.

The Curé was wonderfully inspired when he preached on the feast of his patron, St. John the Baptist. He loved to talk of the tunic of camel's hair, and of how he ate wild honey and locusts. But particularly he loved to speak of this saint's relationship to Our Lady. "Oh, my brethren, what an outpouring of graces in the three months when she remains with her cousin, Elizabeth! How many times did she not take this child into her arms, how often did she not carry it and kiss it? St. Ambrose tells us that the Blessed Virgin was so pure and so holy, particularly since she had conceived and brought forth the Son of God, that she communicated purity to all those who saw her. 'It is impossible,' says this Father, 'to look at her without burning with love for this beautiful and precious virtue. . . .' "

He says that when she held St. John the Baptist as a child and caressed him, she communicated her purity to him. ". . . For in that time Jesus and Mary were, so to speak, but one person. Jesus, in those happy times for Mary, only breathed by the mouth of Mary. The breath of Mary was but the breathing of Jesus."

The Curé loved not only saints but angels: he is inspired when he talks about the holy Guardian Angels on their feast day. He tells

us that directly a child is conceived by his mother, he has his own
guardian angel by her side, and that when we go to church, our
angels walk ahead of us, and our angel watches us during our sleep
and spends the whole night praying for us. "What a joy to know
that when we leave our house, we are never alone on the road!
Men in olden times were so much imbued with a sense of the
presence of their guardian angels that they never saluted anybody
without greeting his good angel also. From that comes the old
custom of saying to a person, even though he is alone, "I salute
you and the company—*je vous salue et la compagnie*." He concludes with a fascinating little anecdote: when the Sovereign
Pontiff says Mass in public, when he says: "The Lord be with you,"
the assistants omit the usual reply: "And with thy spirit." This is to
commemorate the day when, after Pope St. Gregory had said:
"The Lord be with you," it was the angels who replied with resounding voices: "And with thy spirit."

From the rich stores of his reading, his parishioners were regaled
daily with the most wonderful golden legends, overflowing with
the marvellous, almost like spiritual fairy tales. What a child the
Curé was with the simple delight he took in these strange stories!
For instance, about the courtesan of Egypt, St. Thäis, who had
been converted by a monk and lived in great penance; of the
strange doings of St. Mary of Egypt, of St. Simon Stylites perched
on his pillar—he got frozen to it one winter day, and, when his
friends climbed up a ladder and unfroze him, he scolded them
for having interrupted his long ecstasy! Monsieur Vianney told the
legend about the babyhood and childhood of St. John the Baptist,
at the age of eighteen months taken to a wood by his mother, flee-
ing from the wrath of Herod, and leaving the wood at the age of
two, in the care of a multitude of angels who looked after him and
gave him food—for his mother had died.

And then there is the heart-rending and touching story of the
lion saved from a large snake by a crusader of St. Louis, and so
grateful that he followed him everywhere like a lamb. "When this
knight was obliged to cross the sea, the lion, unable to go on board
ship, started to swim. He followed his benefactor until he was lost

to sight under the waves. . . . What an example, my brethren! A
beast losing its life to show its gratitude. And we, far from showing
ours to God, never stop offending Him by sin."

He was never ashamed to speak of miraculous and almost impossible deeds. His excuse was—"The sun does not hide itself for
fear of inconveniencing owls." Then he would speak of the saint
who, burning with the desire to adore Our Lord in the Sacrament
of His love during the night, had only to go towards the church for
the doors to open of themselves and allow him to enter.

His favourite subjects were the Humanity of Our Lord and
His grievous Passion, His presence in the Blessed Sacrament, the
Blessed Virgin Mary, her charm and her uniqueness, Heaven, the
happiness of the saints, the purity of the angels, the beauty of
souls, the dignity of man. At the very end of his life, however, the
subjects did not matter. His voice had grown so weak that his
people could not hear him. He preached by his tears, his inarticu-
late cries, his glances when he turned round and looked at the
tabernacle. He lived more than ever on the heights. And anyway
his own parishioners were already converted.

It was in the early days that he had excelled in painting the
manners and customs of country people. He was a very observant
man, and he could be sarcastic if he chose, yet without breaking
the laws of charity. When he castigates the sin of pride, one can
almost see the young man whom he paints for us, with his watch
in his waistcoat pocket:

"And perhaps he only has the chain. With five sous in his pocket,
you hear him say 'I wonder if it's late,' so that everyone will ask
him to look at his watch, and know he has one. . . ." He speaks of
the father of a family who wants to marry off his children, boasting
in public of his riches. But if you ask him for five sous for the poor
he has nothing. And then a dressmaker, or a tailor, who has made
a dress or suit very well, if he sees his customers go past in the
clothes he has made, says: "That fits extremely well: I don't know
who made it."

Oh yes, he knew his sheep. He loved them, but he had no illu-
sions about them when he first came to Ars—their cheating at

market about their beasts, farm produce and hemp. He knew the fond mammas who got into debt to buy ear-rings, chains, collars and lace-trimmed handkerchiefs for their daughters, and yet had nothing for the poor. He had noted their slightest smiles and gestures. He could make them blush by gentle ridicule. He knew the ways of the malicious gossips: "By a word, a gesture, a smile; by a switch of the head or a little contemptuous air, they make one see the person quite clearly."

He could be as caustic as Our Lord condemning hypocrites as whited sepulchres. How he detests the mean men who spend great sums acquiring more land but won't give anything to the poor! "You are afraid you won't have enough land? Ah, my friend. Wait till you have three or four feet of earth on your head, then you'll be satisfied."

He knew all the young people in his congregation. He knew how girls and men were tempted to unchastity and would doubtless fall into it if they went off to dances together. He used to tell engaged couples that it was a "serious sin" if they were ever alone together, or if they stayed in the same house before marriage! He was sufficiently aware of the temptations of mixed company at Ars to say that boys and girls must not be allowed to climb trees together!

He knew young people who were so contemptible as to grudge a little food to parents who were old and ill, and he advised elderly people never to give up their property before their death.

He was aware that some of the peasants of Ars were cruel to their children. Those cruel mothers sound like Regans and Gonerils: the things they did to their children are too shocking to be related in this book. It must have wrung the Curé's heart—if indeed the poor little mites survived childhood—to see them hobbling along the roads, crippled for life.

He scolded the mothers who did not take proper care of themselves during their pregnancies, whose children, as the result, came before term or were born dead. And the dreadful husbands who so ill-treated their wives that they miscarried.

Those congregations of the saint—what a sight they must have been. In his life of the Curé, Joseph Vianey says: "There came to Ars pilgrims from the furthermost provinces of France—from Brittany, from the Béarn, from Flanders, from the Languedoc. They came from Belgium, England, America. One saw nuns with every sort of coif and peasants with every sort of costume. In one day, a greater diversity of headgear was to be seen than at the fair of St. Jean de Maurienne. But it wasn't only coifs that you saw. Before the delighted eyes of the inhabitants of Ars . . . there passed bishops . . . heads of Orders, generals, prefects, university professors, industrialists, bankers and the bearers of ancient names —the people of Ars, however, were not astonished that talent, power, fortune and noble birth should bow before holiness."

But the Curé cared not a whit whether the company were distinguished or not. He was totally unselfconscious: it was souls he cared about. There is a charming anecdote about a poor beggar who wanted to hear him preach but could not find a place in the crowded church. Monsieur Vianney noticed him struggling. He stopped preaching. He made his way through the crowd, took the beggar by the hand, led him straight to the pulpit, put him inside—right inside the pulpit in front of everybody—and then said, "Ha!" as if he were well pleased.

He had the uncomfortable gift of knowing what his audience was saying about his preaching, and used it. For example, sometimes in summer whole families of glass-blowers from Rive-de-Gier would take their holidays at Ars. One morning several of these workmen were fishing in the Fontblin and, no doubt under the spell of the Curé's last homily, were dreaming of Heaven, of its ineffable joys and of Our Lord's kindness. In the course of conversation, a few of them said that they had no ambition to be in the front ranks of Paradise; as long as they were quite near the door they would be content. At that moment the bell rang for catechism. They left the river and ran to church. What was their astonishment when they heard the Curé take for the text of his instruction the very words they had spoken a short time before, and vigorously condemn the lukewarmness of those Christians who think it too much trouble to make sure of their eternal happiness!

If there were hecklers in the church, the Curé knew how to answer them. One day he was thundering against people who broke the laws of abstinence, and somebody in the congregation cried out: "But it's the usual thing." Monsieur Vianney pounced: "Alas, my friend, it may be the usual thing to eat meat on a Friday; but God won't acquire the habit of taking to Heaven those who despise His law. You will tell me it is the company. Ah, the company, my brethren. The company, eh? People don't force you to it. They don't open your mouths to put the meat inside!"

The Curé had some homely tricks for riveting attention. Sensitive as he was, he knew at once when the members of the congregation had distractions and would call them to order with brief phrases.

"Listen for an instant, and I will show you this. Don't go to sleep, if you please."

"Listen to this very carefully, my children."

"Listen carefully, this is quite interesting."

"Follow me for a moment."

(It all recalls Our Lord's preaching in St. Matthew, Ch. 12, v. 51, when He said to His people: "Have you understood all these things?' and they said to Him: 'Yes.'")

And when he saw people looking very much astonished when he had served them strong meat, the Curé would say to them, "That astonished you perhaps, but not me."

Though he did not achieve literary greatness, and sometimes disregarded the laws of grammar, he had a gift for picturesque, original, personal phrases. Everything he said seemed new and fresh, and we have seen how mordant he could be. With the exquisite tact of a saint, he would try to suit his vocabulary to his peasant audience. Often you find homely words—potatoes, stable dung, hens, turkeys. He even calls the tabernacle "the Christian's larder." He uses His Master's words of every-day life—salt, a lamp, on old article of clothing, wine skins. Often he spoke in the local dialect: for example, "truffe" for potatoes; and instead of saying "no matter how" he would say 'à la bourdifaille,' which is of course completely untranslatable. Montaigne said: "If a French phrase doesn't seem to suit, then use patois." He sometimes employed the effective trick of inventing a dialogue with telling questions and answers.

It is not surprising, with all this, that domestic servants begged their masters to let them go and hear the Curé, even if it meant giving up some of their wages. They could never complain that the sermons had been over their heads, or that they had been bored. Perhaps that is why they forgave the Curé for preaching at them— as when, for example, he castigated those servants who, on their days off, ruined the reputations of their masters by tittle-tattling with other servants. Anyway, they knew that he understood their lot and took their part, for whenever he visited their masters he inquired about the spiritual and physical welfare of the servants. He wanted them to be treated as members of the family, and their spiritual needs to be cared for, because all were equal in God's sight.

Jostling with the homely patois were poetical figures:

"A pure soul is like a lovely rose, and the three Divine Persons come down from heaven to breathe in its perfume."

"God's mercy is like an unleashed torrent. It bears away all hearts in its flood."

"What a cry of joy will there be when the soul is united to its glorified body, to a body no longer a cause of sin or suffering. She will nestle in love's balm, like a bee tumbling about in flowers . . . behold the soul fragrant for eternity!"

Or stark realism: "Imagine a poor mother compelled to let the knife of the guillotine drop on the neck of her child. That is God when He damns a sinner."

It would take too long to point out the autobiographical passages contained in the sermons and catechisms. Comtesse des Garets recalled how he drew charming pictures of his home life—the hospitality his parents gave to the poor, the long evenings during which the servants would work with their masters by the fireside, the devout habits of the family.

Though, as we have said, the Curé was not a literary genius, Monseigneur Trochu can speak of "sentences in the style of Pascal, the strangely abrupt and halting style, elliptical turns of phrase, so full of verve and daring, yet so clear. . . . the closely packed, almost breathless, arguments."

"Outside God, you see, my children, nothing is stable. Nothing, nothing! Life passes, fortune crumbles, health is destroyed, reputation is attacked. We go like the wind. Everything rushes by at a great pace, everything will go like the wind. My God, my God, how much they are to be pitied, who place their affections in all these things! They do it because they love themselves too much, because they do not love themselves with a reasonable love. They love themselves with a love of themselves and of the world, seeking their own good, seeking creatures more than God. That is why they are never content, never at peace. They are always anxious, always tormented, always topsy-turvy.'"

Abbé Raymond took notes at one of the Curé's eleven o'clock catechism lessons. It was a homily on sin. One thing is especially interesting: Abbé Raymond has noted three points at which the Curé wept. First, "Luther used to say to his wife as he pointed to Heaven: 'Look at that beautiful Heaven. We shall never see it.' (As he said these words, tears flowed down Monsieur Vianney's cheeks.)"

Then: "God cannot see sin in a man without repugnance, without horror. The soul in sin is like the decaying carcase of a beast dragged about on a very hot summer's day. It smells bad, it disgusts you, you dare not go near it, you flee from it, you hardly dare to think of it. It makes you feel sick. . . .

"Never to love God in Hell: to hate Him. Oh, my children, what a disaster!" (Fresh tears.)

And then: "Here is the effect of absolution. You've seen, my children, that my candle tonight will stop burning. Where has the flame gone to? It doesn't exist any more. It is annihilated. It is the same with the sins which one has confessed properly, and for which one has received absolution. They do not exist any more. They are annihilated."

He finishes on a note which echoes the little homilies he used to improvise for his shepherd companions when he was a small boy: "Oh my children, let us therefore never commit sin, but let us love God and He will give us His paradise."

The Dominican Père Lacordaire, the greatest orator of his day, who had fired a whole generation of men by his Notre-Dame sermons, came to Ars to hear the Curé preach. When he was asked his opinion afterward, Lacordaire said: "I should like to be able to preach like that village priest."

One cannot conclude this account of the Curé's preaching without mentioning the meeting of these two great men. It took place at five o'clock in the morning of the 4th of May, 1845, when the Curé was fifty-nine and Lacordaire forty-three, before austerities and ill-health had destroyed Lacordaire's remarkable beauty. He was staying at the château. They met in the sacristy and Monsieur Vianney expressed his joy at seeing him. He embraced him warmly, clasped his hands for a long time, and thanked him for his visit with an indescribable smile of happiness. Then he opened all his cupboards and brought out the best vestments, chalice and missal for his guest.

After listening to the Curé preach a sermon on the Holy Spirit, Lacordaire appeared "very much astonished," for there was a great resemblance between their two methods of preaching. Afterwards Lacordaire went up to him and said: "You have taught me to know the Holy Ghost." Then it was the Curé's turn to listen to Lacordaire. He listened most reverently, with a kind of hungry attention. Afterwards he exclaimed: "Ah, today two extremes have met: the extreme of knowledge and the extreme of ignorance."

In the evening the Curé did something quite unusual: he accompanied his illustrious visitor back to the château of Comte des Garets. The des Garets were behind the two as they walked, but kept at a respectful distance as they took the path by the Fontblin stream. Paul de la Perrière gives this account:

"We followed from a distance, respecting this interchange of intimate thoughts. We walked for more than a quarter of an hour along paths hemmed in by hedges, some in bud, others already in flower. The sun had set and twilight was falling. The first notes of the nightingale could be heard and the soft scent of verdant fields filled the air."

Before they parted they gave each other a priestly blessing, each protesting that he was unworthy to do it. And then they embraced with warm affection. When Monsieur Vianney turned away to go, he did so with a movement of brusque decision, as if he were doing violence to himself. He returned to the church with rapid steps. The des Garets and their guest walked back very slowly and in silence to the château.

With his wonderful gift of intuition, the Curé knew, of course, of the terrible mortifications undertaken by Lacordaire, penances of which one hardly dares to speak here because they might be misunderstood. Indeed in more ways than one, here were two spiritual friends. As the Curé said once: "The friends of God always know one another, wherever they meet."

Afterwards a local priest asked Père Lacordaire: "Were you not surprised, reverend father, by the simplicity, or rather the meagre eloquence, of your Ars colleague?"

To this, the great orator replied severely: "The Curé of Ars preached just as a good Curé should. One could wish that all Curés preached as well as he."

In his turn, when somebody told the Curé that Lacordaire's conferences produced more oratorical effects than conversions, Monsieur Vianney said in his defence: "Our fine intellectuals have to be made to admire the beauties of the edifice if they are to be inspired with a desire to go in."

13. *THE CROWDS FLOCK TO ARS*

BEWILDERED ONE DAY BY THE OVERPOWERING HEAT AND THE ENORmous crowds, coming out of his confessional more exhausted than ever before, Monsieur Vianney glanced at some hens which had scratched a hole in the sand of his courtyard and were resting there in the shade of the tree with their heads tucked under their wings. He said: "I think those hens must be very happy. If only they had souls, I should like to be in their place."

All this pastoral work could not fail to be a great cross to a man who was a born contemplative. But then he told a penitent: "God sometimes sends us desires which will never be realized in this world." It is strange how many of the great contemplatives have been called to do terribly hard work for souls. St. Bernard, for example, whose only wish was to hide in his cell, write a commentary on the Canticle of Canticles and pray half the night, was the most travelled monk in Christendom. He was always on the highroads, always called to this and the other council: to Rome or across the mountains to preside at the condemnation of Abelard, to Vézelay to preach a crusade, and to found new houses of the Order.

For Monsieur Vianney, his ministry meant farewell to the delights of nature, to afternoons walking by the Fontblin, saying his Office. He must pass from the contemplation of the little birds, created to praise God, and praising Him, to the sorrowful spectacle of souls made to love God but constantly offending Him.

By about 1825, he observed that he had no free time left. They had come gradually, these great crowds. By the end of his life they were to number a hundred thousand. It was first through the praises of his own parishioners and then through those of parishioners of neighbouring hamlets to whom he had preached missions, that he became known. Gradually these latter left the confessionals of their own priests and came to ask the Curé of Ars for advice. To start with, the other Curés were very jealous; they preached against him in their pulpit and refused absolution to the penitents who had been to him.

It was about this time that his appearance improved a little, for his friends explained to him that it was most unsuitable to wear his patched-up and dirty cassock the whole time, and persuaded him to own two. He kept the better one for great occasions.

In the meantime, the presbytery—in which he lived for only three or four hours out of the twenty-four—became more and more dilapidated. Ivy crept in through a cracked window pane, the walls streamed with damp, there were broken tiles on his bedroom floor. Only with difficulty did the mayor extract his permission to mend the roof. As for his fruit trees—he called them his Bois de Boulogne —he had them cut down, much to the dismay of the villagers. He said they were only a source of temptation to little boys.

This, briefly, was to be his timetable for the next thirty-four years. He rose, with enormous difficulty, at midnight or one o'clock in the morning. Frère Athanase has testified to this daily struggle of the Curé's to get up. "He used to groan: 'One must always begin all over again.'" He would go to the church already clad in his surplice and his violet stole, carrying his lantern with the cracked glass. A dozen women helpers would be there to keep order in the queues and light the lamps. He would then ring the Angelus and wait for his penitents. (Crowds of them were already in the church at this hour.)

He would go on hearing confessions until six or seven o'clock, depending on the season. Then he would go to the high altar to prepare for his Mass. (One must keep in mind that his every movement from one place to another, inside or outside the church, was impeded by the pressure of crowds. Some of their members were appalling nuisances, pulling at his cassock or his rochet to attract his attention—even trying to tear pieces out of his clothing to keep as relics.)

He then said his Mass, with intense recollection; it was a joy to watch his face. Jean Baptiste Mandy said: "Before Communion he would pause for a moment, and he seemed to be speaking to Our Lord. . . ."

After Mass he would bless any objects presented to him. Then he would return to the presbytery and take a little milk. (He had been ordered to do this from 1827 onwards.)

Immediately afterwards, he returned to his confessional and heard confessions until ten o'clock, when he went to the sacristy and there, on his knees, upright, said his breviary. Then he went to the little room on the right of the bell turret to hear the confessions of the sick and other people who could not remain for very long at Ars. At eleven he taught catechism. After this he returned to the presbytery[1] for his slight midday collation, escorted and protected from the crowds by several strong men of the parish. The distance between the church and the presbytery was barely twelve yards, and yet each short journey took a quarter of an hour because of the great pressure of the crowds through which a passage had to be cleared for him. There were the sick on their crutches or stretchers, and children who could not wait in church too long. They would cry out: "Good father, holy father, bless me, pray for me. Pray for my husband, my father." He would address the women in the crowd, even society women, in a good-natured way, as *"ma bonne"* or *"ma petite."* Sometimes, in despair of ever reaching his house from the church, Monsieur Vianney used an innocent ruse. He would take a handful of medals from his pocket and throw them to the crowd, and while they were picking them up he would slip away into the presbytery, locking his door behind him.

In his room he would find a simple meal prepared for him by La Providence. At one fifteen—in the days, of course, when he ate his meal in his own place—he would go over to La Providence, the an-

[1] Before La Providence was taken over by the nuns, of course, he had his midday meal there.

nexe of which from 1853 housed the missionary priests sent by the
Bishop to assist him.[2] He boasted that in the hour which he had to
himself in his own house, he would find time to dispatch his meal
standing up, glance through the many letters which came to him in
the post and which he got Catherine Lassagne to answer, shave,
sweep his room, take forty winks. Was ever an hour of mortal's time
more closely packed?

The few moments he spent with the missionaries were in lieu
of recreation. He would stand by the door and talk with them. Occasionally he would accept some black, unsweetened coffee. Abbé
Toccanier has recorded that during these visits, "he was pleasant,
sprightly and occasionally given to gentle teasing." But of course
he went to them only if there were no sick to be visited.

He would return to church, say Vespers kneeling, and then hear
confessions until five o'clock. After that he would go to the sacristy,
where there were men wanting their confessions heard (some had
been waiting since the morning), or behind the high altar to hear
the confessions of women who were unable to wait in the queue.
There was recitation of the rosary and evening prayers at eight
o'clock. An hour after this, the Curé would go back to the presbytery and talk to a few intimate friends and the missionary priests,
standing by his fire if it were winter. At bed-time, he would escort
his visitors to the door in his usual courteous manner. Then he was
alone at last. But the light in his window revealed to everyone that
he had not gone to bed. There were his prayers, his spiritual reading, his penances. And there was always the Devil! He hardly had
three hours' sleep.

His habit of reading several pages of the lives of the saints every

[2] His experience with the immense crowds which came to Ars to listen to
his catechism instructions suggested to the Curé the idea of extending such
instruction to the entire diocese by means of missions. Around 1850 he began
to collect and save money for this work, and he was instrumental in founding
the missionary society of Pont d'Ain under the auspices of Monseigneur Devie.
Before Monseigner Devie's death the thought came to him that the missionaries of Pont d'Ain might profitably be associated with Ars, where they might
learn from the Curé's example. This plan was carried out by his successor,
Monseigneur Chalandon, in 1853. Monsieur Toccanier, the Curé's assistant,
was one of them.

night before going to bed was heroic. He was so tired, Frère Athanase tells us, that "When he returned from church, last thing, he could hardly manage to walk up the stairs. I have sometimes seen him fall against the wall. He could still joke about his weakness and say occasionally, alluding to an unkind jibe about him, 'Come on, then. The old sorcerer has conducted his business very well today.' "

Very often, even when he got to bed, he could not sleep; then he would gaze with pleasure at the pictures of his saints. He once explained to Madame des Garets, "I am in the company of the saints. At night when I wake up, it seems to me that they look down at me and say 'What's this, lazybones? You sleep on, and we—we spend our time in watching, praying to God.' "

Again, he confided to Frère Athanase, "When I do not sleep, my spirit roams. I am in a Trappist monastery or with the Carthusians. I am looking for a corner in which to bewail my poor life and do penance for my sins."

How extraordinary that after nights like these he could remain so calm during the day, he who was naturally impetuous and quick-tempered! Frère Athanase again tells us, "The holy Curé was bothered in many ways, but nothing seemed to trouble his interior life."

He, who needed sleep so much and got so little, was very tender and fatherly to the women of his parish who used to come to confession at midnight or at one o'clock in the morning after attending one of those night gatherings in the barns. He would say to them: "Go and rest, *ma petite*. You're too sleepy."

After seeing him kneel at the high altar, Catherine Lassagne wrote: "How beautiful, and what an excellent example, to see by the light of his candle this form wasted by penance! He prayed in such a contemplative way, occasionally glancing towards the tabernacle with so sweet a smile, that he seemed to be seeing Our Lord."

A farmer called Jean Tête, the father of ten children, attested: "As to visions, the way I saw Monsieur Vianney smile before the statue of the Blessed Virgin made such a deep impression on me

that I believed he saw her as a living person. And I have seen this
more than ten times."

When the crush of pilgrims was too great, Monsieur Vianney
rose even before midnight. He used to goad himself by promising
himself a few moments of rest during the day.

Of course the centre of his day was his Mass: Monseigneur
Trochu, who collected sheaves of testimonies about it, says:
"Everything in him breathed adoration. One felt that he was not
alone at the altar, but that Jesus Christ and his priest were together
there. His movements, his glances, his posture all indicated that
he was utterly overcome, overwhelmed by desire, hope and love."

At one midnight Mass the choir sang too long. He waited, now
smiling, now weeping a little, to proceed with the Mass. When
afterwards they apologized to him for the delay, he said: "Oh,
time did not hang heavy on me." Once he was asked what he
said when he was holding the Sacred Host—for he had looked
so deeply moved. He replied: "As a matter of fact, a queer idea
passed through my head. I was saying to Our Lord: If I knew that
it would be my unhappy fate not to see You for the whole of eternity, I would not let You go now!"

When at ten o'clock in the morning he recited the Hours from
Prime till None, he would do it uninterruptedly, kneeling on the
sacristy tiles, even if there was a penitent kneeling on the *prie-dieu*
waiting for him. He looked on that short time as recreation. "What
a joy to be able to rest a little in this way!" he would say.

Abbé Alexis Tailhades has reported: "He loved his breviary so
much that in his comings and goings he almost always held it
under his arm. When I asked him the reason for this, he replied:
'The breviary is my faithful companion. I would not go anywhere
without him.'"

A barrister from Lyons who observed him reciting his breviary
said that his eyes shone and he seemed to be breathing a rarefied
air not of this earth. Since in his meditation he had a preference
for the sorrowful mysteries of the Passion and wanted to accompany Jesus in thought on the various stages of His way to Calvary, he had begged Catherine Lassagne to make notes of these

stages in the margin of his breviary. At Matins he honoured the Agony of Our Lord, at Lauds His sweat of blood, at Prime His condemnation to death, at Terce His carrying of the cross, at Sext His crucifixion, at None His death, at Vespers His descent from the Cross, at Compline His burial. These marginal notes can still be seen in the breviary. The Curé said: "The Passion of Our Lord is like a great river flowing down a mountain; it is inexhaustible."

The secret of his unbroken serenity was that although he now had little time to pray, from the beginning of the day he had his plan of campaign: "With my whole being, I try to unite myself to Our Lord, and for the rest of the day I act with the thought of this union in mind." He said: "Faith is when one speaks to God as one would speak to a man."

Perhaps his practice of union with Our Lord was suggested by St. Dorothea, whose story he tells with such enthusiasm in a homily on the mystery of Christmas Day. St. Dorothea tried to spend her days united in spirit to Christ in His earthly life. As she worked, she thought of Our Lord being very tired, and instead of complaining said: "I unite my labours to His with love and resignation. When I am ordered to do something, I picture Jesus Christ, obedient to Our Lady and to St. Joseph, and at that moment I unite my obedience to His." And so on, throughout the day, even to the taking of recreation, when the saint thought of how gentle Jesus Christ was with everybody.

The only person who was able to influence the Curé's conduct in the very least was Catherine Lassagne, and that only towards the end of his life. One morning, after giving catechism, he was so exhausted that instead of going back to the presbytery he dropped into the tiny house next door,[3] where Catherine and Marie Filliat had prepared what was now his usual meal—an egg, a little soup and some vegetables.

"Oh," he whispered, "I can do no more."

"Come, Monsieur le Curé," said Catherine. "Sit down for a moment and I will warm up your milk."

"Oh no," he said, "don't do anything. I need my bed." And he

[3] The little house to which Catherine and Marie retired when the orphanage was taken over by the nuns.

went away again to his house, walking with a more pronounced stoop than usual. Catherine followed him and went upstairs with the cup of milk wrapped in wool. What did she find? Monsieur Vianney, not going to bed but preparing to return to church.

She said. "Monsieur le Curé, take this cup. You will not be able to wait till this evening."

"No, no, I don't want anything."

"Monsieur le Curé, you must take this milk."

The holy man, instead of taking the milk, tapped his brow with his finger to show Catherine that she was pestering him. "Come now," he said, "let me pass."

"Monsieur le Curé," she said, "I will not go."

And in the end she won!

And now we must take a look at some of the people who flocked to Ars, the people to whom the saint gave himself up without any reserve. Monsieur Jean Felix des Garets, after speaking of their immense variety—religious from all orders, members of the secular clergy including all ranks of the hierarchy, lay people from all classes of society, the learned and the simple—says: "Among these last I have seen whole families of peasants arrive in carts from their far-away provinces—even from the mountains of Auvergne...."

An old lady of Besançon recalls that her maid Clémentine, even when she was quite elderly, would spend two days in the queue outside his confessional with a basket of provisions on her arm. Of course in the early days, there was no organized hospitality. In 1832 some nuns who had come to Ars and were unable to find a bed had to improvise their sleeping arrangements with chairs and mattresses in the room given to them by a poor man.

The regular stage coach service began in 1835, with offices at Lyons and at Ars. But it soon became easier to go in boats down the Saône. After a while, more than 20,000 people were coming to Ars every year. The coach was soon superseded by the railway, which sold return tickets valid for a week, for the railway officials knew that sometimes it took fully a week to get to the top of the Curé's queue.

When Comte Prosper des Garets asked the Curé how many big

sinners he had converted during the year, he answered, "More than seven hundred." His heart was full of compassion for poor sinners, in the same way that Our Lady's heart was filled with pity for the crowd of sinners at Lourdes. He would cry out: "Ah, the poor sinners—if only I could make their confessions for them." The tone of voice in which he said this was very moving.

He used to weep for them. One day a sinner in his confessional asked him why he was weeping and he answered: "Because you do not weep enough." When he was criticized for giving priority to people from the end of the queue, he replied that some had come with great difficulty and had incurred great expense. Also, there were some who did not want to be seen and were in a hurry to get back again.

Once, as we have noted, he compared the multitude of the damned to snowflakes falling thick and fast on a winter's day. It is alarming when he speaks of the multitude of the damned, and we are glad to learn that round about 1840 he became less severe in his judgments, owing to the influence of some other priest. However, to a woman overburdened with many children he said: "If you only knew the women who are in Hell for not having given to the world the children they should have given."

Even when he condemned the great, impenitent sinners to whom he could not give absolution, he did it from love. When he cried out: "You are damned," he would burst into tears.

When one pictures him coming out of his confessional to point to somebody at the end of the queue and tell him to come next, one usually imagines the occasions when his action incurred the disapproval of all the others. But there is one charming incident, recorded in the "Annales d'Ars," of the Curé going out to lead a person who had waited eight days out of sheer timidity. She clutched his cassock and slipped along the path which he opened up for her.

He was tender and fatherly to all. Two young priests who were converts from Judaism said of him: "He used to let us hide our faces in his long white hair. We tasted the happiness of steeping ourselves in the atmosphere of a saint."

For many besides these two the experience of the pilgrimage to Ars and of being near the Curé lived in the memory like a fragrance pervading their whole lives.

He once said: "There are some who lose their faith, and see Hell only as they fall into it." He wanted to show it to them before it was too late, and so, like a good surgeon, he used the knife, the cauterizing fire.

Many of those who came to Ars made a general confession of their whole lives. The Curé never hurried them; he made them feel that no one else in the world was of any importance. He gave them his full and complete attention, and afterwards his verdict was quick and sure. No discussion was allowed. The little shutter was closed on them if they started to argue, and he turned to the penitent on the other side.

Occasionally a hardened sinner was persuaded by some kind friend to interrupt a holiday in the neighbourhood and come to Ars, just because all those pilgrims were a curious sight: and then the sinner was trapped! Though the Curé had never seen them before, his eyes would meet theirs; he would turn on them his kindly, severe, penetrating glance.

A certain scholar of Lyons, who had been a sceptic, was taken to Mass at the Curé's church by a friend whom he had encountered by chance. Recalling his experience he said: "We entered the church. My old friend placed me on the seat opposite the sacristy. Presently the door opened, and the Curé of Ars came out, vested for Mass. His eyes met mine; it was but one glance, but it pierced to the bottom of my heart. I felt crushed beneath that look. I bowed down and hid my face between my hands. I remained motionless during the whole of the Mass; then I tried to raise my head, and would have gone out; but as I passed the sacristy, I heard these words: 'Go out, all of you!' At the same moment a hand was laid upon mine, and I felt attracted as by some invisible force. The door was closed upon me, and I found myself face to face with that glance which had struck me to the earth. 'Monsieur le Curé,' stammered I, 'I have a crushing burden on my shoulders.' A voice of angelic sweetness, which seemed unlike any human utterance, replied: 'My friend, you must get rid of it immediately. Kneel down and tell me all your poor life; and Our Lord will take up your burden; for He has said: *Come to me all you who are heavy-laden, and I will refresh you.*' My trouble began to disappear; and without thinking that I was making my confession, I began to tell the holy man all the history of my life, since the day of my first Communion. During the whole time he wept over me, exclaiming from time to time, 'Oh, how good God is! how He has loved you!' I did not weep; but my heavy burden seemed gradually to be lifted off me, and at last I felt as if it were altogether gone."

One single glance of Our Lord's penetrated to the heart of the publican, St. Matthew, and made him leave all to follow Him; the same searching glance brought repentance to St. Peter: "And the Lord, turning, looked on Peter."

There was a man, an unbeliever, who had been brought to Ars much against his will by his wife; she had great trouble in making him come to church. The Curé looked at him fixedly and said: "Why put it off, my child? I will not accept your refusal. You will not leave me before you belong to God."

In 1842, a very important personage—we are not told who—came to Ars. The moment he saw the Curé, he threw his arms round him and held him in a close embrace for several moments. Monsieur Vianney showed neither embarrassment nor surprise. Then he pointed to the confessional and said: "My friend, kneel down and I shall hear your confession." He went back into the world again an ardent Christian.

Monsieur Vianney had his own method for dealing with rather tight-fisted old men. Abbé Monnin recorded this incident. In the course of the year 1842, a man advanced in years came to Ars with his niece, who wished to consult the Curé upon the choice of a state of life.

"My friend," said the holy Curé, "you have come for confession?"

"No, Monsieur," replied he, somewhat disconcerted at the directness of the attack; "I have no such intention. I came simply to accompany my niece; and as soon as she has received your advice, I purpose returning home again."

"No, no, my friend; you must seize the opportunity; it may not return. I am old, and you are not young. In our long life we have witnessed the death of many of our fellows. There are men who reject mercy, and whom mercy in return rejects. Come, my friend, let us not lose time; for time will not wait for us."

"Monsieur le Curé, this is all very true; but my confession will not be the work of a day. I should have to stay here some time, which would cost money."

The holy Curé saw the kind of man he had to deal with, and said with a faint smile: "My friend, do not let this disturb you; when your money is spent, you can apply to me."

"Monsieur le Curé," said the old miser, in a tone of no slight annoyance, and at the same time taking some gold pieces out of his pocket, "I can pay my own way, thank God, and have no need of alms."

"My friend," was the grave reply, "fear not to spend this money for the salvation of your soul; it is the best use you can possibly make of it. Our Lord has said: *What shall a man give in exchange for his soul?* Remain here as long as is necessary for settling the affairs of your conscience, and prepare for confession at once."

In May 1856 took place the unexpected conversion of an eighty-year-old man who had been an habitual blasphemer and who used to call the Curé an old hypocrite. Monsieur Vianney went to see him, threw himself on his knees and wept bitterly, pleading: "Save your poor soul. Save your poor soul." The old man began to weep too, and was converted.

Monsieur Vianney, as we have seen, showed a particular tenderness for orphans and widows. He would weep for them and with them. He would kneel down and pray with them. He was always at his most severe, one notices, with those called to a high level of perfection. For example, there was a woman who was grieving immoderately for the loss of three sons. He gently reproached her for her too human affection and tried to lead her towards a life of greater detachment and more intense spirituality.

The delight of the shriven was almost pathetic to watch. The Curé loved to quote one instance of this. A poor sinner said to him in transports of joy, *"Mon père, mon père,* how happy I am! I would not have missed going to confession for a thousand francs. Until this moment, I had an empty space here." And he pointed to his heart. "You have filled up this empty space. I don't feel it any more. Nothing is lacking. Everything is complete."

One day an unknown Parisian society woman came to Ars out of curiosity. The Curé, meeting her in the village square as he was returning from a sick call, said to her: "Madame, come with me." And having taken her a little apart, he revealed her whole life of sin to her. She was appalled and at first could not speak. At length she said: "Monsieur le Curé, will you hear my confession?"

"Your confession," he replied, "would be useless. I read your soul and I see in it two devils who keep it in chains—the demon of pride and the demon of impurity. I could not absolve you unless you promised not to return to Paris. Knowing your dispositions and your frame of mind, I know that you *will* go back there." He prophesied how in Paris she would fall into a yet deeper pit of vice.

"But, Monsieur le Curé, I am incapable of committing such abominations. Do you mean I'm going to be damned?"

"I do not say that. But from now on, how hard it will be for you to save yourself!"

"What then must I do?"

"Come tomorrow morning. I will tell you."

In the morning, having called the woman to the top of the queue, he said to her: "In spite of yourself, you will leave Paris, and return to that house from which you have come here. Over there, if you want to save your poor soul, you will perform such and such penances."

She went back to Paris without receiving absolution. She committed the sins of which he had spoken. Then, all of a sudden, she stopped short. She fled. She went back to a house she had by the Mediterranean. At the end of three months she was converted.

And then there was thirty-two-year-old François Dorel. He was determined not to be mistaken for a pious Catholic in search of a confessor. He looked gay, ribald even, not at all like a pilgrim. His gun was slung across his shoulders and he had brought his retriever with him. A friend urged him to go to church, but François Dorel said he would rather shoot a few ducks on the ponds near by. When he reached Ars he was met by Monsieur Vianney, who looked in turn at the dog and at the man. Then he said: "Monsieur, it is to be hoped that your soul is as beautiful as your dog."

To cut a long story short, the man confessed his sins and became a Trappist monk.

There was another man who had been involved in a murder case. He went to Ars because his wife was extremely ill and he wanted to consult the Curé. He was slightly misshapen owing to injuries sustained in an encounter with the police, and he had been in prison. To his stupefacation, the Curé (who, of course, had never seen or heard of him before) reminded him of all this. He was converted, and was not ashamed to tell his strange story to all and sundry.

A certain Mademoiselle Farnier of Montchanin, a young girl who walked with a limp, implored the Curé to cure her leg. He replied: "My child, you disobey your mother too often and answer her back. If you want God to cure you, correct that ugly fault." And strangely enough, after she had mended her ways, her leg, which had been too short by ten centimeters, became completely normal, and of course her limp disappeared.

A poor blind beggar girl, Françoise Lebeau, and her mother, walked to Ars all the way from the Saône-et-Loire region, begging their bread and sleeping in stables. When Monsieur Vianney looked at her, he revealed to her a little of the divine mystery which surrounds human suffering. "My child," he said, "you could get well; but if God gave you back your sight, your salvation would be less sure." She understood and went home resigned.

Of course among the crowd of pilgrims there were many beggars, some genuinely destitute but others far from deserving. But even the disagreeable ones were always given a welcome by Monsieur le Curé. He would say: "You never make a mistake when you give to God." He had such a wonderful reputation among beggars that he could never leave the village without being escorted by a whole troop of them.

When the villagers complained of these vagrants to the mayor, and the mayor in his turn complained to the Curé, he replied: "Did not Our Lord say: 'The poor you have always with you?' " And he insisted that none should be turned away.

Ars was the Heaven of poor, neglected, hard-used domestic servants. Monseigneur de Ségur's valet was called Jean-Baptiste Méthol. The bishop always called him by his surname. The Curé gave this valet a statuette of St. John the Baptist and said, "Here you are, child. In memory of me, take this image of your holy patron."

What strange creatures there were in that queue inside the church! For example, the libertine who had come in spite of himself, and who wished with all his heart, as he got inside the church, that he would find the Curé of Ars dead. And the charming young girl brought to Ars by a relation of hers, who, when she was told by the Curé that she would be a nun, exclaimed again and again: "No, no, no!" And he, smiling at those three "noes," repeated, "Yes, yes, yes!"

Some of those who appeared in his confessional brought him great consolation. He said in one of his sermons:

"There was here a *grande demoiselle* from one of the best families in France; she left this morning. She was barely twenty-three. She is very rich. She has offered herself as a sacrifice to God for the expiation of sins and for the conversion of sinners. She wears a belt studded with iron points. She mortifies herself in a thousand ways. Her parents know nothing about it. She is as pale as a sheet of paper. Hers is a beautiful soul, very pleasing to God. It is such souls as hers that prevent the world from coming to an end."

Suffering souls always won his pity. There was an unhappy spinster, infirm, aged, penniless, forsaken by all, almost shattered by numberless afflictions—terrible trials of health and dire spiritual temptations, darkness and undefinable torments of the spirit. She fled to him for a crumb of comfort and went away strengthened. To meet these suffering, heroic souls, must have been a great consolation to Monsieur Vianney.

What a contrast between this spinster and people like a great lady who drove to the door of the church in her carriage. She was in a great hurry and, speaking in an overbearing manner to the women who kept watch outside the confessional, she said she wanted to be at the top of the queue. She said to the missionary in charge that she disliked waiting anywhere; she had waited neither at the king of Bavaria's court nor in the ante-chambers of the Pope. But she had to wait. When at long last she entered the Curé's confessional, she said condescendingly:

"Monsieur le Curé, I have come to make my confession to you."

He replied, with a flicker of his slightly impish smile: "Very well, Madame. Excellent. I have heard confessions often before."

There was a girl who wanted to be a nun and was prepared to leave an old, infirm mother alone in the world. In a pleading tone, the Curé said to her again and again: "Oh, do not leave her, your poor mother. Do not leave her."

Quite apart from his power to convert, the Curé's compassion was immense. He would utter cries of pity when he heard tales of woe, and lift trembling hands to heaven. He would even, with priestly tenderness, wipe away tears. It was not only spiritual consolation that he gave. He could be extremely practical and kind in little material ways. For example, he insisted on a nun accepting a few francs for her return journey, because he foresaw that she would lose her purse. Also, he went out to buy a silk umbrella for the daughter of the widow Fayot, his benefactress from Les Noës, who had come to visit him.

In that tiny church of Ars could be seen a microcosm of humanity, both redeemed and unredeemed. Balzac could have found there an abundant source of material for his *Comédie Humaine*, though he could never have penetrated into the souls of the holy ones.

When one ponders the way certain sins take a stranglehold on the soul, how avarice hardens, and the passions of anger and lust enslave, how malice and envy poison the mind and heart, it is extraordinary to think that sinners ever repent at all. Contrition seems like a miracle.

One of the hall-marks of the hardened sinner is his conviction that all is well with him, that he has not sinned at all: for he has stifled, or even killed, his conscience. But even in the depths of his sins he may through God's mercy be pierced by grace. Our Lord, who shed His blood to redeem him, gives him a flash of light, one necessary moment of illumination in which he sees clearly that he has come to the crossroads and must now choose between Heaven and Hell.

Strange the way Our Lord does things—how He pursues, how He constrains and, so to speak, coaxes. Often it seems that He lets His most devoted servants languish in the desert of aridity and gives unmerited favours to the basest sinners in order to win them over. As in the parable of the prodigal son: no banquet was prepared for the son who had stayed at home. "My son, thou art always at my side, and everything that I have is already thine; but . . . thy brother here was dead, and has come to life again; was lost, and is found."

At length, shriven and full of new resolutions, the Ars pilgrims leave the church. One can imagine them going back to Lyons on the bus or in the boat along the Saône or in the new train. One would tremble for them, frail in their new-found virtue, if one forgot the abundance of God's grace, staying them in the temptations which are bound to come. The avaricious, the cruel, the proud, the dishonest, all touched and changed by grace: hundreds and hundreds of souls wrested from the Devil's power by one humble country Curé who thought himself a fool!

St. Augustine said, "It is a greater miracle to convert a sinner than to raise a man from the dead." And that is why we have considered the miracles of spiritual healing in this story before the bodily ones. When Monsieur Vianney noticed one day that his prayers for a miracle of physical healing had been granted, he was so appalled, so dumbfounded, that he hurried across the square holding his head in his hands. Abbé Monnin tells us that the sick came in crowds to Ars—the lame, the blind, the deaf, the epileptic, the mad; all kinds of infirm people came from distances of several hundred miles, often on foot, upheld by invincible confidence.

In February 1857, a pathetic pair appeared at Ars—a poor woman carrying her eight-year-old boy, who could not walk. For twenty-four hours she pursued the Curé from place to place with the obstinacy of despair. Everybody around was touched by her wretchedness. Monsieur Vianney blessed the child again and again and tried to console the mother. When they had both gone back to the hovel where they spent the night, the boy said to his mother: "Mother, will you buy me a pair of clogs? Monsieur le Curé promised me that I should walk to-morrow." She bought the clogs.

What was the amazement of everybody the next day when they saw this little boy running about the church like a hare, crying out, "I'm cured! I'm cured!" Monsieur Vianney merely said drily: "St. Philomena should have cured this little child in his own home."

Then there was the young man from the Loire region, who had been injured in a fall from his horse. He was bent in two, with his head between his knees. His affliction was a perpetual martyrdom. They brought him to Ars. Monsieur Vianney told him to ask St. Philomena for a miracle. The two men who looked after him put him to sit in St. Philomena's chapel every day. Little by little, he

began to straighten up, and at the end of two months, without the
help of any doctor, he had been completely cured.

In 1854 came Mathilde, a little girl from Grenoble. When she was
five, an older companion had picked her up by her ears, and all the
muscles of her neck were torn. She could no longer hold her head
up. She was brought to Ars by her parents. They heard Monsieur
Vianney's Mass. All of a sudden, the great silence at the elevation
of the Host was broken, as the child held her head up and cried,
"Oh, Mamma, I'm cured! Look!"

What a source of embarrassment it must have been to the humble Curé to hear these children crying out: "Look, Mama, I'm
cured"; to see the crippled throw away their crutches and shout:
"Look! I can walk!" Do the saints know that they are saints? How
is one to preserve humility amid such universal acclaim?—for
without humility no one can save his soul.

Now Monsieur Vianney was well aware that one does not need
to tell untruths in order to be truly humble; humility and truth are
one. His curate, Abbé Raymond, who watched him for years, sometimes without enthusiasm, concluded that Monsieur Vianney knew
quite clearly that the pilgrims came for him. And it is at this point,
when his fame became a threat to his humility, that Pauline Jaricot
returned to his mind. When he had gone to see her in 1816 with
Monsieur Balley she had first spoken to him about St. Philomena.
But his real devotion to the virgin martyr began in 1830. When
people asked him for miracles of healing, he would simply tell
them to pray to St. Philomena. He hoped thus to turn the pilgrimage to his confessional into a pilgrimage to St. Philomena's shrine.

In 1834 Monsieur Vianney acquired a minute relic of the saint.
"Acquired" is a polite word, for in reality, to achieve his ends, he
committed, in the French phrase, "a pious larceny," though the
reader may think the word "pious" ill-chosen. This is how he did
it.

Hearing that Pauline Jaricot had a relic, the Curé asked Catherine Lassagne to visit Pauline Jaricot in Lyons. The two girls prayed at Pauline's little shrine of St. Philomena, and then Catherine, greatly daring, asked Pauline whether she would be so kind as to give her a tiny fragment of the precious relic. Her wish was granted. She hurried back to Ars and told Monsieur Vianney. His first gesture was to hold out his hand for it. He was painfully disappointed when she refused point-blank to give it to him and said she was taking it back to the orphanage.

"Oh, Catherine, Catherine," he groaned. Then, insinuatingly, he said: "You will give me my dear little saint, won't you?"

"No, no, I shall keep her for myself," Catherine replied. "Mademoiselle Jaricot will give you another."

For several days on end, Monsieur Vianney renewed his demands. He received the same reply. But he made a plan. In the meantime he pretended to put the whole matter out of his mind.

Then one day all of a sudden he appeared at La Providence. He seemed in a tearing hurry. He even looked as if he had run there.

"Catherine, where's Catherine?" he cried. "I must see her at once."

Catherine appeared in all haste.

"Quick, quick, Catherine, give me St. Philomena's relic at once," he said. "I need it immediately."

Catherine did as she was told. Monsieur le Curé must have his reasons for behaving thus, she thought—a soul to convert, a sick person to heal. But the next day, when she asked for her relic back again, he replied, rather impishly, "This time I keep it, the relic of my dear little saint. My poor Catherine, you will be obliged to go and fetch another one from Lyons. I have to stay here, where St. Philomena chains me with all my penitents."

"Monsieur le Curé," Catherine pleaded. "Give it back to me. I beg you."

"St. Philomena will bless the charitable Christian who has given me her relic," he said.

"Oh," cried Catherine, "I am sure that when she hears what

has happened, Mademoiselle Jaricot will see to it that my treasure is returned to me."[1]

Catherine always said that he had not examined his conscience on this point; moreover she accused him of laughing at the grief he caused her.

Abbé Toccanier, when he was a witness for the Curé's beatification, recounts a conversation he had had with him. He said: "Monsieur le Curé, there is a rumour going around against you."

"And what is it, comrade?" he asked.

"It seems that you have forbidden St. Philomena to perform any miracles here," said Abbé Toccanier.

"That's true, my friend," the Curé answered. "It makes people talk too much. These miracles bring too large crowds. I begged St. Philomena to cure souls here, as many as she wants, but as for bodies, she must heal them further away. . . ."

As Monseigneur Trochu writes in his charming book on St. Philomena, "Our virgin martyr had died young. The Curé d'Ars knew this, and it is doubtless for that reason that he treated her with charming familiarity, with exquisite impudence correcting her as one corrects a child. He scolded her for performing too many miracles and he scolded her as well, one must admit, when she performed no more miracles. . . ."

At the end of his life Monsieur Vianney, speaking in confidence to Baronne Alix de Belvey, whom he knew to be extremely discreet, said: "I was troubled, as I wanted to know the will of God about the new church. Should we put all our resources into this building scheme and sacrifice the work of parochial missions? As I was praying, St. Philomena appeared to me. She had come down

[1] In 1835, when Pauline Jaricot was cured of serious heart trouble by a relic of Philomena, the Pope gave his assurance that he would canonize her. In 1836 Pauline returned to France and housed her relic in her little chapel on the hill of Fourvière. In 1837 Philomena was canonized. Early in 1837 the Curé inaugurated a chapel to St. Philomena in the church of Ars and in July 1838 Catherine Lassagne, who was mortally ill, was cured by her intercession. This was the first chapel dedicated in France to the young Roman martyr. The Curé had managed to win the race against his friend Pauline!

from Heaven, beautiful, luminous, surrounded with a white cloud. She said to me twice: 'There is nothing more precious than the salvation of souls'—by that she meant the work of the missions."

"As he spoke," the Baronne said, "Monsieur Vianney was standing, his eyes were raised, and his face was glowing in the memory of this vision; it seemed to draw him into ecstasy all over again."

The Curé's renowned confessional is still in the chapel of St. John the Baptist, that chapel of which he had said, "Brethren, if you knew what had happened in this chapel, you would never dare to come into it . . . . I will tell you no more."

Priests tell us that the sheer physical strain of sitting in one position all day listening to confessions is a terrible ordeal. They emerge from a long session fit for nothing, almost tottering with exhaustion. The Curé was in addition very sensitive to cold. (As spring drew near, he seemed to thaw out, he greeted the warm spring breezes with delight.) His little church was an ice-box in winter; terrible draughts used to come through the door, bitter east winds which had swept across the Alpine snows. There was no form of heating whatsoever.

During a particularly severe winter, one of the missionary priests played a trick on him. Very craftily, when the Curé was away, he placed a sliding board under the confessional, and just before Monsieur Vianney was due to arrive he would slip in bottles of boiling-hot water. Monsieur Vianney was entirely deceived. He said with great tenderness: "How good God is! During this bitterly cold winter, my feet have always been warm."

Some other devoted friend, knowing that sitting such long hours in one position made his bones almost pierce his skin, so that he was sometimes raw, tried to line his confessional with little cushions. But when the Curé saw these he tore them all out and scattered the shreds far and wide.

Perhaps his sufferings were worse in hot weather, for then there was really no means of keeping the place cool, and the ventilation was bad. Also, greater numbers were packed into the church in summer than in winter. The stench alone must have been intolerable, for the penitents had been up for hours during the night, with no opportunity to bathe or put on fresh clothing, and there were many sick people and beggars. It was an ordeal both for priest and penitents.

But his physical sufferings were nothing compared with the mental agonies he endured. Here was a man whose life was so innocent that he learnt about serious sin only in the confessional, a man who was pierced through and through with God's beauty, with His understanding, with His love for men, yet was constantly hearing the avowal that this great love had been defiled: he saw men who had been created in the image of God, and then he contemplated Christ, disfigured by their sins. Hour by hour he saw all the marks of sin on human faces. Is it surprising that he should exclaim so often, "My God, how heavy time spent with sinners hangs on me! Oh when will I be with the saints?"

14. *MONSIEUR VIANNEY AND THE CONSOLATIONS OF A MYSTIC*

PÈRE POULAIN SAYS IN HIS BOOK *The Graces of Interior Prayer*, Chapter 28, paragraph 18: ". . . the holy Curé d'Ars . . . was several times questioned adroitly with a view to ascertaining the nature of his prayer; he always eluded his inquirers. But they had indirect proof of his being in a mystic state by seeing him at prayer or hearing his prophetic words, or hearing the loving exclamations that he was unable to repress, such as: 'One never gets weary in prayer.' 'The hours glide past like minutes.' 'It is a foretaste of heaven, all this.' 'There are some priests who see Our Lord every day in the Mass.' Or again, 'After Communion the soul revels in the balm of love like a bee amongst the flowers.' 'After Holy Communion we are conscious of something extraordinary, a sensation of well-being that pervades the whole body. It is Our Lord who communicates Himself to us.'"

Never was a mystic more crafty in eluding the traps set to discover his spiritual secrets. And yet one or two remarks which he let slip open wonderful vistas of his mystical experience. Those with listening ears, when they heard him preach about Heaven in transports of joy, must have guessed that he had seen the heavens opened.

Abbé Monnin testified that he never spoke of the divine favours of which he was the object. He says: "The questions which were put to him about this obviously troubled and tired him. To fend them off he used to pour himself out in outbursts of love for God, or in entrancing details of the lives of the saints; he spoke about the saints as if he had known them. Thus it is from the lips of a certain number of witnesses and not from his own that we have been able to learn something of the secrets of his mystical life."

There was one occasion, however, when he was taken by surprise. He arrived one day at the orphanage with a glowing face. "What a grace!" he exclaimed in the presence of Catherine Lassagne. "What a joy, what an extraordinary thing!"

Catherine was thunderstruck. "Where?" she asked him after a moment.

"In church . . . in church . . ."

But he would say no more.

Monseigneur Trochu suggests that perhaps he had seen in church that procession of the saints of which he spoke on another occasion to Soeur Catherine Lacon. He could never forget it.

But it was at Mass that he was most apt to betray himself. (He told the orphans they must never look at the priest at the altar.) A nephew of Mademoiselle d'Ars told a priest that as the Curé said Mass: "His eyes became like flames, lighting up his whole face." One morning he said to Catherine Lassagne: "Oh how hungry I was during Mass. When the time for making my Communion came round, I said to Our Lord, 'My God, feed the body and the soul,' and my hunger disappeared completely."

Abbé Toccanier says everybody at Ars believed that the Curé enjoyed the visible presence of the Saviour in the Eucharist. He confessed to Abbé Toccanier: "After the consecration, I forget myself as I hold Our Lord in my hands."

A more precise description is recorded by Catherine Lassagne. The Curé said: "When Our Lord is on the altar during Holy Mass, directly one prays for sinners, He darts rays of light towards them, to reveal their miseries to them and convert them."

One day when he thought he was alone in the kitchen Jeanne-Marie Chanay, the orphanage cook, heard him sigh and say, "*Tout de même*, I have not seen God since Sunday."

He started when Jeanne-Marie asked him: "Before Sunday, then, you saw Him?"

But he did not reply.

Towards 1850, in one of his catechism instructions, he said, "There are priests who see Him every day in the holy Sacrifice of the Mass."

A certain Abbé Tailhades came to Ars determined to learn more about the Curé. He was prevented from revealing anything he had learned by being ordered to hold his tongue as a penance by Monsieur Vianney, but he lived to be a valuable witness. (We have quoted his testimony before.)

One day, during an hour of intimate conversation—for the Curé really loved him—Monsieur Vianney talked to Abbé Tailhades about his first years as a priest at Ars and spoke of that time as a period of extraordinary graces.

"At the holy altar I enjoyed wonderful consolations: I saw God," he said.

"You saw Him?" asked Abbé Tailhades.

"Oh, I would not say that it was in a perceptible, palpable manner . . . but what a favour . . . what a favour!"

Soeur Marie Françoise came to his confessional in Holy Week, either of 1849 or 1850. When she had finished her confession, she said to him: "What does God want of me, *mon Père?*"

"Ah, my child," said the frail, sweet voice behind the grille. And then for the space of five minutes he seemed to be talking to himself in an unknown tongue. Anyway, she did not understand it.

"Astounded, I looked at his face. He seemed beside himself. I thought he was seeing God. Judging myself unworthy of remaining in the presence of so great a saint, I withdrew, very much afraid."

At about half past one on a morning in March 1852, a holy young nun, Soeur Clothilde, entered his confessional. Only one candle lit that corner of St. John the Baptist's chapel, but when Monsieur Vianney opened the confessional grille, he appeared to her all clothed with light. He was bathed in an unearthly glow. When she had made her confession, she said, *"Mon Père . . ."*

"Make your confession," murmured the saint.

She did it again from the beginning. Then she said, "*Mon Père* . . ."

"Make your confession."

"But I have nothing more to say."

She received absolution in the end. She had been in the confessional for about an hour. When she left, he looked quite ordinary again.

In 1849 a Mademoiselle Marie Roch of Paris, who was enduring great spiritual suffering, entered his confessional and was amazed to see two great fiery rays springing from his face. His features were, so to speak, eclipsed by this intense light. She was quite sure she was not the victim of hallucination and equally sure that the sun had not penetrated into that dark chapel.

Our Lady was the great love of Monsieur Vianney's life. We recall that Jean Tête, the farmer with ten children, noticed how Monsieur Vianney smiled at the statue of the Virgin Mary in such a way that one felt he was seeing her alive. The extraordinary thing about his visions of Our Lady is that they were sometimes shared with others. (Unlike the apparitions at Lourdes, for example, which St. Bernadette alone saw.) Here is the incident as it is described in Monseigneur Trochu's pamphlet on Catherine Lassagne:

"On May the 8th 1840, which incidentally, was the birthday both of the Curé and of Catherine Lassagne, a certain very devout pilgrim, Mademoiselle Etiennette Durié, who was suffering from a painful tumour, went to see her friend Catherine Lassagne in the early afternoon. She was bringing alms for the Curé. This whole scene is easy to reconstruct.

"Etiennette has taken her meal at La Providence. Since it is Monsieur le Curé's habit after his quick meal to visit the orphanage, the alms-collector has only to wait for him there. But the church clock has struck the half hour after midday, and the saint has not appeared. No doubt he has gone directly from the presbytery to the church. Catherine and Etiennette go to the church and inquire of one of the helpers. This woman herself seems very puzzled. No, Monsieur Vianney is not in his confessional; he has not been seen to leave his house. 'The safest thing,' suggests Catherine, 'is to go and wait for him at the foot of his stairs.' Catherine ushers Etiennette into the little courtyard in front of the presbytery. More waiting . . . . One o'clock strikes. Monsieur le Curé is still in his room. Is he ill?

"Catherine, who is occasionally allowed to clean the place for the saint, has a key to the presbytery. She opens the door and makes Etiennette go ahead of her. At the bottom of the staircase the two visitors look at one another inquiringly. Would it be discreet to go up? But here their difficulty is resolved: there is a sound of talking. Monsieur le Curé has a visitor. At such an hour it is most unusual. But what is even stranger is that a lady has gone up to talk to him in his room. The feminine voice is sweet and clear and the words are pronounced so distinctly that our two daughters of Eve, having impulsively gone up the staircase a little way, can hear the dialogue.

" 'What do you want?' they heard the visitor say.

"Monsieur Vianney answered in a tone of trustful tenderness. 'Ah, my sweet Mother, I want the conversion of sinners, the consolation of the afflicted, the relief of my sick people. . . .'

"Pale with shock, Etiennette and Catherine looked at one another: no doubt at all, this Lady was . . . she whom the church calls 'the refuge of sinners, consolation of the afflicted, health of the sick' . . . the Blessed Virgin.

"In the meantime, the Curé of Ars was continuing his prayer. 'In particular I ask for the relief of a person who has suffered for a long time and who wants either to die or to be cured!'

"Etiennette and Catherine, mounting softly, had reached the landing of the first floor. 'It's about me!' said Mademoiselle Durié half to herself, and she went into the room, for the door was ajar. Catherine did not dare to cross the threshold. However, she too saw the heavenly visitor and heard her voice. She saw standing in front of the chimney piece a lady of average height clothed in a dress of dazzling whiteness sown with golden roses . . . her brow was encircled by a crown of stars, shining like the sun."

Of her own feelings Catherine never spoke. Etiennette, as she tells us, "remained for a moment as if she were beside herself," and then, going on her knees, she burst out: "My good Mother, do take me to Heaven!"

"The apparition replied in her pleasant voice, 'Later.'

" 'Ah, but it's time now, Mother.'

"As for the Curé of Ars, he remained standing by his table, his hands clasped on his breast, his face radiant, his gaze fixed. He had not come out of his rapture even when the Virgin was gone. Fearing that he was dead, Etiennette went to him, still on her knees, and plucked at a fold of his cassock.

"He said, 'My God, is it You?'

"She said, 'No, *mon Père*, it is I.'

"Then he came to himself.

" 'But where were you, *mon Père*? What did you see?' she asked.

" 'I saw a lady.'

" 'So did I. Who was this lady?'

" 'If you speak of it,' said Monsieur Vianney severely, 'you shall never cross my threshold again.' "

"Etiennette said: 'Shall I tell you, *mon Père*, what I thought? I thought it was the Blessed Virgin.'

" 'And you were not mistaken. So you saw her?'

" 'Oh yes, I saw her and I spoke to her. But now will you tell me what state you were in when I thought you were dead?'

" 'Oh, no! It was because I was so glad to see my Mother!'

" 'My good father, it's only owing to you that I have seen her . . . When she comes back, do consecrate me to her, and then she will offer me herself to her Divine Son.'

"The servant of God promised, and added, 'You will be cured.'

" 'But when, *mon Père*?'

" 'A little later. Don't ask me so much.'

"Then, more gently, he added: 'The Blessed Virgin, St. Philomena and I, we're well acquainted with one another.' "

This last remark suggests that apparitions were not rare occurrences in his life. One recalls what he said to a visitor: "You would not dare to put your foot on a certain tile, if you knew what had happened there."

Catherine must have drawn back on to the landing when Etiennette entered the room. Anyway, she never mentioned the event until 1875—that is, sixteen years after the Curé's death.

Marianne Renard, the daughter of the Curé's housekeeper who lived next door, testified to another such event. It seems that a woman who had come to Ars went into church very early in the morning. She noticed that the sacristy door was open. Looking in, she saw the Curé talking to a beautiful lady dressed in white. She waited, not daring to interrupt. After a while, Monsieur Vianney noticed her hesitating before the door and said: "Why didn't you come in at once?" She replied, "But *mon Père*, you were talking to a lady." He said nothing. When she came into the sacristy at last, the lady had gone. But how? for there was no door other than the one by which she herself had entered, and she had not seen the lady leave.

In 1856 François Bourdin, a youngish man of the Ain region, having failed in business, had lost his faith and was yeilding to thoughts of despair. At length he decided to go to confession to the Curé of Ars. He was frightened out of his wits when the Curé said, "My son, you are damned."

He made seven consecutive confessions, but on the morning of the eighth day, as he was about to go to Holy Communion, he suddenly felt anxious and wanted to see the Curé again. So he waited one more day. Towards evening of the next day he entered the church and knelt down in his place near the sacristy door.

"At that moment Monsieur Vianney was not seated on the bench where he heard confessions. He was standing with his back turned to the door, holding a conversation with a lady, a little taller than himself, who also was standing. She was dressed in pale blue, and was marvellously beautiful in appearance. The Curé of Ars had not noticed François Bourdin. Only the lady had glanced at the new arrival, with a look of tenderness. This mysterious conversation lasted for about half an hour, but without any sound of words. During that time, the man remained kneeling at the *prie-dieu*, his head in his hands. He felt as if an immense weight were being lifted from him and he was conscious of a real impress of grace on his heart.

"All of a sudden the priest took the penitent by the arm. Bourdin got to his feet. He looked for the vision. She had disappeared, though no door had been opened. Instead of sitting down near him to listen to him, the Curé of Ars dismissed him gently, saying: 'Go, my friend, go in peace. You are surely in God's grace.' "

In the year 1900, when Bourdin was almost eighty, he told the whole story to his parish priest, who wrote it all down. The priest tells us that this old man was universally esteemed for his piety and virtue. His testimony was not open to question.

In his little book on St. Mary Magdalen, Lacordaire speaks of the gift of tears: "It is God who causes these tears in ecstasy." Whenever the Curé made the Stations of the Cross in his church, his frame was shaken by sobs; when he gave Holy Communion at the altar rails, very often his eyes were streaming, and his chasuble wet with tears. Towards the end of his life, he could never preach on the Eucharist, or on the love or kindness of God, or on the joys of Heaven, without weeping.

He was seen twice by two sound, calm witnesses, to rise and float into the air in ecstasy. On the supernatural plane, this being raised up (technically called levitation by spiritual writers) is explained by Pope Benedict XIV in his treatise on the Canonization of Saints: "By divine power, the body may be raised on high . . . which gift is a certain imperfect participation in the gift of agility which will be bestowed on glorified bodies."

When St. Teresa of Avila speaks of this from experience she says: "It seemed to me, when I tried to make some resistance, as if a great force under my feet were lifting me up. I know of nothing with which to compare it."

Abbé Poulain mentions it in his fascinating Chapter 13 of *The Graces of Interior Prayer*. He says that there are three phenomena which may occasionally accompany ecstasy. First, the body rises up into the air: this is what is termed levitation. Second, it is enveloped in a luminous aureole. Third, it emits a fragrance.

"When the body is lifted up into the air, it often becomes as light as a feather, so that a breath is enough to set it in motion and to cause it to float like a soap bubble.

"There is no fixed rule with regard to the height to which the body ascends. When St. Francis of Assisi had withdrawn to Mount Alverna, his only companion being Brother Leo, his confessor, this latter saw him lifted up sometimes to a man's height from the ground, and sometimes above the highest trees, and at others so high that he was no longer visible."

We have two testimonies from Ars. On Whit Monday, the 28th of May, 1849, a young girl, Mademoiselle Annette Chrétien, who later became a nun, was consulting Monsieur Vianney in the sacristy about her vocation, when all of a sudden she saw him join his hands, lift his eyes heavenwards, then "rise about a foot above the ground." He remained like this for a quarter of an hour. "When he touched the floor again, he made a prediction of marvellous clarity, which was later fulfilled."

During the process of canonization, a chaplain to some Carmelite nuns swore on oath that the following had happened: "My brother, the Curé of Saint Vincent, of Chalon-sur-Saône, was at Ars one day with me. In the evening, while the servant of God was leading the prayers, we were facing the pulpit. Towards the middle of these devotions, just as Monsieur Vianney was reciting the act of Charity, my brother, whose eyesight was very good, saw him ascend little by little until his feet were above the edge of the pulpit. My brother looked around him and did not notice any astonishment in the others present. He kept silent, but directly he came out of church, he could no longer keep secret the prodigy which he had seen with his own eyes. He spoke of it openly and enthusiastically."

In his most interesting chapter on ecstasy, Abbé Poulain distinguishes between ecstatics and neuropaths. He rightly calls attention to the fact that, in most mystics, we find the powerful organizer side by side with the strange dreamer—for example, he says: "Ecstatics have written books which give proof of immense work, both of erudition and composition, and consequently of great strength of will." We may rule out any trace of hysteria or neurosis in the Curé's case by referring again to the testimony of his doctors already quoted (in Chapter 9). His devoted physician Dr. Saunier made this declaration at the process of beatification: he spoke of his patient's serenity of ideas, delicacy of perceptions, soundness of judgment and views, and his total self-possession.

And now we come to a strange, mysterious incident at which unbelievers may scoff, and which the sceptical may dismiss as pure illusion. It is referred to in a letter, undated, from Jeanne Clairet of Villefranche-sur-Saône, addressed to one of the Curé's successors and still preserved in the Ars archives.

"Monsieur le Curé, I consider it my duty to inform you that being in Ars on the 2nd of July, 1856, and having been unable to address myself to the saint in confession because of the multitude of strangers who surrounded his confessional, I intended at least to throw myself at his feet and beg for his blessing. Therefore, having managed to get near this admirable man, I was trying to take his blessed hand to kiss it respectfully, when he took it away from me, saying, gravely but with great courtesy: 'Oh, do not take my ring!'

"At the same moment, I noticed a thing which I had never seen till then—on the fourth finger of his left hand an extremely brilliant gold ring.

"Thus he had indeed received, because he was worthy of it, the signal favour which several other saints had received."

Other great saints who received betrothal or marriage rings include Blessed Henry Suso, the Dominican, and St. Teresa of Avila. It is the proof that the saint has arrived gradually, and after being purified by many trials, to what the mystical theologians call: "that calm and durable union which is named Transforming Union, and which seems to be the uttermost limit of mystical union."

This serene Transforming Union is called by the mystical theologians "Spiritual Marriage." The most moving description of its raptures has been written by St. John of the Cross, who experienced it when he was imprisoned by the unreformed Carmelites in a dank, dark cell in the monastery of Toledo. For weeks he was left there, wearing a verminous shirt, scourged in public three times a week in the refectory, deprived of the sacraments. Only during one hour of the day did a ray of light penetrate his dungeon, enabling him to read his breviary. But throughout this time he was flooded with spiritual joy. His soul was wedded to Christ, the Bridegroom, and his pain seemed to him of no account. And when he came out again, broken in health, but radiant in spirit, he was able to write that great treatise, that love-story of mystical theology, his commentary on the Canticle of Canticles. Only those who have endured spiritual fang and flail with great courage are thus rewarded. "Many are called, but few are chosen"—"Often," said St. Teresa, "through lack of courage."

Père Poulain says in Chapter 19: "The transforming union is a mystic state containing three principal elements.

"The first, a union that is almost permanent, persisting even amidst exterior occupations, and this in such a manner that the two different operations do not interfere with each other.

"Two. A transformation of the higher faculties as to their manner of operation (hence the name of Transforming Union).

"Three. Generally a permanent intellectual vision of the Blessed Trinity or some Divine Attribute."

Père Poulain says in paragraph 22: "It may happen that the spiritual marriage begins with a ceremony and rejoicings. But these are passing facts which must not be confounded with the marriage itself which is a permanent state.

"For example, in certain lives of the saints we read of the interchange of rings, of angelic chants, etc. These circumstances are not necessary, and, further, they may just as well symbolize simple espousals or other unions.

"In the Old Testament as well as in the New, God's love for mankind, and particularly His relations with the Synagogue or the Church, are often represented by the symbol of the relationship between bridegroom and bride. Likewise from the first ages of Christianity, Christian virginity has been called a marriage with the Divine Spouse."

We have already quoted a passage from Monsieur Vianney's catechism instructions in which he inadvertently disclosed the stage of the spiritual life which he had reached; it bears repeating: "O beautiful life, beautiful union of the soul with Our Lord! . . . the inner life is like an ocean of love into which the soul plunges. God holds the soul, when she has reached this state, just as a mother clasps the head of her child to cover it with kisses and caresses. Our Lord is hungry for her."

The Curé was indeed able to rise from the love of visible things to the invisible! The tenderest experience he had known in the world had been the love and caresses of his mother at Dardilly. And now this love was echoed by the all-mothering love of God. In one of his catechism instructions on humility, he said: "We must pray like guileless four-year-old children, who tell their mother everything."

15. *TEMPORARY TRIUMPH OF THE DEVIL: MONSIEUR VIANNEY'S THREE ESCAPES*

St. John of the Cross tells us that during the Transforming Union the soul has to endure trouble and affliction in its lowest part at the hands of the Devil, but that all this ceases in the state of Spiritual Marriage. The Curé d'Ars was an exception to this. We know he suffered from the Devil's attacks until about six months before his death in 1859. He became so used to it all that he came to treat the Devil as a great joke.

As we have noted, the Devil started his antics in 1824. But by 1840, sixteen years later, he had made no headway. His tricks during that time had been like the practical jokes of some feeble-minded schoolboy. Now we must realize that the Devil is a fallen archangel, with an immense archangelic intelligence, far greater than that of any human being; his subtleties are greater than any of ours. In view of this, the silliness of his early pranks is surprising. But that was just a smoke-screen. Having failed to exhaust the Curé, the Devil now tried to pierce him where he was most vulnerable, to destroy his hope in God. He knew that nothing he could do would lessen the Curé's humility, but this humility itself could be turned into a weapon against him. Monsieur Vianney despised himself and doubted that he would ever be capable of serving his beloved Lord as he should. The Devil began to play upon these doubts to strain him to the breaking point.

The Devil had failed to make his life impossible by wearing him out with fear during the night hours. He had failed to conquer the Curé by bodily exhaustion, though he knew that exhaustion could engender despair, that profound sadness to which Monsieur Vianney already was exposed by the spectacle of the boundless depths of man's sinfulness. Night after night the Curé reached the limit of his endurance. It was not that he lived in despair, so much as in fear of despairing. He was tormented by the thought that he might fail to possess for eternity that glorious, loving presence of God.

Père Lefèvre, writing in *Etudes Carmélitaines,* says: "The psychology and the folklore of the nineteenth century in the West conceive a Satan of sonorous presence, and it is thus that he manifested himself to Monsieur Vianney."

Those terrible crashes and rumblings, or those nerve-racking tiny sounds, repeated throughout the night, had no effect on Monsieur Vianney's soul, though they might make his eyes start out of his head and his cheeks turn ashen. No. Satan lurked in his hiding place to prepare a more subtle snare, a more crafty ambush. He lay in wait to deceive him spiritually. So he tried to penetrate him with a sense of his unworthiness and urge him to flee from Ars in despair.

If Monsieur Vianney had fled, it would have been because he had lost his trust in God's love. Strange that the saint should ever have felt temptation when he was living in the blossoming heart of Love. As so many of the stages of the spiritual life are not as definite and clear-cut as the mystical text-books would have us think, but often overlap, perhaps when he was at the height of the Transforming Union he was still occasionally experiencing some shadows of the Dark Night.

That is the only explanation for Monsieur Vianney's three strange flights from Ars.

Catherine Lassagne tells us that he used to pray: "My God, make me endure everything You will, but give me the grace never to fall into Hell." And he would pass through terrible alternations of fear and hope, and plunge into that Dark Night of the soul in which he thought that God had left him for ever.

Catherine has told us in her *Petit Mémoire* that he remained in his parish for forty-one years, always against his will. He said in one of his early sermons that he did not want to die a curé, because he knew of no saint who had died in this post. "I wish I could have two years before me to weep over my poor life . . . Ah, then it seems to me that I would love God very much." He was always writing to his bishop, asking to be released, but of course the bishop would not hear of it. (In fact, when in 1835 the Curé turned up at an autumn retreat for priests, the bishop told him he did not need a retreat, but must go back to Ars at once and look after the souls flocking to see him.) When the bishop's visit was expected at Ars, the Curé, looking very happy, would whisper into some friend's ear: "Monseigneur will come. Monseigneur will come. And then I will ask him you know what."

We remember that when he could not sleep he pictured himself as a Trappist or as a Carthusian. "I am seeking for a corner in which to weep for my poor life and do penance for my sins." He was a born contemplative, and in thus crushing his longing for solitary prayer he was gaining great virtue and merit.

In this whole mysterious story we must not forget the element of physical exhaustion. In 1835 he was paying for his youthful "follies." The terrible facial neuralgia, toothache and acute stomach pains remained to torment him even after he had moderated the austerities which caused them.

One dark night in 1840 he was overwhelmed by the desire for solitude and contemplation. He left his rectory and went some distance on the road to Villefranche. But a sudden thought gave him pause in his flight. "Am I really doing the will of God now?" he asked himself. "Is not the conversion of a single soul worth more than all the prayers I can offer up in solitude?" He turned at once and went back to his work.

His physical energies continued to decline. In 1841 he made his will. In 1843, when he was fifty-eight, came a breakdown. On the 6th of May he suddenly collapsed in church. Doctors were called and he was put to bed.

Even in such a moment his sense of humour did not desert him. He whispered to an attendant, "I am engaged at this moment in a great combat."

"Against who, Monsieur le Curé?"

"Against four doctors. If a fifth one appears—I'm dead."

During this illness he had terrible nights, troubled by nightmares. He said in the morning, "Last night I thought I heard the demons' triumphant cries. 'We've got you, we've got you! He is ours!'"

However, to cut a long story short, his life was saved by praying to St. Philomena, and everybody in Ars believed that his "dear little saint" had appeared to him. But during his convalescence trouble began in earnest, the Devil began really to torment him. Monsieur des Garets once found him sitting on his bed, weeping bitterly.

"What's the matter with you?" he asked.

"Oh," replied the Curé, "nobody knows all the tears I have shed on this bed. Since the age of eleven I have been seeking solitude . . ." He ended on a sob: "And it's always been denied me."

Until this time, the Curé had had no assistance with the work of the parish, but as a consequence of his illness a priest from Savigneux who secretly aspired to become Curé of Ars, one Abbé Raymond, was coming with increasing frequency to help out.

After his recovery, the numbers of pilgrims coming to Ars were greater than ever. The poor saint was tormented with a desire to slip away just for a few weeks from the crowd of penitents besieging his confessional; the thought that Abbé Raymond might carry on without him added to the immense pressure of the temptation. He wrote a letter to his bishop; he wrote to his brother François telling him to expect him quite soon at the Dardilly farmhouse; and on the night of the 11th–12th of September he fled from Ars for the second time.

But not without saying farewell to La Providence. That was his undoing, for Catherine and the others could not keep his secret. They told other parishioners, who were at once on the alert around the presbytery. A little after one o'clock in the morning they heard somebody slip through the garden hedge. It was he, carrying his breviary and a little parcel. Seeing the people on the watch, he began to run, poor man, and they ran too. This is the account of Abbé Monnin:

"Some wanted to speak to him again, others to make him bless their objects of devotion. He continued on his way without taking any notice. He carried under his arm a packet containing some linen folded in a large pocket handkerchief and his little purse. He gave the packet to a young man who wanted to accompany him, but as the young man was in his working clothes and returned home to smarten up a little, he never caught up with Monsieur Vianney until he had reached his destination. He was replaced by faithful Pertinand, the schoolmaster. They walked on foot as far as Dardilly to the family house, owned by François Vianney . . . When he arrived, his feet were all torn and bruised. He felt ill and was obliged to go to bed."

It is a wonder he did not lose his way, for during his long years in the confessional new roads had been cut, all strange to him. Once he said to Pertinand suspiciously, "Jean, you're betraying me." The walk had taken seven hours and they had recited the rosary ten times. He had gone several miles out of his way to avoid disturbing the Trévoux bridge-keeper at that hour of the night.

One can imagine the tears and dismay of the orphans and indeed of the whole parish. The church was empty, the church which had been filled day and night with pilgrims. Everybody was quiet and lifeless. Had it not been for the Angelus ringing, someone re-marked, one would have thought one was in a parish of infidels. When Monsieur des Garets preached in church on the virtues of their departed Curé, everybody burst into tears.

In the meantime, at Dardilly, François was having a terrible time. He protested: "If he remains here, I'll be obliged to ask for help. I am no longer the master in my own house." What had happened?

On the evening of the 16th, twenty-three young men of Ars had walked through the night, reaching the Vianney farmhouse at dawn. François and his wife refused to open the door. All of a sudden the young men looked up. Here was their dear Curé at the window, calling the visitors up. He had been awake all night, of course. He made them come into his room. He recited the rosary with them, then took them to church and said Mass for them. After that, blissfully unaware of the probable inconvenience to his sister-

in-law, he begged them to stay to breakfast, but they had the sense
to refuse. They went back that evening.

While his brother and his children were working in the fields, a
pretty young niece remained at home to open the door. Her uncle
the Curé particularly asked her to welcome any pilgrims, and not
to let anyone go back without offering him some refreshment.

Quite soon, people from Ars began appearing in a horse-drawn
bus especially chartered for that purpose. The niece tells us:
"Briefly, that day, the crowd was so great that we could not perform
the duties of hospitality properly. We only had our meal after
Vespers. The holy Curé sat down to table with his family, but
consented to eat only a cooked pear, in spite of all pleadings. However, he talked a lot and told us many edifying stories. . . ."

(His family used to say that when they ate at his table at Ars,
they lost their appetites as on a First Communion Day, so entrancing was his conversation.)

In spite of the interruptions, it is easy to imagine Monsieur
Vianney's happiness at returning home for a short time after all
these years, and recalling all the happy times he had spent there.
Of course the dear little grey donkey which had reached thirty was
now dead. And it would have been unwise, in view of the great
numbers of visitors, for the Curé to go out and look at the oak tree
and the old apple tree under which they all used to take their
midday siesta. He stayed indoors, looking at all the familiar objects, the clock under which he had made his first confession, the
kneading trough where his mother had made bread, the oven
where he had dried the beggars' wet garments, the table at which
he had shared his soup with them, the bed in which he had been
born, with the picture of Mary Immaculate still above it. Every
corner was filled with memories of his mother.

It is a pity that apparently he could not go to Montmerle and
recall memories of his prayers in the old cleft willow tree, and the
sermons preached to shepherd lads.

The inconvenience to his family caused by the great crowds
coming from Ars made the Curé think of finding another retreat.

The Bishop had forbidden him to leave the diocese but said that he might go to the village of Beaumont if he were still firm in his desire to leave Ars.

On Monday morning, September the eighteenth, the two brothers rose in the darkness before dawn and took the Albigny road. Monsieur Vianney was on one of the farm horses, with François holding the bridle. When they reached Albigny Monsieur Vianney said to his brother: "I can continue my way on foot." He said good-bye to him and entered the hamlet alone. There he met Abbé Raymond, who had undertaken to conduct him to Beaumont. Around thirty miles from Dardilly, Beaumont is isolated amidst the pools of the Dombes region, surrounded by immense stretches of flat marshlands. It has a famous shrine to Our Lady, and a tradition that she restores to life children who have died before baptism.

On the morning after their arrival at Beaumont, both priests said Mass, the Curé with the intention of finding out God's will for him. When Abbé Raymond returned to the sacristy, even before he had removed his chasuble, Monsieur Vianney said to him: "God does not want me here."

"Where do you wish to go then?"

"Let us return to Ars."

Abbé Raymond got a carriage for the return journey. Poor Monsieur Vianney wept now and then, but he never stopped praying. From Ambérieux he made the journey on foot. He had found the carriage tiring, as indeed it would be to anybody who was used to walking everywhere. He must have felt as if he were going back to a prison house. Good-bye, solitude. Good-bye.

At Savigneux, Abbé Raymond advised him to go into the church to pray and rest a little. Meanwhile he made plans for the return to Ars. He sent this message ahead: "Monsieur le Curé is coming back. He will be there in an hour."

At Ars, the moment they heard this news, the villagers rang the church bells as if it were a great feast day. Even the corn threshers in their work-a-day clothes came hurrying to join in the universal jubilation. Though he had only been away a week, how they had

ached for his return! This is Catherine Lassagne's account of his
home-coming:

"Let us bless and praise the Lord! Yesterday, at five in the
evening, the whole parish was still under the burden of sorrow. We
were seeking our Saint, whom we feared we had lost for ever. A
quarter of an hour afterwards the bells rang out a joyous peal; all
hurried to the market-place to see the holy curé arrive, dragging
himself along with difficulty, leaning on his pilgrim's staff, and
accompanied only by one priest. The people all crowded round
him, laughing, crying, nearly stifling him with their joy and gratitude. As for himself, he stopped and smiled at their madness. 'It
was all lost then,' said he. 'Well, now it is all found again.' Prosper
des Garets had hurried to the spot; the saint embraced him with
the delight of a father who has found a lost child. He does not
conceal his satisfaction. He is pleased with everything and everybody; pleased with the Blessed Virgin, who gave him the inspiration to return to his flock. . . .

"I saw him for a moment afterwards. There was peace and joy
in his eyes and in his voice, and, as he told me, in his heart. . . ."

Catherine Lassagne concludes by asking herself what is the
secret of the Curé's astonishing celebrity. She knows it is neither
his talent nor his learning nor his eloquence nor his charm, nor
anything exterior. But it is "the eminent holiness of a poor priest,
gentle and humble of heart."

Monseigneur Trochu says that round about 1844 or 1845 the
Curé of Ars attained the heights of holiness. Were his earthly
troubles over? Far from it! In 1845 Abbé Raymond came to him
as a curate on a permanent basis. He remained with him eight long
years, until 1853. Although he was a good priest, he became a thorn
in Monsieur Vianney's flesh.

To start with, he did not appreciate his Curé. He thought his
preaching not eloquent enough. And then he was ambitious; he
himself, as we have said, wanted to become the Curé of Ars. He
must have been blind indeed not to realize that if it were deprived
of Monsieur Vianney, Ars would no longer be Ars.

Monsieur Vianney emerged from this ordeal with flying colours.

There is ample proof of this in the letters he wrote to the bishop about his assistant. Abbé Raymond was twenty years his junior. He had been born at Fareins in the Ain district. While he was in the seminary the Curé of Ars had paid for his upkeep, and he had even, it seems, given him his first cassock. He had been named Curé of Savigneux (less than two miles from Ars) while still a young priest. On the days when Monsieur Vianney was supposed to go to the clergy meeting at the Château d'Ars and could not leave his confessional, he appointed Abbé Raymond to sit at the head of the table in his stead. Of course one can imagine how delighted Abbé Raymond would be. He was an active, zealous and enterprising priest, and from 1845 onwards, as the Ars parochial register proves, it was he who was responsible for the baptisms, marriages and burials of the parish.

When he finally severed connections with Savigneux to come to Ars to relieve Monsieur Vianney of the overwhelming pressure of parish work, he refused to give up his old title of curé, although at Ars he was only an assistant, and would sign the register "Raymond, Curé."

The first unpardonable thing he did was to ask Monsieur Vianney to give up his bedroom to him, and lodge in one or other of the guest rooms. Abbé Vianney did so very meekly, although at that age, even if one is a saint, it is very hard to give up one's little habits and one's usual background. True, Monsieur Vianney had endured much in that room at the hands of the Devil. But there was the remembrance of heavenly visitations too. It must have been very hard to give it up. Nevertheless he did so with his usual gentleness.

When the parishioners heard of this, no doubt through the Curé's occasional housekeepers, they protested so loudly that Monsieur Vianney had to go back to his room. Abbé Raymond moved out into the village.

Then Abbé Raymond, who was determined not to be thwarted in any other way, said to Monsieur Vianney: "You have too much to do in the confessional. Leave the preaching and catechism lessons to me. For you the confessional, for me the pulpit." And from then on, a quiet little altercation went on, for the saint did not agree with this suggestion at all. The saint's confessor, Abbé Beau, was forever hearing echoes of these painful arguments. Catherine Lassagne has written:

"He tried to hold out a little against a character so much opposed to his own, but he saw that it only irritated him the more, so he resigned himself to listening to him, consulting him on all sorts of matters—in a word, to following all his orders as closely as possible."

The Curé of Ars, of course, had just as determined a temper as his curate. But he was the first to give in, out of virtue. When he went out into the village, the crowds cried out, "It is he! It is he!" And yet he lived cheek by jowl with a curate who thought nothing of him. But Monsieur Vianney very soon began to consider his curate as his best friend and greatest benefactor. After his death, the curate used to speak of "the tender and fatherly affection" with which Monsieur Vianney had surrounded him. If occasionally Monsieur Vianney lost patience in secret, and played with the idea of finding somebody to replace him, he looked upon these wishes as stray impulses. When the bishop, hearing of his trials, sent some one along to Ars to enquire about the curate's behaviour, the Curé said to him, "Oh leave him. Leave him with me. He tells me home truths." One can see how saints take their revenge by taking a glance at all the references to Abbé Raymond in Monsieur Vianney's letters to his bishop. Here is a letter of 1848:

"I say nothing about Monsieur Raymond to your Eminence, except to mention all the kindness he shows me and the good he does. He deserves a great place in your kind heart. Do not listen to those malicious tongues. . . ."

Here is a letter of 1852 in which he says of Monsieur Raymond: "I want to tell you, Monseigneur, that I very much wish to keep Monsieur Raymond, because he does a lot of good, especially to strangers . . . I am most attached to him. He has a kind heart."

A month later: "Monseigneur, the greatest pleasure that you could give me would be to put off the departure of Monsieur Raymond."

It is very rarely that those bitten by spiritual envy repent, so the good testimonials Abbé Raymond gave his Curé after his death are particularly precious; they are, so to speak, wrenched from him, to his own undoing.

A way out of the situation seemed to offer itself in September, 1853. The people of Ars had begun really to dislike Monsieur Raymond, for he was not easy to get on with, and they were longing to see him go. Monsieur Raymond himself, thick-skinned though he was, must have guessed that he was unpopular.

Abbé Poulain, in the twenty-fourth chapter of *The Graces of Interior Prayer*, has a most interesting thing to say about the trials which beset the faithful. "I have seen very religious persons who try to cure themselves of irritability. They have been unable to succeed. They doubtless lacked the prolonged effort and humility that were necessary. I think that a miracle is required to overcome these temperaments. St. Francis of Sales, who was naturally rather fiery, ended by being a model of gentleness; but he was a saint." He might have added, as another splendid example, the Curé of Ars, who was born with an extremely violent nature and a caustic tongue. (We have already noted the occasion when, suppressing his anger, he came out in a rash.)

Now Monsieur Raymond helped him to put the finishing touch to this wonderful virtue of patience. As Father Vincent McNabb once said, there is a special "finish" about the sweetness acquired by fiery-tempered people, a finish not to be found in naturally gentle natures. Catherine Lassagne considered Monsieur Raymond as "sent by God to exercise the patience of his servant." Comte des Garets noticed how Monsieur Raymond looked upon himself as the Curé's tutor, how lacking he was in tact and judgment. One can imagine the feelings of Catherine when her saintly Curé was turned out of his bedroom and sent to sleep in the damp, dark room on the ground floor. Baronne de Belvey said that Abbé Raymond treated the Curé "with harshness and without any consideration for his age and his holiness." The only thing one can say to excuse him is that he did not realize how much he could make Monsieur Vianney suffer. He kept reproaching the Curé for never telling him anything, and said that he was trying to organize the pilgrimage as he thought best. The Curé's confessor said: "He even went so far as to contradict him publicly in the pulpit." The Curé really did look upon him as a cross, for once in Holy Week, when he had been persuaded to write to the bishop asking for a new auxiliary, he went behind the altar, read the rough copy which had been written for him, then tore it into four, exclaiming: "I had been meditating how Our Lord carried His cross during these holy days. I could do as He did."

And when at long last the bishop had sent Monsieur Raymond elsewhere, the Curé d'Ars wrote the Abbé a very kind letter: "You have been so useful to me. You have rendered me so many services that you have my heart in chains." Monsieur Raymond continued in blissful ignorance of how the Curé had once wished him gone. In fact, when he was replaced by Monsieur Toccanier, he thought that the Curé was upset about it. "Monsieur le Curé was very fond of me."

This new priest, Monsieur Toccanier, was thirty-one in 1853, the year of his appointment, and he looked very strong. His method of preaching, which was simple and lively, resembled the manner of Monsieur Vianney, and he was very kind and agreeable. In fact, just the right person. He became one of the saint's most devoted friends and an invaluable witness during the beatification process. Monsieur Vianney grew to love him so devotedly that when he was away for three weeks in 1854 because of an epidemic of cholera, he missed him terribly. Monsieur Toccanier, most anxious to see the Curé again after this absence, presented himself in front of the confessional where the Curé had been penned in since midnight. Monsieur Vianney came out at once and embraced him tenderly. "Here you are then, my good friend," he said in a whisper. "I'm very glad. The time seemed so long to me. I was thinking that the damned must be very unhappy in Hell, eternally separated from God: we already suffer so much on earth when we are far from the people we love."

One likes to think of this young priest spoiling his Curé a little.

There is, for example, the record of a new breviary which he brought him when he went to Paris.

Long years after, before his death, in 1883, Abbé Toccanier recalled: "One day I asked the Curé of Ars to give me a 'leg up' when he was in Paradise. 'Yes, my friend,' he answered, 'I will tell God to let *mon camarade* come in.'"

Abbé Toccanier was named assistant at Ars on Monday, August the 29th. Catherine Lassagne seems to think that Monsieur Vianney did not yet know of the appointment when on the 21st of September, a Thursday, he said to her, as she was giving him his midday meal: "I have been thinking, this time I ought to go. My brother-in-law, Melin, who lives in the parish of Saint-Irénée is expecting me. I will go on Monday evening. Keep that to yourself."

"Oh, Monsieur le Curé, you mustn't go away," said Catherine, and she reminded him of his last attempt at escape ten years before, and the behaviour of the crowds when he returned.

On the Saturday afternoon, the Vicar-General came to Ars accompanied by the Abbés Raymond and Toccanier. The new priest was installed the following day at High Mass.

Towards eight o'clock on that same Sunday evening, Catherine asked Monsieur Vianney's permission to tell his secret to Marie Filliat, who would be discreet. He replied, "Just as you like." After a while the two women came to him in tears, but it was no good. They left the presbytery and stood talking in whispers at the garden door. "What shall we do?" said Catherine. "Feeble as he is at his age" (for he was then sixty-seven), "he will never be able to walk to Lyons. You, Marie, will carry the basket of provisions. But supposing he falls ill on the journey? He will need a carter to lead the way."

"But there is no man here who could help us at this moment."

Just then the sacristan, Frère Jérôme, passed by. In two minutes he had learned their secret. Of course he could not keep it to himself. He went off to tell Frère Athanase, and both went to knock on Monsieur Toccanier's door. He was then sleeping in the annexe to La Providence.

Monsieur Vianney had said that he was going to his brother-in-

law in Lyons. That was a ruse. A friend of his, Abbé Colin, founder
of the Society of Marists, had recently added on to his house at La
Neylière a monastery following a modified Trappist rule. A room
had been prepared there for Monsieur Vianney. This is Abbé
Toccanier's account:

"You may judge of my surprise when I heard the good Brothers'
story; I could hardly bring myself to believe them. 'Mount guard in
front of the presbytery,' I said, to them, 'and if Monsieur le Curé
attempts to escape, call me.' At midnight I heard three hurried
knocks at my door. I was lying on my bed fully dressed.

"I stood in the square with the two Brothers, spying on the movements of our holy Curé, who could be observed in his room because
of the light of his lamp. And he was taking his hat, his breviary and
his umbrella. 'Let him come down,' I said to the Brothers. He came
down and joined Marie Filliat and Catherine Lassagne, who were
to accompany him. We listened carefully. 'Are you ready?' he asked
as he came down. 'Well then, let us go.'

"He came out followed by Marie, who carried the provisions,
and Catherine, who held a lantern in her hand. All of a sudden we
placed ourselves in front of him. He looked severely at Catherine,
who burst into tears. 'You've betrayed me,' he said. Frère Athanase
said at once. 'Where are you going, Monsieur le Curé? You want to
leave us? Very well, we will ring the tocsin.'

"'And,' added Frère Jérôme, 'we will follow you in procession.'

"'Do so,' replied Monsieur Vianney, curt and resolute, 'and let
me pass.'"

Monsieur Toccanier whispered to the two Brothers, "Let's stay
behind to follow him." However, Frère Jérôme took the lantern
from Catherine's hand, and while pretending to guide Monsieur
Vianney in the darkness, he led him, not towards the little bridge
over the Fontblin, but in a different direction. The Curé soon saw
he was being tricked. And now he was followed by quite a procession—and by no means a silent one. The women pilgrims who were
awaiting him near the bell turret and the parishioners who had
been awakened by all this were calling for their confessor and their
pastor.

When he got to the Fontblin bridge, he said: "Let me pass, let me pass," in a tone of real anguish. Then Monsieur Toccanier was inspired. He snatched the Curé's breviary from under his arm, gave it to Catherine Lassagne and told her to be gone, and not come back. The Curé cried out, "Give me back my breviary!" But then he beckoned to Marie Filliat. "Keep on walking, I will say it when I get to Lyons."

"*Et quoi,* Monsieur le Curé, you will spend the hours of the day without saying your Office? A fine example!"

The Curé said: "I have another breviary in my room—Monseigneur Devie's."

"Let's go back and look for it," suggested Abbé Toccanier.

They turned back, but they had gone scarcely a few yards when the bell began ringing in the church tower. It sounded doleful in the silence of the night. The Curé knelt down to recite the Angelus. "Having risen to his feet," relates Abbé Toccanier, "the Curé d'Ars went forward with great strides. He rushed into the presbytery and went upstairs to his room, which I entered along with him. On the way, Frère Athanase had passed the word to me that the Mayor had been warned and was coming. In order to give Comte des Garets time to arrive, I was mixing up on the bookshelves the eight volumes of the great breviary in octavo—a precious souvenir of the old bishop, who had died quite recently. As Monsieur Vianney was putting his hand on the volume for the season my eyes fell on a portrait of Monseigneur Devie hanging on the wall. I remembered that the prelate had already prevented other flights. An inspiration came to me. 'Monsieur le Curé,' I said firmly, 'do you see Monseigneur Devie looking at you crossly from Heaven? If one is bound to respect one's bishop's wishes during his lifetime, one should do so all the more after his death. Remember what he said to you ten years ago.'

"Disturbed by these words, Monsieur Vianney answered with the naïveté of a child threatened with his father's reproaches: 'Monseigneur will not scold me. He knows my need to go away and weep over my poor life.' And without waiting any longer, he seized the great breviary bound in green morocco and went down the stairs." At the turning, the Curé nearly collided with Comte des Garets, now arrived to add his persuasions to those of the others. But Monsieur Vianney seemed scarcely to listen to the protestations of this old and faithful friend. "His face was drawn, sad and almost desperate." Monsieur des Garets was left with the impression that he was acting under the influence of a presentiment of death.

In the meantime the villagers, awakened by the sound of bells, thought that there was a fire, or that burglars had been discovered; they all got up and came out into the streets. Some clutched pails, some pitchforks or sticks as they rushed about in the dim lantern light. Joseph Vianey has a most realistic description of the scene in his biography of the saint. He says that some of the villagers were even armed with scythes and guns, and they were all crying out repeatedly, "Monsieur le Curé, Monsieur le Curé," and then, in chorus, "Stay with us!"

When Monsieur Vianney at last appeared, they barred his way into the street. He kept saying, "Let me pass." Catherine Lassagne was deeply moved by the scene: it was so like the taking of Our Lord in the Garden of Olives, she said. Michel Tournassoud, the village shoemaker, tells us: "I was posted at one of the street gates. Monsieur le Curé took me by the arm, half smiling, half weeping, and moved me aside. But he could not get the gate open."

And then the women penitents who had been praying in church that he should remain, all came out and, mingling with the men in the square, fell on their knees before him and said: "*Mon père*, before you go, finish hearing my confession. Oh, good father, do not leave us." And it is here that Abbé Toccanier triumphed by saying the right thing.

"What, Monsieur le Curé—you who know the lives of the saints off by heart—are you forgetting the zeal of St. Martin who cried, after he was already assured of his crown: 'I will not refuse my work . . .'?"

At this point, Monsieur Vianney went back to the church and entered the sacristy. When the crowd saw that he had put on his surplice and was going towards his confessional, he was unable to walk because he was swept up and carried there in triumph.

Abbé Raymond said that this was one of the greatest trials of the Curé's life, but when they spoke to him about it afterwards all he could say was: "I behaved like a child."

As Monseigneur Trochu has pointed out, this flight is "painful, mysterious and troubling." And yet as Catherine Lassagne said: "In taking flight, he thought that he was doing the will of God."

Monsieur Monnin tells us that several witnesses reported: "The Curé of Ars showed in his thought, his voice, the movement of his lips, the expression of his face, usually so serene and agreeable, a mixture of irony, sadness and bitter resentment against everything which had never been seen in him before and which astonished everyone."

A short time afterwards he got a letter from a priest explaining to him that his desire for solitude was a temptation of the Devil: this made a deep impression on him. The only difference in his life after this attempted flight was that he got to church much earlier and stayed much longer in his confessional.

One night in 1854, towards half-past eleven, a carriage drawn by two horses stopped near the church. Two men got down and waited at the sacristy door for Monsieur Vianney. When towards midnight he appeared, one of them seized him by the arm and said,

"If you want to go, there's a carriage all ready."

But, disengaging himself, he replied: "I haven't got my bishop's permission."

Then he went quickly into the church.

What a mysterious visit! Who were those strangers? It sounds very like the Devil and his flunkeys.

At Christmas of that same year, 1854, Monsieur Vianney had alarming news from Dardilly. His elder brother, François, was dangerously ill. But it was impossible to go to him at Christmas. In the New Year, however, he made an attempt to visit him. This is described in a letter which Abbé Toccanier wrote to the bishop.

"It seems that on the 26th of January his nephew was pressing him to go to Dardilly, and he took the Curé in a carriage. But he was not used to carriages and he was already ill with a mysterious complaint which could not be diagnosed. When he had got about sixteen kilometres or so from Ars, he said, 'I can go no further. I feel I'm collapsing.' The roads were covered with snow and ice: he had already felt sick and been obliged to walk some of the way. He had a fit of trembling as he reached Parcieux. When he realized that he would never get to Dardilly, he thought: 'My poor brother.'" Monsieur Toccanier, who had accompanied them, went to Dardilly with the nephew to offer what comfort he could.

"When Monsieur Vianney was returning, he met the omnibus which was coming from Ars and going back to Lyons. It was full of disappointed pilgrims. When they saw him, they all got down and let the bus go back empty; they escorted Monsieur Vianney to the village and followed him into church. And that bus had been full of hardened sinners. Indeed, there were some who had not been to confession for forty years."

François Vianney, who was a good man and a devout Christian having much in common with his brother, died on Good Friday, April the 8th of that year, 1855. On Holy Saturday, of course, the Curé could not dream of going to the funeral, with all the duties in the confessional: he stayed there for eighteen hours that day. Thus circumstances prevented him from putting his resolve never to leave Ars again to the test. Catherine Lassagne writes: "He was resigned even to that . . . It is likely that in the month of January God permitted his excessive fatigue, in order that he should not fall into the trap . . . It is thus that God's will is done in spite of the plots and plans of man."

16. *MONSIEUR VIANNEY'S CHARM*

SOME OF THE MOST CHARMING PICTURES OF THE SAINTS GIVEN TO US by their biographers show them in moments of innocent recreation: St. Ignatius Loyola with his lame leg, dancing a jig to entertain a sick novice; St. Thomas More teasing his plump, flute-playing wife and his monkey. St. Jean-Marie Baptiste Vianney seems, in the natural sense, never to have had any recreation at all. The whole direction of his extraordinary vocation seems to have been to deny —even to annihilate—the most legitimate needs of a human being, however holy, however God-centred. And it must be remembered that this degree of austerity was practised not in the desert, not in the monastery to which he constantly longed to withdraw, but in the active apostolate of a parish priest, in a parish, moreover, to which he drew souls by the thousands. By the laws of the human nature he treated with such contempt, the final result should have been: death. Instead it was what Dom Chauvin, in his study of the subject, says that holiness is: love. Monsieur Vianney had become, in every look, in every gesture, love incarnate.

To repeat the testimony of the graphologist who examined his handwriting: "He has had to fight his passions . . . to triumph over them. . . . What energy he has spent in this struggle! All this has become sublimated for him. This handwriting shows an extremely violent nature, but also a real saint, one of the most attractive saints possible."

One could almost define his personality as that of a priest forged in the furnace of the Heart of Jesus.

Towards the end of his life, what was the impression he gave? Although we have quoted others, Monseigneur Trochu's description of him does not seem redundant here: "Monsieur Vianney was a little below the average in height. Towards the end of his life, his bent head and stooping shoulders made him appear shorter still.

"His face had become very thin and, so to speak, worn away. 'Narrow and tapering from the cheeks to the chin,' wrote a journalist of the time, 'his face was heart-shaped.' His complexion, slightly swarthy in early childhood, then browned in the sun and open air, had become deathly pale during those interminable sessions in the confessional. Early on, deep wrinkles, the sacred scars of his watchings, of his heroic exhaustion, furrowed his cheeks. His thick, straight hair, which he wore . . . rather long at the back, never went quite white.

"Brow high, wide and serene; eyebrows well-defined, his blue eyes, shadowed in their caves of bone, glowed with a strange, unearthly brightness, their gaze guileless but deep, intense, piercing. Abbé Denis Chaland said: 'He seemed to guess my thoughts; when his glance met mine, it pierced to the depths of my soul. I knew a person who confessed to being frightened of it.' On occasion his eyes were as brilliant as diamonds. Even as one was conversing with him, one was struck by this look, intent, it seemed, on the things of the next world. . . . In repose, it was veiled by a gentle, resigned melancholy: it was at such times, no doubt, that his thoughts travelled from God, offended by men, to those who offended Him."

It was as if his body had lost all importance for him; it had become almost immaterial, a light vesture letting the soul shine through.

His immense reputation was grounded on his kindness. Benoît Trève, an observant farmer of Ars we have mentioned before, said: "If one had not honoured him as a saint, one would still have loved him as the gentlest of men." That wonderful look of his became one of limpid sweetness when it was fixed on a child.

There was a six-year-old boy who didn't like learning to read. When he heard that the Curé had given good advice to his brother (in that gentle voice with the unforgettable break in it), he said, "I want to go and ask Monsieur le Curé if I must learn to read." He ran out to him from the crowd.

"Monsieur le Curé, must I learn or may I play?"

"Play, child. It is suitable to your age."

He was reserved with little girls, but undoubtedly he loved them. He treated their occasional audacities with utter benevolence. Once in his orphanage he was just finishing the catechism lesson when a little girl, standing on tiptoe, plucked a hair out of his head. All he said, with a smile, was: "Little one, love God very much."

Love God who loves us; that was at the heart of his priesthood. To a woman brought to the point of agony from an inflammation of the nervous system, he said: "Poor child, how you have suffered! How much God loves you! Love Him in return."

People in financial difficulties used to come to the Curé for advice. There is the rather touching story of Fiacre Ouvry, a little pedlar from Auvergne. He had been abroad on the highways since he was a child of twelve, making a precarious living selling needles, holy pictures and suchlike in France, Italy and Germany. He was illiterate, but he knew the main thing, his catechism, and was very devout. When he was in his early twenties, between the years 1850 and 1855 (the exact date is uncertain), he was passing through Ars, and he went three times to the Curé's confessional. The Curé became interested in him. He said. "It's a mistake to travel about like this, taking root nowhere. You could find some better way to live than that."

"But Father," he said, "I must make a living somehow."

Then the Curé remembered something he had seen at La Louvesc when he was a young man—men and women chatting on their doorsteps as they made rosaries. He suggested that the pedlar should do this work, in a home of his own.

"But Father," the pedlar objected, "this work is unknown in our part of the world."

"Well, you will introduce it," the Curé said. "And you will be successful. Your industry will bring money to the whole countryside, for it will grow, and your family will prosper as long as they are faithful to the practice of their religion."

Fiacre Ouvry took his advice, and everything came to pass as the Curé had promised.

Of course, like all other beings, Monsieur Vianney felt strong natural antipathies towards certain people, but one caught only a glimpse of it, Maître Camille Monnin tells us, "in the lightning flash of his eyes."

He was totally unconscious of himself. When he saw one of those grotesque pictures of him which were sold in the hamlet for a few sous, he would laugh and say gaily, "Do look! Wouldn't you say I was on my way out of the tavern?" Or, "Yes, it's me all right. See how stupid I look!"

He was convinced that he was like Bordin—the village idiot. He said he looked like a cross between a turkey and a goose. He went to endless pains to avoid being painted or sketched. When the great artist Cabuchet came to hear him preach and was hiding a little wax model behind his hat in church, he said: "Monsieur, what are you doing over there, to give me and other people so many distractions?"

When he saw the statue of himself adoring the Blessed Sacrament—the model for that magnificent and moving work of art now in the chapel enshrining his heart—he relented a little and said, "Well, that certainly isn't a *carnaval*." (The *carnaval*—the great painted dummy carried in the Mardi Gras procession—was what he said he looked like.)

Indeed this authentic image of Cabuchet's is about the most moving representation of a saint's face imaginable. Its adoring gaze, lost in God, is a reflection of God in His beauty. And in fact the Curé's constant, ardent gazing at the Primal Being who is ever old and ever new had renewed his own youth in a curious way. Even wrinkles were effaced in the ecstasy of his prayer. (They tell us that Cabuchet had no difficulty in keeping the Curé under observation when he was praying alone before the Blessed Sacrament, for at those times he was oblivious to his surroundings and never noticed any movement about him.) There is a sort of upward sweep of the whole body, the face and the hands, like that eager movement in the pulpit when the wind of enthusiasm caught him up and even his clothing seemed to be swept by a Pentecostal breath, the mighty, rushing wind of God.

And yet to those without the seeing eye, Monsieur Vianney could be most unprepossessing. One strange woman who came to Ars dared to say aloud to a friend that he looked like a caricature, and somebody else exclaimed in his hearing, "Why, is *that* he?" And he turned round, smiled sweetly, and said, "Oh, yes, only *that*. Unlike the Queen of Sheba, who was surprised by seeing more than she had expected, you are surprised because you are seeing less." (Strange that the same remark was made about St. Bernadette—"Is *that* Bernadette?")

Indeed he must have been a wretched spectacle on many occasions. He had a habit of forgetting his umbrella. One day he had got caught in such a terrible icy downpour that he thought it prudent to call on a farmer friend of his on the way home. The farmer nearly wept at the sight of him. He took him in at once and made him change in front of a blazing fire.

It was a good thing that his friends were often on the watch. One day during a heavy shower, Frère Athanase saw him as he passed the Brothers' house. He was without an umbrella or even a hat. Frère Athanase hurried out and managed, with difficulty, to catch up with him.

"Where are you going, *mon camarade?*" asked the Curé.

"I am bringing you an umbrella."

"Bah, I'm not made of sugar," he retorted and burst out laughing.

Oh! that big three-cornered hat of his which one can still see in the presbytery in a glass case, that hat which he seldom put on his head but still carried long after it had lost its shape and even its crown. And we must always picture him with his breviary under his arm.

Although he showed little outward sign of it all, one must not neglect to take into account the terrible physical pains he endured all the while. For example, he had acquired a double hernia from the violence of his activities in the pulpit. Sometimes he suffered from fits of giddiness, owing to lack of fresh air and exercise. He had terrible toothaches (Pertinand, the schoolteacher, had to extract his teeth with pincers). We have already spoken of the facial neuralgia he contracted through sleeping on faggots in the damp kitchen, but he had in addition frightful migraines—torturing in the confessional in hot weather, when the church became like a Turkish bath. He had to listen to confessions with a wet compress on his forehead. The heat gave him an inkling of the oppression of Hell. And then on those stifling days when a storm was brewing, all this heat would make him feel sick and he could keep going only by inhaling vinegar fumes from a little flask.

One must recall that under his cassock he wore penitential chains and a hair shirt, and there must have been a sharp increase of the pain caused by these devices when he was pressed and jostled by the crowds. And yet he never showed it.

His great energy was mostly nervous. He could not have been muscularly strong, considering the kind of life he had led for so many years. It is extraordinary that a man of such great sensitiveness should have been able to endure that appalling nervous and physical ordeal for so long and yet gain the mastery of his nervous system and retain that marvellous emotional equilibrium.

Charity, at the heart of his courtesy, had shaped his manners to a great, almost aristocratic, stateliness. This impressed a young man of noble birth so much that he questioned Frère Athanase about the Curé's origins and was amazed to learn that he was a peasant without education:

"I was most struck by the exquisite courtesy with which Monsieur Vianney received me. When I went into the sacristy, he greeted me most graciously; he showed me the *prie-dieu* and did not sit down until I was kneeling. When I had finished my confession, he was the first to rise; he opened the door for me, said goodbye and then very politely let in the penitent who came after me."

When Frère Athanase replied that the Curé of Ars behaved like that towards everybody, the other said, "I understand. He is a saint. He has the charity which is the source of true courtesy."

We remember what a bad host he was to his brother and sister in the early days at Ars, but old age mellowed him in that respect. When he entertained the local clergy, he used to imitate his good Monsieur Balley and give them excellent fare, well served, taking great trouble over it all, though he himself ate nothing. And it is touching to learn that his guests forgot to eat because the conversation raised their thoughts to heavenly things.

No picture of him would be complete without a few words about his wit. One day when he had been brought to the end of his tether by a woman who would not stop talking, he said to her: "My daughter, in which month of the year do you talk the least?" And he added with a smile: "It must be February, because there are three days less in that month."

He was an enchanting mixture of artlessness and subtlety. He was really very intelligent, and with his keen powers of observation he could easily have been unkind in his small talk. His lips have a slightly sarcastic quirk. Instead he was charmingly gay in conversation. Sometimes his remarks were pungent and even mischievous, but his witty sallies never wounded anybody because of the playfulness of his manner and the delightful facial expression which accompanied them. One of the des Garets girls asked him for some relics, and he replied, "Make some for yourself."

Once, after the great mission of Trévoux, someone gave him a present of some velvet breeches. He gave them away to a beggar he saw shivering with the cold. When he was asked afterwards at Trévoux what he had done with them, he replied light-heartedly: "Oh, I made very good use of them. A poor man borrowed them from me; it was a loan without security—(à fonds perdus)."

Some priests who had wholly accepted the legend of his "ignorance" wrote to the bishop denouncing him for undertaking spiritual direction in cases for which his theological training was inadequate. The letter came into the Curé's hands and he added his own signature to the others in his best handwriting.

Then there was the grand lady queue-breaker, exclaiming as usual that she was not used to waiting anywhere, even at the Vatican. He bowed to her and said with a smile: "I am very sorry,

Madame, but you will have to wait at the confessional of the poor
Curé of Ars."

Once an impertinent stranger went up to him and said, "It seems,
Monsieur le Curé, that you see the Devil." He looked at him very
hard and replied, with a smile, "Yes, I see the Devil."

No, the Curé was no fool. His bishop, Monseigneur Devie, said
of him, "I don't know whether or not he's well educated, what I
do know is that he is enlightened." He used to wish that all his
clergy had *"un petit grain de cette folie"*—a tiny grain of that madness.

He was never taken in by the crowd of visionaries and adven-
turers who flocked round his confessional and tried to reap financial
benefit by begging in his name. Although always extraordinarily
patient with stupid people, he took precautions against the nuisances, who could be ridiculous or even shocking. With regard to
one of these he said to the woman who kept the queue outside his
confessional in order: "Deliver me from that person. Send her
away. She's to be pitied." So he could be firm when necessary.

The Curé of Ars is, as far as we know, the only country curé—
indeed, perhaps the only canonized saint—who ever auctioned his
private belongings to the rich in order to get money for his
charities. And then, he said gaily, if selling his old rags did not
suffice, they would send him to the jail of Toulon. He sold as many
of his possessions as he decently could, even, as we have seen, some
of his sermons. And when he had nothing more to give beggars, he
gave his kindness. Many ragged vagrants were brought up to his
own bedroom. In the winter he would light a fire for them.
Catherine Lassagne says: "As he warmed their bodies he tried to
warm their souls by the fire of Divine Love." Jean Pertinand, the
schoolmaster, adds: "He used to call them 'my friend' in such a
gentle voice that they went away comforted." He would say: "How
happy we are that the poor come to us in this way. If they did not
come, I would have to seek them out, and there is not always time."

The people who bought his belongings paid high prices for old
shoes, cassocks and surplices, foreseeing, no doubt, that they would
be precious relics when he was gone. He was once reduced to

auctioning a tooth, his humility, as Abbé Monnin explains, yielding, in this case, to charity, which is the first of the virtues. (It was an old shoelace of his, kept by a beggar woman in a sixth-floor attic, which was instrumental in performing the first miracle, necessary for the introduction of his cause.)

Poor Catherine complained that he gave away his sheets and napkins; in desperation she locked the linen away, and only gave things out one by one as he needed them.

On the 25th of July 1852 Monseigneur Devie was succeeded by Monseigneur Chalandon. Three months after his accession this young bishop appeared in the church of Ars, holding in his hand a canon's mozetta of black and red silk trimmed with ermine—a gift for the Curé. The Curé was compelled to put it on. He looked, says Comtesse des Garets, like a criminal brought to the scaffold with a rope round his neck. One can picture the stupefaction of the bishop when the Curé wrote, ten days later, to tell him that he had sold the cape for fifty francs needed for his charities. "I was pleased with this price," he said.

In August, 1855, he was given the rank of Chevalier in the Imperial Order of the Legion of Honour. Abbé Toccanier was delegated to present him with the Legion of Honour insignia in a beautiful box. The Curé thought at first that it was some relic he was being offered. When he broke the seal and found it was only a decoration from Napoleon III he exclaimed: "Is that all it is?" and taking the cross in his hand he gave it to the bishop's delegate, saying: "Here, my friend, take as much pleasure in receiving it as I have in giving it to you." The only time he ever wore it was in his coffin.

17. *MONSIEUR VIANNEY'S FRIENDS*

MONSIEUR VIANNEY'S FLIGHT FROM THE PARISH OF ARS IN SEP-tember, 1843, had in one respect consequences which did not ap-pear until 1848, when the direction of his orphanage of La Provi-dence was taken from Catherine Lassagne and handed over to the Sisters of St. Joseph of Bourg. It was in 1843 that the bishop first realized how dependent the orphanage was on the Curé for its very existence: his absence even for a short time might mean that La Providence would be without food. Also, he wanted the institu-tion to survive after the Curé's death. There had, moreover, been complaints from some of the village people that Catherine Las-sagne had not kept the place clean and neat enough. Poor woman, she had no time for housework. Funds were too insecure. The Curé was always having to beg. The Curé, of course, accepted the bishop's decision without a murmur, although it came as a terrible blow to him.

He gave Catherine Lassagne and her rather trying companion, Marie Filliat, a tiny house (it is still standing) next to the presby-tery, where they attended to the church linen and the sacristy. They also prepared meals for the Curé—though this of course was no great labour. Catherine did as much as she could to help the pilgrims.

The months of transition at the end of 1848 and the beginning of 1849 were distressing for all concerned. It was painful for the Curé, even though he had reached the heights of sanctity, to alter his habits. Though he never complained, one could see that he was suffering. How he missed his dear orphans who had helped him by their prayers! The nuns were a little dismayed when they saw the extent to which the house had fallen into neglect and disrepair. Quite apart from all the scrubbing that needed to be done, the walls were damp and some were crumbling. Masons had to be called in.

Mademoiselle Marthe Miard, who kept a shop for devotional articles in the hamlet, said that she thought the Curé was saddened by the renovation of La Providence, the uncompromising order and cleanliness which were introduced; he thought it detracted somewhat from its original poverty. "However," she said, "he never showed the slightest bitterness about it."

But there were two great results from this. Through his total obedience to his bishop the Curé was now able to devote more time to the ever increasing flood of pilgrims coming to his confessional. And what was one small orphanage compared to the thousands of souls he saved? Catherine, who had really been very much overworked all these years, was now rewarded by seeing more of her saint, as she called him, and was able to write, very carefully and diligently, her *Petit Mémoire*, putting together all the facts she had noted about his day-to-day life. But one cannot say that she became his spiritual friend. Both she and the Curé lived on such heights that they had no need of friendship, spiritual or otherwise. Anyway, the Curé had his little St. Philomena. But one suspects, all the same, that Catherine's presence in the background and her rare understanding of spiritual things must have been a joy to him.

Through living in the atmosphere of a saint, Catherine had experienced a lifting of her mind's horizons. She saw, beyond the daily problems of a small village lost in the Dombes, the spiritual need of the whole continent of Europe, troubled by wars and revolutions. She and her orphans had done penance to expiate scandals, and to "catch" great sinners. Now after so many years of service, she lived in poverty. Her special joy was decorating the high altar, for she loved to be close to the Blessed Sacrament. Whenever she managed to save any money she would give it to the poor. She had become such a good nurse that the village people would always call for her when they were ill; they knew that, like the Curé, she would bring much comfort. Once she had to apply her nursing skill to the Curé. He had fallen downstairs and cut his leg, and it had become infected because he wrapped it in an old rag. Catherine saw him limping and dressed the cut properly.

In 1839 Abbé Tailhades said to her: "It is a saint, and a great saint, that you have with you. If you survive him, you will be called on to bear witness." And he advised her to keep a record of all the marvellous things that were happening at Ars. So on Thursday August 29th of that very same year Catherine Lassagne began to keep a diary. Here are some of the entries:

August the 18th, 1841. "Monsieur le Curé told me yesterday that the Devil sang in his chimney like a nightingale."

"15th of September. Monsieur le Curé advised me to widen his palliasse because the Devil was in the habit of throwing him out of bed. 'I have not seen him,' he added, 'but several times he seized me and hurled me out of bed.'"

In the end Catherine put all her notes together, bought a fat notebook and started to write her "souvenirs." (While she was still at La Providence she used to work at it in the evenings, after the orphans had gone to bed.) She made three drafts. The first began towards 1843, ended in 1855; in 1860, after the death of the Curé, she added several touches to her original manuscript. This she offered "to Mary my tender mother . . . I hope that you will obtain for me from your divine Son the grace of recalling to mind so many subjects of moral enlightenment, found in your good and faithful servant, in order that I may profit by them." Her principal source of information is always Monsieur le Curé himself. It is like a refrain recurring at the beginning of every paragraph, "I have often heard Monsieur le Curé say. . . ." Monseigneur Trochu has observed that the reader hears the echo of her kind voice in the simplicity of her words. This unlearned farmer's daughter knew how to convey the essence of an event in a few words. For example:

"The greatest cause of the ever increasing flow [of pilgrims] was Monsieur le Curé himself with his prayers for the conversion of sinners. The grace he obtained was so powerful that it sought them out, leaving them not a moment's rest."

In her description of the flight of September 1853 she says that when the poor Curé found he had been caught out, he said again and again: "Let me go," and she adds: "It seemed to me by the sound of his voice that he was weeping."

As Monsiegneur Trochu says, "How precisely she has observed! How she has relived that dramatic scene!—the leaves of the elder trees touched with red by the lantern-light, the confused shouting of the men who surrounded the holy Curé. . . ." Her finished manuscript is signed with her initials and dated the fourth of February, 1867.

As we have already observed, Catherine had a cross to bear in her old friend Marie Filliat. Marie had neither tact nor good sense. She never appreciated Catherine and had no understanding whatsoever of the Curé. Catherine had need of great patience when they lived together in the little house next to the presbytery. Marie would do nothing to help the pilgrims; she detested cooking and housework and grumbled so much about it that Catherine did all the heavy work about the house. Abbé Toccanier said, "Catherine is Marie's servant without Marie's realizing it."

But when Marie died Catherine grieved deeply for her.

How strange it is to recall that in her girlhood Catherine had prayed that God would take the Curé away from Ars, she found his direction so unbearable. To think of the patience she must have had: "When I brought him anything, I always prepared myself beforehand to be sent away." Well might she say, with a sigh, to Marie: "My God, how difficult it is to serve a saint!" She should be made the patron saint of all priests' housekeepers.

Catherine survived the Curé by twenty-four years, living until 1883. Even after she had reached seventy, her face was fresh and unlined. She was much sought after by the pilgrims to Ars, who regarded her as a kind of living relic of the saint. They would crowd around her, saying, "Here is the one who saw the Queen of Heaven" (referring, of course, to the apparition concerning which we quoted Etiennette Durié's testimony).

The Curé of Ars had once said to a certain Brother Gabriel: "Oh, the friends of God understand one another very well!"

Besieged as he was by the souls of sinners, repentant and unrepentant, Monsieur Vianney found much consolation in the holy persons whose lives touched his. Pauline Jaricot is not the least of these.

In her girlhood Pauline's beauty was of the type which aroused sentimental admiration at that time. She was tall, majestic and gracefully proportioned; black hair framed her oval face, and her dark eyes were most expressive. She was equipped by both beauty and wealth for a worldly life in the society of her day. At the age of seventeen, however, having emerged from a stormy period of sentimental attachment, she began to lead a life of extraordinary self-denial.

In order to make reparation for the sins of neglect and ingratitude committed against the Sacred Heart of Jesus, she established a union of prayer among devout servant girls, called the Réparatrices du Sacré Coeur de Jésus-Christ. From among these girls she solicited offerings for the foreign missions, at the rate of a penny a week. The Society for the Propagation of the Faith, which today collects money for the missions from every diocese in the world, was founded, as the result of her efforts, in 1822.

In 1826 she founded the Association of the Living Rosary. Each Sunday they had their meeting at her house on the Fourvière hill. Apart from their devotion to the rosary, the group had the object of spreading good books and religious articles. The members were mostly poor girls—weavers, factory workers, spinners, housemaids.

The rapid development of industry had produced severe economic problems in Lyons, which were complicated by the new-born socialism that was itself the outcome of the dire poverty in which the working classes lived. It was Pauline's ambition to organize a happy Christian life for a nucleus of workmen's families, whose wretched condition filled her with pity.

For a time her work prospered, and she succeeded in effecting a complete transformation in the lives of great numbers of the workers. In 1841, the Curé of Ars, with his strange intuition, fore-

saw Pauline's troubled future. He sent her one of his most loved
orphans, one Françoise Dubois, whose devoted heart he knew well.
"I am going to send you to a mother who will have great need of
you," he said. "You must serve her in all her needs."

When Françoise reached Lyons, Pauline took her in her arms,
kissed her and gave her work in the kitchen. Thus began many
years of devoted service on the part of Françoise, who was thereafter called Maria. The Curé had sent her at just the right time, for
Pauline's troubles were beginning.

Her plan for the relief of workmen's families had been undertaken with the utmost prudence, but she had entrusted her financial
affairs to a pious hypocrite, Gustave Perre, a plausible rogue with
"Jesus" and "Mary" always on his lips—just the sort to deceive a
guileless woman and go off with her money. The other members
of the household were quick to distrust him. One woman refused to
go to chapel when he was there. He (a daily communicant) always
knelt beside her at Communion, and she detested his very presence.
But Pauline was wholly deceived. To make a long story short, he
got hold of her capital and squandered it. From then on, the
humiliating cross of debt entered her life. What made the situation
more appalling was that some of her creditors were poor working-
people who had entrusted her with all their savings. Thereafter she
became a beggar, making her way even as far as England to plead
for funds.

Between 1850 and 1852 her health broke down. She grew im-
mensely stout, with the obesity of illness. Her heart was weak, and
her legs were ulcerated. Her energies were depleted and she was in
constant pain. In February 1853 she had to apply for poor relief
from the parish of St. Juste. Her letter to her chaplain describes her
destitution:

"We cannot afford to have any fires this year, and must be content with a footwarmer each. The short days have cut down our
practical work of sewing and vestment-making to almost nothing,
for oil is so dear that we are obliged to reduce the number of our
lamps to one in the chapel and one in the kitchen."

One of her daughters said: "We often went to the market with one franc or one franc twenty-five centimes, to buy food for five persons." A Monsieur Dru who came one day to talk business with her was reminded of the worst meal of his life, eaten in a Trappist monastery. The meal he ate in Pauline's house was even worse.

People of the Lyons working classes, seeing her living in a large house surrounded by a beautiful garden, did not believe in her poverty and accused her of avarice. They could not grasp the fact that the property was no longer hers. When beggars were sent away without alms, they threatened her and called her a miser.

Her affairs reached the point where her own debtors would not pay her what they owed her. People had got into the habit of saying, "Mademoiselle Jaricot is ruined. Her debts are so enormous that it's no use paying her small sums, they would only be swallowed up."

Paul Claudel wrote, in a poem about her life:

> It must be good to feel something heavy on one's back,
> Something weighty and inflexible, and the path we are to
>   take all traced out . . . .
> The exactly right cross for us is the one made to our
>   measurements,
> Just enough to be too much; and the sweet sign that it
>   is for us, is that any other would seem preferable . . . .

It looked, from the outside, as if everything were failing in Pauline's hands. But the Curé of Ars saw the meaning of her life. One day, preaching on the subject of suffering, he interrupted his sermon to say: "Ah, brethren, I am acquainted with someone who knows how to accept the Cross, and a heavy Cross, and how to bear it with love! Mademoiselle Jaricot."

In March or April 1859 the Curé, who had not been to Lyons for many years, received a visit from Pauline of which we have an account from Elizabeth Ste. Marie Perrin.

One bitter day towards the end of winter, Pauline's troubles were weighing on her so heavily that she felt she could not go on, and she suddenly had a longing to see the Curé. Maria wondered whether Pauline was strong enough to make the journey, but when Pauline said "I must get out of Lyons for a little while" she agreed to take her. So they set off. At Villecourt, where they hired a carriage for the last few miles of the journey, it began to snow. The driver refused to set out, and put his horse back in the stable. They were in despair of completing the journey when a baker from Ars offered them a seat in his cart.

They made slow progress along the frozen road—the snowstorm was blinding—and arrived stiff with cold. The Curé ran out to greet them, and he had to summon two men to help Pauline down from the cart. He was shocked by her appearance, and since his little room was scarcely warmer than the world outside he set to work, with Maria's help, to light a fire in the grate. But the wood and straw he brought from his shed were damp, and all they produced was smoke. He went down on his knees to blow at the fire, while Pauline protested, "Dear Father, let it alone. I'm used to the cold. All I want is to be warmed up inside by hope and love. That's all I've come for."

So the Curé sat down and they talked. He was looking very frail but oddly joyful. His death was only a few months off, and no doubt the thought of it was not far from him. Pauline told him how overwhelmed she was by the debts she saw no possible way of paying. The Curé said that she must not worry, she could not do the impossible, and she must not mind what was said or done to hurt her reputation in men's eyes; God saw the justice of her case. He told her how once when he desperately needed money for La Providence he had suddenly found a big package of it on his table. "That is what you want. A big package like that dropped from heaven. But Grappin won't allow it. Trust in God, whatever may happen. In Heaven you will understand the whole thing."

Then they began to talk about the love of God. They had hardly noticed the time going, when suddenly they heard feet on the stairs: the Curé's penitents had come to look for him.

The visit must end. The Curé looked about for something to give Pauline and picked up a little cross on which was written: "God is my only witness, Jesus Christ is my model, Mary is my support.

I ask nothing else but love and sacrifice." Pauline's pleasure in the gift delighted him. He gave her and Maria his blessing, adding St. Philomena's name to the divine names, and the women left.

They never met again. Monsieur Vianney died in August of that year. Pauline lived until 1862.

And so we bid farewell to Pauline Jaricot of Lyons, broken in health and fortune, disgraced in the eyes of the world, tragically changed from the lovely young woman who gave the Curé of Ars his Philomena: but in the eyes of Heaven one of the greatest of the holy beggars of the Church.

Blessed Pierre-Julien Eymard, too, came to Ars and received the saint into the Third Order of Mary. The Curé used to refer to him as "my saint." To see an extraordinarily lifelike statue of him, lost in adoration before the Blessed Sacrament, we have only to go to the entrance to the Spanish chapel in the Avenue de Friedland in Paris. (He is the founder of the Blessed Sacrament Fathers, a society devoted to honouring Christ's hidden presence in the Eucharist and of the Servants of the Blessed Sacrament, a congregation of cloistered nuns who carry on Perpetual Adoration.) The bond between the two priests was inevitably strong: both with a special devotion to the Holy Eucharist; both called to the life of prayer from childhood (Blessed Pierre-Julien had begun to follow his mother to Benediction when he was a toddler). Circumstances favoured Pierre-Julien's contemplative vocation; his priestly life burnt itself out in ecstatic worship.

The "holy man of Tours," the widower Léon Dupont, known for his devotion to the Holy Face, was another who came to see the Curé. (His little house in Tours has been turned into a chapel and great graces have been received there.)

In *Diversity in Holiness*, Father R. H. J. Steuart, S.J., says of him: "He resembled the Curé d'Ars in his peculiarly keen perception of the devil as the active individual agent of all the wickedness in the world, and also in the half angry and contemptuous, half humorous, way in which he spoke of him or addressed him:

and, like the Curé, he experienced many revengeful and terrifying assaults from that quarter. For him, too, Satan was a person, malignant beyond utterance, evil, cruel and relentless, possessed of immense cunning, foresight, and resource, and unceasingly active in every detail of social and private life—yet with it all a fool and unspeakably contemptible."

Like the Curé, too, he was intensely conscious of the evils of blasphemy and the profanation of Sunday which were rife in France after the Revolution, and he felt called to atone for them by a life of penance.

He paid his visit to Ars in 1846: "When he arrived at the church, the Curé was just leaving it, surrounded as usual by a packed throng of pilgrims. But he singled out Monsieur Dupont at once, and making his way straight up to him, stood for a moment looking him earnestly in the eyes, then raising his joined hands, 'Ah, my friend, how well it will be with us two when we find ourselves in heaven together singing the praises of God!' "[1]

Quite soon after he had been forced to give up La Providence, the Curé succeeded in bringing the Brothers of the Holy Family to Ars to take charge of the village school for boys. They began their classes on March 10, 1849. Frère Athanase was the Superior. He too became a well-loved friend. He was only twenty-five when he came to Ars, small of stature, holding himself very straight. His eyes, under heavy brows, could look with severity at his pupils when necessary. The saint said of him, "He is a real religious." His faithfulness to the rules of his Institute was remarkable. He delighted in telling anecdotes about the Curé, but if he were in mid-sentence when the clock struck the hour he would stop short, saying, "It's time for me to say my Office" or "It's time for my spiritual reading," then gravely take leave of the company without a moment's delay.

Monseigneur Convert, one of the Curé's successors in the parish of Ars, said that Frère Athanase's liturgical sense was perfect; he had trained the children with such care that the bishop, Mon-

[1] *Diversity in Holiness:* Sheed & Ward, London and New York, 1937.

seigneur de Langalerie, said he should be taken as a model by the clergy of the diocese. "Brother Athanase is a living and impeccable ceremonial!" he said.

He was much loved in the parish. When he had been there fifty years a banquet was given in his honour to which forty-one of his old pupils came. Towards the end of his long life he became the mayor's secretary. He was a delight to the villagers and the pilgrims as a living source of anecdotes about the Curé. He was sympathetic and interested in his visitors and he could make a peasant forget his anxieties in laughter.

Frère Athanase had observed the Curé attentively for many years, and we owe many interesting details to his testimony at the beatification inquiry. He says of the Curé saying his Mass: "His face was so beautiful when he was celebrating! I thought I was seeing another Saint Francis de Sales." And it is he who tells us how the saint used to look at the Host, weeping and smiling in turn: "He seemed to speak to Him. Then the tears started again, and then the smiles."

It was Frère Athanase, too, who discovered in the Curé's room, well hidden behind the bed curtains, the discipline of chains which had "visibly served."

He had reached the age of eighty-eight when he died in June, 1912. Even during the last solemn ceremonies of his deathbed, attended by Monseigneur Convert, he was talking about his favourite subject: his beloved Curé.

Another friend was Frère Jérôme, twenty-nine years of age when he came to Ars. He lived a further twenty-six years in brotherly peace with Frère Athanase. He had been a working tailor in Savoie before entering this teaching Order, and at Ars he was put to caring for the sacristy and the altar linens. At the same time, he was responsible for the garden and the kitchen.

He took his turn in controlling the crowds outside the confessional and managed to keep order with untroubled good nature. He worked from seven o'clock in the morning until between eight and nine at night, when the doors of the church were shut. With all the visiting priests, there was a great deal of work to do in the sacristy. Comtesse des Garets once said with pride, "The other day there were seventeen Masses. Our little church has become a cathedral."

Frère Jérôme was proud of his occupation. He escorted the saint everywhere, protecting him from the crowds. He wrote to his sister: "For part of the day I am near the good Curé. I take him to his house, which he would never be able to reach unaccompanied, everyone crowds around him so much."

It was he who, when the hour of Mass drew near, would fetch Monsieur Vianney from his confessional and help him to cross the narrow nave from the chapel of St. John the Baptist to the sacristy. (This always took several minutes.) It was he too who, a little before eleven o'clock, would help him to settle down in the little low pulpit for the catechism lesson, and then put back the barrier which protected him from the crowds. After catechism he led Monsieur Vianney back to his presbytery: this is depicted in Paul Borel's fresco in the church.

Often he watched the saint at his meals and saw his mortification with regard to food. One day Monsieur Vianney was holding in one hand a cup of milk in which a little chocolate had been melted, and in the other a piece of dry bread. First he would take a mouthful of bread and then take a drink of chocolate. Frère Jérôme exclaimed: "Monsieur le Curé, it would be far better if you dipped the bread in the milk."

"I know that," he replied.

It was Frère Jérôme who had the privilege of holding the Curé in his arms when he was dying.

And, of course, there were the Curé's devoted parishioners. Mademoiselle Colombe d'Ars died around Christmas 1832, and he was saddened at the sight of her empty pew. But then her place was taken by Comte and Comtesse des Garets with their great brood of children. The letters which have been preserved show Monsieur Vianney full of gratitude for the Comte's loyal assistance in the needs of the parish and of affection and esteem for the man himself.

When a soul has sacrificed all human friendship, God gives it back a hundredfold in this life. One cannot but think that with all his detachment, with all the pressure of his astonishing activity, the Curé of Ars was rewarded by the friendship of those whose lives touched his even briefly. To him might be applied the words of one of these, the Holy Man of Tours: "The best and most useful way of sharing the life of those from whom one is, to one's own regret, separated is to advance on the way of perfection. Souls who do not love one another in God cease to be in contact directly they are parted; there is no distance for those who have God as their centre."

18. *SOME STRANGE CASES OF SUPERNATURAL INSIGHT*

ONE COULD FILL THREE VOLUMES BY MERELY COLLECTING FASCI-
nating instances of the Curé's gift of prophecy. This is a strange
and puzzling gift, by no means rare among the saints.

On July 26, 1570, St. Teresa of Avila in the Spanish Carmelite
convent of Medina saw a vessel on the high seas which was taking
forty Jesuits to Brazil attacked by a Calvinist corsair ship. She witnessed the slaughter of the priests and then saw them entering
Paradise. She described this vision to Father Balthazar Alvarez.
A month later, it was confirmed when the news reached Spain.

On the 7th of October, 1571, Pope Pius V at his prayers in
Rome saw the battle of Lepanto in which the Ottoman fleet was
destroyed by the forces of Don Juan of Austria.

Pope Benedict XIV, writing on the canonization of saints, says
that an extraordinary grace which they receive, apart from miracles, apparitions and revelations, is, "the gift of knowledge and
wisdom and the gift of prophecy." Now the power of spiritual
intuition possessed by the Curé of Ars which was the wonder of
all who knew him is related to this gift of knowledge, wisdom and
prophecy.

Throughout this story we have perhaps been struck especially
with one thing; that the Curé's eyes pierced and knew, like His
Master's eyes. Instances of how he knew all about his penitents
are legion.

A young girl who came to him seeking advice about her voca-

tion as a nun said: "May I confide in you? You do not know me."
"I do not know you, child?" he replied. "I read your soul as if
I had heard your confessions all your life."

It was as if the story of that soul, like the stories of countless
others, were unfurled before his eyes. He knew exactly how many
years had passed since a person had made his or her last confession. He also knew the sins or the anxieties the penitent was seeking to hide from him. One day a servant named Marguerite asked
him how he knew a certain thing about her, and he replied:
"Your guardian angel told me."

Once a widow in great grief came to consult him on the fate of
her husband, lately dead. She saw him shrink back into his confessional, and for five minutes he seemed to be holding a conversation with someone unseen. She could hear the sound of words but
not the words themselves.

Canon Saudreau, a specialist in these matters, has ranked some
intuitions of the Curé of Ars among "phenomena of an angelic
order." He explains that before the Fall Adam and Eve had this
infused knowledge from God and could produce purely spiritual
acts in the manner of angels . . . "They had illuminations which
were very like those received by pure spirits. . . . When a faithful
soul is raised to that angelic state, it can embrace a vast horizon
with a single glance of its intelligence . . ."

These things are in the nature of intellectual visions. The Curé
of Ars saw with the eyes of the soul, in the manner of disembodied
spirits. When a stranger asked him who his master in theology
had been, he replied, "The same as St. Peter's."

Pope Benedict XIV says, "This knowledge and wisdom, which
come from the Holy Spirit and have for their principal object
nothing less than salvation, appear to be the reward and fruit of
the liveliest faith. . . . It is not the natural result either of temperament or of circumstances, but is the effect of a predilection of the
spirit of love, which is pleased to enrapture a holy soul, lifting it
for several moments above human nature . . ."

In an extraordinary way, for example, the Curé knew of dis-
asters in advance. He saw the cannon ball that killed him striking

young Johanny des Garets at Sebastopol. He saw a man commit suicide by leaping from the parapet of a bridge into a river, and at the same time knew of the saving act of contrition he made between the bridge and the water.

With regard to the manner in which revelations came to him, a remark he once made to Abbé Toccanier is of great interest. He said: "I once said to a certain woman, 'So you are the one who has left her husband in the hospital and refuses to go to him.' 'How do you know that?' she asked. 'I never told it to a soul.' I was more surprised than she was. I imagined that she had already told me the whole story."

Here is a story which reads like a thriller. It was recounted in 1873 to one Madame E. . . by her maidservant. When the girl was nineteen, she wanted to earn her living, and had set out for a domestic agency at Lyons. On the way she stopped at Ars. Monsieur Vianney caught sight of her in church, listening to his catechism class. He paused for a moment and said directly to her: "Come and see me in the sacristy afterwards. I have something to tell you."

"When the catechism class was finished I went to find him. 'You will leave for Lyons,' he told me, before I had said anything to him. 'Know, my child, that a great danger lies in wait for you. When you are involved in it, think of me and pray to God.'

"We arrived at Lyons, and for three days I found nothing. Then I went to an agency. Two men were waiting there. I explained my business to them. 'Ah,' said one of them, 'you're looking for a situation? It just so happens that I am looking for a maid.' When we had made our arrangements, he added, 'But my wife must see you first. Come this afternoon at three o'clock.' (He lived at La Mulatière.)

"So I went at the time arranged. *Mon Dieu,* how long the road seemed to me! At last I arrived at the point where the Saône joins the Rhône. There were boats and workmen about. But at a certain turning I found myself in a lonely spot where there was only one house. I saw my man on the threshold. He was making signs to me to come along. . . All of a sudden I was seized with a terrible fear. I remembered the words of the Curé of Ars, and I called on God and fled as fast as my legs would carry me. In the meantime, the man—the wretch—had dashed out in pursuit of me and was trying to throw a lasso around my neck . . . He was unsuccessful and had to stop when some bargees appeared.

"Since then I have found out that I had nearly fallen into the hands of the too famous Dumollard, the 'murderer of chamber-maids' . . . When this criminal was arrested, I had to testify against him at the assizes . . . and but for the Curé of Ars. . !"

In 1854 the Curé was visited by William Bernard Ullathorne, the Catholic Bishop of Birmingham, England. The bishop after-wards related: "I was speaking of prayer for England, and of the sufferings of our poorer Catholics on account of their faith, and he was listening, his eyes nearly closed, when suddenly he opened them and turned their singular light in all its brightness full upon me, and breaking in on the narrative in a way I shall never forget, with the manner of one giving a confidence, he said: 'But I believe that the Church in England will return again to its ancient splen-dour.'"

Baronne de Lacomble came to Ars in great anxiety because her eighteen-year-old son had fallen in love with a girl of fifteen, and she thought they were both too young to marry. The journey took three days by coach. She went into the church. The Curé, as if he knew that she had but a short time in Ars, came out of his chapel, went up to her, looked at her and then whispered in her ear: "Let them marry, they'll be very happy."

One day in 1858 a tall girl with an arrogant manner and a provocative look came to Ars as a sightseer. She was only twenty but was already living a licentious life. At midday Monsieur le Curé came out of church, smiling at the children and the sick. All of a sudden he stopped smiling. He had seen Louise Gimet— for that was the girl's name. He went up to her and said in a hoarse whisper: "Woe to you! You will do much evil." Then, in a gentler voice, he said: "But Our Lord in His mercy will have pity on you . . . you will be converted because of the devotion you still have for His divine Mother." Then he left her.

(It was perfectly true that once in a street in Lyons, hearing a young man make a vulgar remark about Notre Dame de Fourvière, she had turned on him and given him a resounding buffet with the back of her hand.)

These are the facts of Louise Gimet's career, still far in the future when the Curé saw her. During the revolution of the Commune in March 1871 after the Franco-Prussian war, she went about disguised as a man, wearing high boots and carrying a great sword, and was known as Capitaine Pigerre. She became a famous *pétroleuse*—that is, she used to pour gasoline down the drain pipes of houses and set fire to them. She was one of the assassins of the Archbishop of Paris; she struck him on the head with the butt of her rifle, then trampled on his dead body. After that, she became ringleader in a general murder of priests. (One of these priest victims had no fewer than seventy-two bayonet thrusts.) She confessed that she killed thirteen priests in all. She was caught and condemned to death. However, the Superior of the nuns in charge of the female inmates of the St. Lazare prison obtained a commutation of the death sentence. This fine nun used to say to that satanic woman: "I want your soul, and I will have it."

Louise Gimet remembered the words of the Curé of Ars. She read a collection of sermons by a priest who had been one of her victims and began to wonder how she could have had such a hatred for priests. She was converted and for twenty years lived a life of mortification and sacrifice. She finished her days at Montpellier, completely transformed in character and utterly devoted to the Virgin Mary, whose medal she wore around her neck. She asked for the privilege of attending to the dying so that she could speak to them of the divine mercy, of which she had so much experience. When she was asked on her own deathbed whether she were afraid, she replied: "I have thrown myself into the arms of His mercy. What have I to fear?"

The Curé knew when some pilgrim had not brought enough money on the journey and would make up the difference out of his own pocket. He knew when a servant had left her master's house during his absence without permission, and warned her when to return.

There was poor little orphan Marie-Antoinette Rigollet, who was fourteen in 1851. She was very unhappy with her stepmother and decided to run away from home. On the 4th day of October she arrived in Ars at four o'clock in the afternoon without a sou. The next day, Sunday, she was dizzy from lack of food. A beggar woman went up to her and said: "Here you are, Mademoiselle, this silver piece is from Monsieur le Curé. You are to go to the hotel which is quite near here. You will have some soup and eat your dinner." Marie-Antoinette started to refuse the coin, but the beggar woman pressed it on her. "He told me that you would refuse, and he made me promise to make you accept it. Here, take it. Take it."

The saint persuaded the little girl to go back home, and she was perfectly happy after that.

There is the strange story of Madame Mercier, a farmer's wife of the Ain district. When she appeared in Monsieur Vianney's confessional, he said to her: "How long are you going to stay here?" She replied, "Until tomorrow, *mon Père*." He said to her, "No, no, go today. There is a snake in your house." She hurried home. In her absence her husband had put the palliasse of their bed to air in the sunlight. This palliasse was stuffed with the leaves from corn stalks. He had put it back in her bed before she returned. She found everything in the house clean and shining. She began to wonder what the Curé could possibly have meant about a snake. All of a sudden she saw a movement in her bed, and a huge snake slid out. Some farm labourers who heard her cries came and killed it.

Two young girls came to the Curé and he prophesied that some disaster would overtake one of them. And indeed on their way home this girl was bitten by a viper. She died on the spot. (The woods near Ars are filled with vipers and it is dangerous to sit in the glades.)

One can only say that this extraordinary gift was bestowed on the Curé of Ars as a grace from God to help in his ministry. He could spare only a few moments to each penitent, and he could never have given the right advice had he not been enlightened by the Holy Spirit. His consideration of their problems took only a moment; the answer—exactly right—came in a few words. If a good person in no need of his advice came to his confessional he would say: "Go, child, you have no need of my assistance," and then give his blessing.

Paul Claudel said that a mother does not know the tenderness, patience, ingenuity and even physical strength she has until a child comes to lay claim to it all. So it was with this man of a naturally impetuous and irritable disposition, tormented by a longing for solitude, who was like a mother to these great crowds, no physical need too small for his care as he led their souls to Heaven.

19. *MONSIEUR VIANNEY ESCAPES FROM ARS*

MONSIEUR VIANNEY REGRETTED THAT HE NEVER HAD TIME TO WRITE about *les délices de la mort*—the delights of death. He foresaw the exact day of his own. How he must have longed for it, "that night which unites Lover and Beloved," as the liturgy for Holy Saturday says. It was the bridal feast for which his Lover had given him a ring invisible to all others except the one woman who saw it.

Abbé Monnin said, "The conversations which we had with him within the last two months of his life remind us . . . how the last thoughts of a heart filled with the love of God are like the last rays of the sun, brighter and more intense before they disappear."

His surroundings were a curious contrast to his youthful spirit; the presbytery, as we have said, had become more dilapidated year by year. The plaster was falling from the walls, tiles were missing from the floor of his bedroom. The woodwork round the windows was cracked, and the window-panes were falling in. A thorn bush had even taken root in the kitchen fireplace and grown up there. But what did it matter when he spent only about three hours out of the twenty-four in his house?

And all the time he longed for Heaven: "My God, how time spent with sinners drags for me! When shall I be with the saints?" —it is the refrain of his exiled life. The only alleviation of his condition came when, six months before his death, the Devil stopped haunting him. One might hope that he could then have slept, but a persistent dry cough made sleep impossible.

The crowds pushed him about as much as ever, but he never gave any sign of impatience, although his terrible fatigue showed on his face. Abbé Toccanier would say, when he saw him so calm: "Monsieur le Curé, in your place the angels would get cross." A curé of Grenoble Cathedral whom Monsieur Vianney called "my cousin" watched him for hours being jostled by the crowds, and he said he was constantly smiling, unfailingly gentle. When in the confessional he applied a compress to his aching brow, it was not so much to relieve the pain as to be able to attend better to his penitents.

To the very end he was mortified in little things. For example, he would never lean his elbows on anything when he knelt in prayer, he would not flick away a fly. He mortified the most ordinary curiosity.

He could take the discipline less often now, because he had to wait till the old wounds were healed before he could strike again. Madame des Garets said that one could tell from the clumsiness of his movements and the stiff way he walked and stood in the pulpit and at the altar that his body was loaded with penitential devices.

His stomach had shrunk so much from fasting that once when his bishop made him eat a reasonable amount at a banquet he nearly died. One might imagine that his frugality would have become second nature to him early in life, but Comte des Garets, who watched him for many years, declared that to maintain this degree of abstinence cost him an immense effort.

Whenever the crowds saw him, they used to cry out, "It's he! It's the saint!" How could he remain humble amidst all this applause? We have the answer in a confidence he once made to his penitent, Baronne de Belvey: "My daughter, never ask God for the full knowledge of your wretchedness. I asked for it once and obtained it. If God had not upheld me, I would have fallen instantly into despair."

He told Frère Athanase that God left him enough insight into his nothingness to make him understand that he was capable of nothing. He was only a tool in God's hands.

And here was this man held in high honour by thousands of people from all over Europe; his bishop called him a saint and had made him a canon; the Emperor had decorated him with the Legion of Honour; here he was caught out by Catherine Lassagne darning the knee of his trousers! She stood stock-still on the threshold of his room, and he said with a laugh: "Eh, Catherine, you thought you would find your Curé, but you came upon a tailor."

He did not realize that when people stole his personal belongings it was because they thought him a saint. One day after a mission his breviary had disappeared. He exclaimed, "It's extraordinary, I thought everybody was converted . . . . And look, somebody's stolen it."

One day, preaching on the Assumption of Our Lady, he said that she had reached the age of seventy-two. (That was about his own age at death.) "Yes, my brethren, if the Mother of God were to die, she could die no other way than in a transport of love. Oh lovely death, oh blissful death, oh death so much desired!"

In March 1859, five months before his death, a journalist, Georges Seigneur, came into church towards four o'clock in the afternoon. At intervals of about ten minutes he heard a sob coming from the confessional. At first he thought it was a cry of fatigue or pain, but later he realized that it sounded like a cry of love, "like a soul stifled by this world . . . trying to open a way towards Heaven."

He had become so weak that he was now forced to have a little milk at bedtime. In order to get himself up in the morning he had to give himself three or four strokes of the discipline. He didn't spare himself anything even at the end; he would say that he could rest in the next life. His short nights were made a torment by his cough. ("It is a nuisance," he said. "It takes up all my time.") He turned and tossed on his board, bathed in sweat. Once he said to Frère Athanase: "I would have liked to go on sleeping this morning, but I didn't linger over getting up. Saving souls is so important." He said to Abbé Toccanier, "Oh yes, sinners will finish off the poor sinner."

In the afternoons, he found it terribly hard to keep awake, and sometimes he would doze off for a second or two. He never betrayed this to the pilgrims, but at the end of the day he would sink down on a chair, and once Jeanne-Marie Chanay heard him say in a gay voice: "Oh, really, this is beyond a joke."

The last half of that month of July, 1859, was a time of appalling heat. The church was so like a furnace that the penitents had to keep going outside for relief. On Friday the 29th there was thunder in the air and great yellow storm clouds were piling up on the horizon. The Curé felt weaker than usual when he rose that morning. At eleven o'clock, before his catechism class, he asked for a small glass of wine and drank a few drops of it out of the hollow of his hand. He could no longer make himself heard from the pulpit, but the very sight of him was a sermon in itself: the adoring glances he turned towards the tabernacle, the cries of love from his parched throat, the tears on his cheeks.

At the end of the day, Frère Jerome found him so near collapse that he had to help him into bed. An hour after midnight, he was shivering in spite of the stifling heat. Catherine Lassagne, sensing that the end was approaching, had not gone to bed but was sitting up in the next room. When he knocked on the wall, she came at once. He whispered: "It is my poor end. You must fetch the Curé of Jassens." His confessor appeared almost at the same time as Dr. Saunier, with the dawn.

This time the penitents waited in church in vain. It was the first time he had failed them. The doctor said that if only the heat would abate, he could be saved. But the storm which would bring relief had still not come.

And then—extraordinary, almost incomprehensible!—some of the penitents came to his bedside to make their confessions.

For the first time in his life, he was docile in illness. He swallowed all the medicines which were given him and even allowed his attendants to put a good mattress on his hard palliasse. The only time he complained a little was when one of the Sisters of St. Joseph flapped the flies away from his sweat-covered face. He said in a whisper: "Leave me my poor flies. . . . Nothing troubles me but sin. . . ."

The diabolical temptations, the fear, the despair which have afflicted some saints at the approach of death did not trouble the Curé of Ars. He had said: "How good it is to die when one has lived on the Cross."

Soon Frère Athanase had to guard the door against the penitents who were outside, sobbing. He allowed them to peep in as they knelt on the threshold. Somebody guided the saint's hand, so that he could bless them. Comte Villier, who was amongst those privileged few, testified: "I saw him in bed on the last day of his life. He was as gentle and peaceful as an angel."

He fixed his dying gaze on all the children of Comte des Garets.

Some of the devoted people of Ars, hoping to bring a little coolness to the house, hung lengths of wet cloth all around it from the roof.

The Curé lay quietly on his bed for four days. His confessor described how his glance was fixed, turned upwards towards heaven. "It seemed that he was in contemplation, and I think that something extraordinary was happening in him."

At one point he said: "I have thirty-six francs left, ask Catherine to give them to Monsieur Saunier . . . and then tell her to ask him not to come back again. I would not be able to pay him."

When the Viaticum was brought to him, tears sprang into his eyes. He was asked why he was weeping, and he said: "It is sad to make one's Communion for the last time."

After that, the priest from Fareins helped to watch by his bed. This old priest said to him: "Monsieur le Curé, you are with God."

"Yes, my friend," he said with a heavenly smile.

"Tomorrow we are keeping the feast of the Translation of St. Stephen's relics. That saint, when he was on earth, saw the heavens opened."

And then the priest from Fareins tells us: "Monsieur Vianney raised his eyes heavenward with an extraordinary expression of faith and happiness. He spent the whole day in that same state of serenity and contemplation."

"We shall see Him! We shall see Him face to face!" he used to exclaim.

On the 3rd of August, Monsiegneur de Langalerie, the Bishop of Belley, appeared at seven o'clock in the evening. Abbé Monnin tells us that he was "out of breath, in a state of great emotion, praying aloud as he pushed his way through the kneeling crowds."

The Curé recognized his bishop and smiled at him.

On that Wednesday night of August the 3rd, towards ten o'clock, he seemed to be sinking. At midnight young Abbé Monnin was at his bedside, saying the prayers for the dying, very slowly. Dawn came: the feast of St. Dominic, Thursday the 4th of August, 1859. He was lying very quietly in the arms of Frère Jérôme. A storm was breaking violently over the village, and lightning flashed in the room. At the very moment when Abbé Monnin was pronouncing the words: "*Veniant illi obviam Sancti Angeli Dei et perducant eam in civitatem coelestem Jerusalem*"—"May God's holy angels come to meet him and bring him into the heavenly city, Jerusalem," Jean-Marie Baptiste Vianney, Curé of Ars for forty-one years, gave back his soul to God, peacefully, without either agony or transport of love, in great simplicity.

Soon the road was crowded with pilgrims, on foot or in carriages. A great mass of people filled the village square. Everybody was in tears. "My feelings were the same as theirs," say Abbé Monnin, "and my brother and I wept together." For the first time in many years the Angelus bell rang at dawn.

He had died serenely in the midst of a storm.

> Storm flakes were scroll-leaved flowers, lily showers—
> sweet heaven was astrew in them.[1]

No longer the fang and flail of men's sins scourging his Lord, no further torment of despair, but hope:

> Hope holds to Christ the mind's own mirror out
> To take His lovely likeness more and more.[2]

[1] From "The Wreck of the Deutchland" in *The Poems of Gerard Manley Hopkins:* Oxford University Press, New York and London, 1937.
[2] *Ibid.*, a fragment.

He is reunited for eternity to the Queen of Heaven, whom he had known on earth:

> Be thou then, O thou dear
> Mother, my atmosphere;
> My happier world, wherein
> To wend and meet no sin;
>
> ....
> Stir in my ears, speak there
> Of God's love, O live air,
> Of patience, penance, prayer:
> World-mothering air, air wild,
> Wound with thee, in thee isled,
> Fold home, fast fold thy child.[3]

As the bells tolled the death-knoll from the church steeples of all the neighbouring hamlets, Frère Jérôme, who had been wandering about the church, grief-stricken, saying again and again, "He is gone," suddenly cried out with utter certitude: "He was a saint!" And at once he was at peace.

Monsieur Vianney had left instructions that his body was not to be prepared for burial; he wanted to hide the scars of his terrible penances. But his wishes were not obeyed, and his fellow priests, reverently performing the last rites of filial love, learned "the secrets of the King" and marvelled at them.

On the 16th of August, Monsieur des Garets' brother-in-law wrote from the Château du Pin to his niece Beatrice: "Our one subject of conversation is the poor Curé of Ars, especially in the evening when we talk about him under our great lime trees. The clear sky, covered with stars, the milky way, the beautiful moonlight, all help to raise the soul to God, our thoughts to him. What rejoicing he must find in heaven now that he has left his poor church, his confessional, his chapel of St. John, his presbytery, his

[3] From "The Blessed Virgin Compared to the Air We Breathe" in *Ibid*.

poor bedroom, his poor bed; now that you weep for him and the pilgrims wait for him in vain; now that the Angelus, which used to ring at one o'clock in the morning, rings like all other vulgar bells at sunrise, since he is no longer among you!"

EPILOGUE

And now he rests awaiting the resurrection of the body, incorrupt in his beautiful shrine in Ars, amid bronze lilies and roses, surrounded by statues of St. Philomena, St. John the Baptist, St. Francis Regis, St. Francis of Assisi and St. Benedict-Joseph Labre.

When his exhumed body was first shown to the people of Ars on April the 2nd 1905, nearly forty-six years after his death, many of the aged burst into tears and said, "Oh, it is really he!"

In 1862 Monseigneur de Langalerie established the ecclesiastical tribunal to inquire into his life, virtues, writings and miracles. A few of the two hundred meetings took place in the chapel of the Château d'Ars. (It is now, alas, crumbling to ruin.) There were sixty-six sworn witnesses, people like the Abbés Raymond, Toccanier, Monnin, Beau; Catherine Lassagne, Jean Pertinand, the schoolmaster, Frère Athanase; Baronne Alix de Belvey; Dr. Saunier; a boyhood friend from Dardilly; Jérôme Fayot from Les Noës, who said with a sob: "I loved him like a brother." The carter, André Verchère, the gardener, Jean Cotton, and Antoine Mandy, the mayor's son. Marie Ricotier, who had had the foresight to buy his possessions for relics; his old sister, Marguerite (she lived to the age of ninety-one and recalled many of the vanished scenes of his childhood); Marthe Miard, whose new white collar the Curé had wanted to buy for his cat.

In 1872 he was declared Venerable; Pius X, in 1905, declared him beatified and made him the patron of all priests having charge of souls in France. Finally on May 31st, 1925, the Feast of Pentecost,

Pius XI canonized him in St. Peter's, amidst a crowd of around 70,000 people from all over the world. In 1929 he made him patron of all parish priests in the world.

Marvellous to think that in that immense crowd at St. Peter's stood sons and grandsons of the sinners Monsieur Vianney had converted. Pope Leo XIII said: "The Curé of Ars is the religious glory of France." It may well be that France, or indeed Europe herself, would never have risen from the carnage of world wars and revolutions if that shabby little priest had not converted so many thousands of her people beforehand.

We who have not had the privilege of being present at his canonization, but have simply read his life and visited his country, let us take this humble French curé to our hearts. That is what the saints are for, it gives them happiness and pleases God. St. Jean Vianney wants to enter our lives as a father, as a friend, to preserve us from eternal perdition, to guide us to the practice of Christian virtue and to the contemplation of Christ. Though his penances are inimitable for most of us, we can at least learn to have the faith he had, faith which he once defined as "speaking to God just as one would speak to a man."

To live in the company of the Curé of Ars for long is a perilous adventure; one risks being caught in his trap. For the first time, perhaps, one may cease to presume about one's salvation and tremble at the thought of Hell. Or, having under his ascetic guidance learned to take repentance for sin more seriously, one may read the lives of the saints and learn to love them as he did. Or hunger for Christ in Communion may consume us as never before. Or in imitation of this innocent priest who loved Mary from childhood, we may begin to love and know this tender Mother—Mary, whom the Church calls "Gate of Heaven." If we do what her Son bids, she will laugh for joy as He turns the water of our lives into wine and bid us sit and be merry in Him at a bridal feast greater than Cana's.

A NOTE ON BOOKS

It was well-nigh impossible, for various reasons, for me to gain access to the original archives dealing with the Curé of Ars: even learned priests have been unable to do so. I have therefore been obliged to get much information at second hand, which is against all my principles and all my training. It is true that Monseigneur Trochu kindly gave me permission to make use of his references, which he had extracted from the sworn testimonies of the canonization process, but this did not equal, for me, the thrill of finding things out for myself by reading the original manuscripts. Heaven sent me two other generous and learned priests, Abbés Pagnoux and Balavoine, the former engaged at that time in writing his own great book on the Curé: *L'Apôtre de la Confiance en Marie*. Their advice and assistance was invaluable to me.

My other sources were:

Mgr. H. Convert.   *Catechismes du Saint Curé d'Ars*. Emmanuel Vitte. 1920.

Abbé Alfred Monnin.   *Esprit du Saint Curé d'Ars*. Librairie Tequi. Paris.

    (Undated; first edition was 1864.)

    Le Curé d'Ars, vie de M. Jean-Marie-Baptiste Vianney. 2 vols. Douniol. Paris. 1861.

    The Curé of Ars. Burns, Oates & Washbourne. London. 1862.

    (Various excerpts from Abbé Monnin's accounts and from the Curé's sermons

are quoted from this English translation.)

Mgr. F. Trochu.   *Autour du Curé d'Ars.* Emmanuel Vitte.
Lyons and Paris. 1949.
Catherine Lassagne. (A pamphlet.) Im-
primerie de Trévoux. 1953.
L'âme du Curé d'Ars. Emmanuel Vitte.
Lyons and Paris. 1928.
Le Curé d'Ars, predicateur populaire.
Emmanuel Vitte. Lyons and Paris. 1950.
The Insight of the Curé of Ars. Westmin-
ster. Newman. 1957.
Les intuitions du Curé d'Ars. 3 vols. Em-
manuel Vitte. Lyons and Paris. 1952.

Joseph Vianey.   *Le bienheureux Curé d'Ars* (1786–1859).
Lecoffre. Paris. 1905.
Blessed John Vianney. Benziger. New
York. 1906.

Jean-Marie Vianney.   *Sermons du Saint Curé d'Ars.* Vols. 1 & 4.
Gabriel Beauchesne. Paris. 1925.

My most grateful thanks are due to Burns, Oates & Washbourne
for allowing me to make my own translation of passages from Mgr.
F. Trochu's *Le Curé d'Ars,* of which they publish the authoritative
translation, *The Curé of Ars,* in England; and to The Newman
Press, the publishers of the American edition. I thank The Newman
Press also for permitting me to use my own translation of passages
from *Les intuitions du Curé d'Ars,* of which they publish the English translation, *The Insight of the Curé of Ars.*

I wish to thank Oxford University Press for their kind permission to reprint selections from *The Poems of Gerard Manley Hopkins,* and Kegan Paul, Trench, Trubner & Co., Ltd. for their kind
permission to quote excerpts from *The Graces of Interior Prayer,*
by A. Poulain, S.J.